CHOOSING WHITE-COLLAR CRIME

For more than three decades, rational-choice theory has reigned as the dominant approach both for interpreting crime and as underpinning for crime-control programs. Although it has been applied to an array of street crimes, white-collar crime and those who commit it have thus far received less attention. *Choosing White-Collar Crime* is a systematic application of rational-choice theory to problems of explaining and controlling white-collar crime. It distinguishes ordinary and upperworld white-collar crime and presents reasons for believing that both have increased substantially in recent decades. Reasons for the increase include the growing supply of white-collar lure and noncredible oversight. *Choosing White-Collar Crime* also examines the generative world of white-collar criminals, their decision making, and their criminal careers. The book concludes with reasons for believing that problems of white-collar crime will continue unchecked in the increasingly global economy and calls for strengthened citizen movements to rein in the increases.

Neal Shover is Professor of Sociology at the University of Tennessee, Knoxville, where he teaches courses in criminology, white-collar crime, and criminal justice. He is author of *A Sociology of American Corrections* (1979), *Aging Criminals* (1985), *Enforcement or Negotiation? Constructing a Regulatory Bureaucracy* (with Donald A. Clelland and John P. Lynxwiler, 1986), *Analyzing American Corrections* (with Werner Einstadter, 1989), *Great Pretenders: Pursuits and Careers of Persistent Thieves* (1996), and co-editor (with John Paul Wright) of *Crimes of Privilege* (2000). His work has appeared in *Social Forces; Social Problems;* the *British Journal of Criminology; Criminology; Crime, Law and Social Change*, and numerous edited collections.

Andy Hochstetler is Associate Professor of Sociology at Iowa State University, where he teaches courses on crime at the graduate and undergraduate levels as well as a course on inequality and stratification. He writes on white-collar crime, prisoners, criminal decision making, and recidivism. His work has appeared in numerous edited collections and journals including *Criminology; Social Problems; Journal of Contemporary Ethnography; Crime and Delinquency; Justice Quarterly; Journal of Criminal Justice; Deviant Behavior;* and *Crime, Law and Social Change*.

CAMBRIDGE STUDIES IN CRIMINOLOGY

Edited by

Alfred Blumstein, *H. John Heinz School of Public Policy and Management, Carnegie Mellon University,* and David Farrington, *Institute of Criminology, University of Cambridge*

Other books in the series:

Life in the Gang: Family, Friends, and Violence, by Scott H. Decker and Barrik Van Winkle

Delinquency and Crime: Current Theories, edited by J. David Hawkins

Recriminalizing Delinquency: Violent Juvenile Crime and Juvenile Justice Reform, by Simon I. Singer

Mean Streets: Youth Crime and Homelessness, by John Hagan and Bill McCarthy

The Framework of Judicial Sentencing: A Study in Legal Decision Making, by Austin Lovegrove

The Criminal Recidivism Process, by Edward Zamble and Vernon L. Quinsey

Violence and Childhood in the Inner City, by Joan McCord

Judicial Policy Making and the Modern State: How the Courts Reformed America's Prisons, by Malcolm M. Feeley and Edward L. Rubin

Schools and Delinquency, by Denise C. Gottfredson

The Crime Drop in America, edited by Alfred Blumstein and Joel Wallman

Delinquent-Prone Communities, by Don Weatherburn and Bronwyn Lind

White-Collar Crime and Criminal Careers, by David Weisburd and Elin Waring, with Ellen F. Chayet

Sex Differences in Antisocial Behavior: Conduct Disorder, Delinquency, and Violence in the Dunedin Longitudinal Study, by Terrie Moffitt, Avshalom Caspi, Michael Rutter, and Phil A. Silva

Delinquent Networks: Youth Co-Offending in Stockholm, by Jurzy Sarnecki

Criminality and Violence among the Mentally Disordered, by Sheilagh Hodgins and Carl-Gunnar Janson

Corporate Crime, Law, and Social Control, by Sally S. Simpson

Companions in Crime: The Social Aspects of Criminal Conduct, by Mark Warr

Situational Prison Control, by Richard Wortley

The Criminal Career: The Danish Longitudinal Study, by Britta Kyvsgaard

Violent Crime: Assessing Race and Ethnic Differences, edited by Darnell Hawkins

Gangs and Delinquency in Developmental Perspective, by Terence P. Thornberry, Marvin D. Krohn, Alan J. Lizotte, Carolyn A. Smith, and Kimberly Tobin

Early Prevention of Adult Anti-Social Behavior, edited by David Farrington and Jeremy Coide

Errors of Justice, by Brian Forst

Rethinking Homicide, by Terance D. Miethe and Wendy C. Regoeczi

Understanding Police Use of Force, by Geoffrey P. Alpert and Roger G. Dunham

Economic Espionage and Industrial Spying, by Hedieh Nasheri

Marking Time in the Golden State, by Candace Kruttschnitt and Rosemary Gartner

The Virtual Prison, by Julian V. Roberts

Prisoner Reentry and Crime in American, Edited by Jeremy Travis and Christy Visher

Choosing White-Collar Crime

Neal Shover

University of Tennessee, Knoxville

Andy Hochstetler

Iowa State University

CAMBRIDGE UNIVERSITY PRESS
Cambridge, New York, Melbourne, Madrid, Cape Town, Singapore, São Paulo

Cambridge University Press
40 West 20th Street, New York, NY 10011-4211, USA

www.cambridge.org
Information on this title: www.cambridge.org/9780521662178

First published 2006

Printed in the United States of America

A catalog record for this publication is available from the British Library.

Library of Congress Cataloging in Publication Data

Shover, Neal.
Choosing white-collar crime / Neal Shover, Andy Hochstetler
   p.   cm. – (Cambridge studies in criminology)
Includes bibliographical references and index.
ISBN-13: 978-0-521-66217-8 (hardback)
ISBN-10: 0-521-66217-6 (hardback)
ISBN-13: 978-0-521-66554-4 (pbk.)
ISBN-10: 0-521-66554-x (pbk.)
1. White collar crimes. 2. Commercial criminals. 3. Criminal behavior – Decision
making. 4. Rational choice theory. I. Hochstetler, Andrew. II. Title. III. Series:
Cambridge studies in criminology (Cambridge University Press)
HV6768.S55 2005
364.16′8 – dc22   2005017961

ISBN-13   978-0-521-66217-8 hardback
ISBN-10   0-521-66217-6 hardback

ISBN-13   978-0-521-66554-4 paperback
ISBN-10   0-521-66554-x paperback

For Riley Marie Shover

N.S.

For Nell Hochstetler

A.H.

Contents

List of Figures and Tables

Preface

In November 2001, both the world's largest newspapers and electronic media were filled with stories about the collapse of Enron Corporation and speculation about likely criminal charges for some of its officers. That crime was committed there was little doubt, and, largely because of it, some 20,000 Enron employees eventually lost entirely or saw a severe reduction in their retirement financial accounts. Criminal proceedings against and negotiated guilty pleas by some of Enron's former top managers began soon afterward. Andrew Fastow, the Enron chief financial officer who contrived many of the deals that enabled his employer to hide from investors and shareholders the enormity of its debt, was one of the first. On January 12, 2005, he pleaded guilty to federal charges and later was sentenced to ten years imprisonment. Like him, Kenneth Lay, Jeffrey Skilling, and other high-ranking officers were indicted and faced trial on criminal charges. Criminal proceedings will continue for years. Enron was not the only major corporation caught out for crimes on a massive scale; its crimes were duplicated by predatory and criminal behavior by management of WorldCom, HealthSouth, Tyco, Xerox, Adelphia, and others.

For those inclined to look for it, evidence of pervasive and widespread white-collar crime has rarely been more plentiful. Even the casual consumer of the mass media almost daily encounters reports of outrageously harmful or destructive crime committed by privileged citizens and large corporations. Few white-collar crimes are as complex or costly as media coverage of these sensational cases might suggest; the media generally single out for attention the most gluttonous offenders and the most egregious crimes. But the picture gained from coverage of regional and local events by newspapers in smaller cities is no less disturbing. The crimes of Enron, similar crimes committed by other organizations and individuals, and media reports highlight the concern shared by many citizens that white-collar crime has reached dangerous levels.

This epidemic developed even as the nation witnessed a corrective shift in the way most people think about street criminals and the most promising ways to deal with them. For more than three decades, political leaders have embraced and promoted assiduously the notion of crime as *choice*. The fundamental assumption of this approach is that criminal acts are products of decision making in which individuals examine and assess available options and their potential net payoffs, paying attention particularly to the possibility of arrest. The notion of crime as choice is cited approvingly by many academics, policy makers, and crime-control managers, and it has spawned a host of bromides about crime and the most appropriate responses to it. Elected officials and citizens have come to understand that indulgence and permissiveness breed crime, and that offenders must be shown that "decisions have consequences." Few doubt the wisdom of communicating to all who contemplate criminal choice that if they "do the crime, [they] do the time." There is a timeless quality in the interpretations, applications, and lessons of rational-choice theory that commands attention.

The no-nonsense conventional wisdom speaks not only to management of offenders but also to the environments that attract them. Observers place themselves in the mind of rational offenders and imagine, for example, how they might see some neighborhoods as more attractive than others. Places with high rates of disorder and crime are places also where offenders sense tolerance for uncivil behavior. Broken windows that go unfixed invite only more broken windows. The lesson is that there can be no public refuge for vice and no tolerance even of minor forms of criminal activity. It sends the wrong message and thereby increases the likelihood of offending. On the crime-prevention front, the promise of crime-as-choice theory is relief from an impressive range of criminal behaviors, everything from loitering to armed robbery.

More important than its function as underpinning of contemporary approaches to crime control, crime-as-choice theory is a general theory of criminal conduct; its depiction of the criminal decision-making process and its propositions about curbing crime are applicable to all offenses. This book is intended as a straightforward demonstration of how rational-choice theory applies to the problem of explaining and controlling white-collar crime. Doubtless this will strike some as misguided; depiction of white-collar criminals as calculating actors may not sit well with them or with sympathetic interpreters of their conduct. Both prefer interpretations that are less voluntaristic and more blameless. In addition to the potential crime-reduction benefits of crime-as-choice theory, it seems appropriate that privileged criminals not be permitted to market exculpatory explanations for their crimes while their poor and minority criminal cousins are held to the standard of rational actors.

Although we draw from a variety of materials in the pages and chapters that follow, the data available to investigators of white-collar crime pale in quality and comprehensiveness beside data available on street crime. Inevitably, what can be learned easily about white-collar crime and criminals whether from available data or from use of well-established research techniques is patchy and of uncertain validity. The most important problem this presents is inability to measure with even a modicum of comprehensiveness and confidence the volume of white-collar crime.

The complications begin but do not end there; investigations of white-collar crime are beset by disagreement over fundamental conceptual issues, and decades after pioneering research on the subject, investigators still contend with these. Considerable time and energy have been invested in efforts to resolve these controversies, but progress has been nil. Where white-collar crime is concerned, figure and ground are easily blurred and seen, therefore, in more than one way. We believe that conceptual disagreements should not impede efforts to better understand and confront white-collar crime, but in chapter 1 we touch on some of these disagreements. Rational-choice theory gives reason to believe that white-collar crime is increasing substantially, but data limitations make impossible a straightforward test of this assumption. Consequently, the strategy employed here is to examine and document changes in conditions that theoretically predict the level of white-collar crime. Variation in lure, oversight, and the supply of motivated offenders, concepts at the heart of crime-as-choice theory, is described in the chapters that follow and documented where possible. Readers are on notice, however, that our theoretical reach and analysis perhaps cannot be applied evenly to all white-collar criminals.

Chapter 2 examines temporal increases in the supply of lure, one of the principal sources of variation in the rate of white-collar crime. In chapter 3 we explore the class, family, and organizational backgrounds of those who choose to exploit lure. Chapter 4 describes oversight and argues that its credibility has failed to keep pace with the burgeoning supply of white-collar lure. Chapters 5 and 6 examine the dynamics of white-collar criminal decision making and careers in white-collar crime. These matters have captured the attention of investigators and policy makers alike, and no treatment of crime can ignore them. The analysis concludes in chapter 7 with discussion of victims of white-collar crime, the frustrations they face dealing with unresponsive control agents, and why state responses to white-collar crime generally are tepid and ineffective. We argue that determined efforts will be required if the odds of runaway increases in white-collar crime are to be minimized.

Acknowledgments

The list of organizations and individuals who assisted us in one way or another to complete this project is a long one, and we are pleased to thank them publicly. Heith Copes, Mark Berg, Katie Elam, and Evelyn Blane served capably and cheerfully as assistants at various times while it was in gestation. Michael Benson graciously made available copies of interviews he conducted with ordinary white-collar offenders, and reading them helped us gain additional insight into their perspectives and decision making. Harry Dahms's knowledge of the contemporary literature on the state and globalization is as impressive as it was indispensable for our efforts. Conversations with Heith Copes, Alicia Cast, and Teresa Tsushima helped clarify conceptual issues and saved time in the library. Rachel Burlingame brought to bear her expert typing skills and thereby helped us push the project to completion. Gil Geis, the undisputed authority on matters of white-collar crime, read a draft of the manuscript and spurred us to do better. We appreciate very much his concern and comments. Richard Wright, Peter Grabosky, Stephen Cernkovich, Jeffrey Ulmer, and Annette Lareau read portions of the manuscript and provided critical feedback. Matt Potoski and Aseem Prakash shared with us expertise on organizational culture and reassured us about our treatment of this concept and explanation for white-collar crime. Patrick Langan, at the Bureau of Justice Statistics, and Guy Blackwell, Assistant U.S. Attorney for the Eastern District of Tennessee, directed us to or provided materials we otherwise would have had difficulty locating. Linda Maxfield at the United States Sentencing Commission made available statistical reports and assistance interpreting them.

The Criminal Justice Initiative at the University of Tennessee provided support, as did the College of Liberal Arts and Sciences at Iowa State University, which awarded a faculty development grant to Andy Hochstetler. A broad outline of the project was conceived while Neal Shover was a visiting scholar at the Centre for Tax System Integrity, Research School of Social Sciences, Australian National University. Valerie Braithwaite made possible this opportunity.

As with all the projects of our lives, completion of this one would not have been possible without the support, constancy, and good cheer of Beth Hochstetler and Jeanie Shover. It pleases us to make this known to all.

CHAPTER ONE

White-Collar Crime

The closing decades of the twentieth century saw dramatic change in the way policy makers and elite academics talk about crime and what should be done about it. In place of the deterministic accounts of its sources that had enjoyed support for decades, they turned to and advanced an interpretation of crime as *choice*. Seen in this way, aggregate-level crime rates are determined by the supply of opportunities for crime and the number of individuals willing to exploit them. As to the further problem of explaining why only some do so, crime-as-choice theory resurrects an answer advanced by philosophers nearly two centuries ago: they choose. As with all choices, criminal ones are said to be preceded by a decision-making process in which individuals assess options and their potential net payoffs, paying attention particularly to potential aversive consequences. The possibility of arrest and punishment presumably is prominent among these. When viewed through the lens of crime-as-choice theory, crime unambiguously is purposeful and calculated action.

Rational-choice theory gained unrivaled dominance not only as explanation for variation in crime but also as justification for a changed emphasis in crime-control practice. It was pointed out that because the so-called root causes identified in some theories of crime supposedly are beyond the reach of meliorative action by the state, a more appropriate focus is policies and practices meant simply to increase the risks of choosing crime (Wilson, 1975). Programs grounded in theories of deterrence and incapacitation took center stage, and the emphasis shifted to initiatives that would increase the odds and severity of punishment. The net cast by the state to ensnare and control

1

miscreants simultaneously was widened, and its mesh was thinned (Garland, 2001).

A mountain of research and statistical reports can be cited to document these developments, but suffice it to say that across the United States police were given new powers to search out and pursue more aggressively criminal suspects. Sentencing laws were also revamped to provide for mandatory and increasingly severe penalties. The nation witnessed a dramatic increase in arrests and criminal convictions. Three decades of growth in the U.S. prison population, for example, add up to an overall increase of some 500 percent since 1973. In the eyes of some public officials and policy makers, this is an important reason why rates of serious street crime declined substantially in the years bounding arrival of the new millennium.

On the crime-prevention front, in place of broad strategies aimed at reducing poverty and inequality, the new focus became policy initiatives implemented in narrowly circumscribed geographic locales against specific types of crime (Clarke, 1995). In the British Home Office, for example, a stream of studies and publications examined the effects of manipulated situational elements on offenses as diverse as car park crime, household burglary, and theft of natural gas by residential tenants. Among the lessons learned from this research are that simulating occupancy when homes are deserted reduces the odds of household burglary, and improved lighting in public places can lower the incidence of some types of crime. Known as *situational crime prevention*, this approach is said to be applicable to all types of crime (Felson and Clarke, 1998).

As a general theory of crime and crime control, the appeal of rational-choice theory is belief that it explains significant variation in all crimes across time, space, populations, and individuals. Thus far it has been applied principally to street crime and its perpetrators but only sparingly and unenthusiastically to white-collar crime in its immense variety (Braithwaite and Geis, 1982; Shover and Bryant, 1993; Cohen and Simpson, 1997; Weisburd, Waring, and Chayet, 2001). The promised crime-control benefits of the theory, therefore, have yet to be extracted and exploited adequately where it is concerned. The effort is undertaken in the pages that follow.

The project's premisses are few and straightforward. They begin with belief that all criminal decision making makes up a single field of study, and that much of what has been learned in studies of street criminals and their decision making almost certainly is paralleled in white-collar criminal decision making. There are good reasons to believe that white-collar criminals generally behave more rationally than street offenders; the latter routinely choose to offend in hedonistic contexts of street culture where drug consumption and the presence of other males clouds judgment and the ability to calculate beforehand. Many white-collar workers by contrast live and work in worlds that promote, monitor, and reward prudent decision making. They are significantly older to boot and more capable, presumably, of exercising the greater care and caution of persons with some maturity.

It is a mistake, however, to focus interest narrowly on the effects of threat and punishment on decisions by individual offenders. There is the general deterrent effect to consider. When the state looks the other way or responds with apparent indifference to white-collar crime, those tempted to violate the law are emboldened. The moral and educative consequences of state response to white-collar crime merit greater attention as well. Official punishment is not meant to be nor is it a neutral event. It signals to others important lessons about moral values that underpin many criminal laws; citizens take cues about the seriousness of behaviors by observations of how it is treated by state officials. This is one reason many white-collar criminals escape the public condemnation that generally comes from seeing crime as willful choice. Beyond narrow and technocratic policy issues, moreover, application of rational-choice theory to white-collar crime is consistent with lay notions of fairness; currently, materially disadvantaged and disreputable offenders bear the greatest burden of crime control. In light of its astronomical if inestimable costs, systematic application to white-collar crime of a theoretical approach that has gained backing by citizens and policy makers alike for its realistic and hard-nosed interpretation is past due.

As a guide to policy making, the bedrock assumption of rational-choice theory is belief that "when punishment is not only uncertain but altogether improbable, crime rises precipitously" (van den Haag,

1975:70). Expressed as advice to parents, teachers, and legislators alike,

> the way to improve behavior is to provide rules, teach precepts, offer good examples, and enforce the law. The answer to bad behavior is to hold people accountable and if necessary to punish them. Simply offering a course on theories of responsibility isn't sufficient. You don't change a [criminal's] behavior by making him take an ethics course. You change it the old fashioned way, by telling him to stop and why; and if he doesn't stop, you force him to stop by the power of the law, if necessary. It's not complicated, but it requires resolute action and tough mindedness. (Bennett, 1992:165)

The call for tough action has been extended to the problem of curbing white-collar crime also:

> [W]e believe that some nonviolent, first-time offenders . . . belong in prison. White-collar criminals, those who commit fraud, those who extort or embezzle, and those who conspire or cover up can be just as deserving of punishment as any street predator. And we suspect that most Americans – most people who believe in equal justice under law – agree with us. (Bennett, Dilulio, and Walters, 1996:101)

Before we turn to sketching and examining critically predictions about white-collar crime grounded in rational-choice theory, we briefly review continuing controversy over the crimes of privileged citizens and appropriate policy responses.

WHITE-COLLAR CRIME

It is ironic that the designation *white-collar crime* does not appear in statutes or in state regulations yet has become securely rooted in lay and scholarly lexicons. In everyday parlance, it is understood and used to denote a type of crime and that differs fundamentally from street crime. One way it is different is its obscured and innocuous appearance. Street crimes typically are committed by confronting victims or entering their homes or businesses, but most white-collar crimes are committed by using guile, deceit, or misrepresentation to create and exploit for illicit advantage the appearance of a legitimate transaction. Many have the look and feel of the ordinary. Others are committed by abusing for illicit purposes the power of organizational position or public office. The crimes committed by white-collar criminals are dissimilar also in the ways they develop and harm others. From the abruptness and violence of some to the slow-to-develop nature and widely diffused harm caused by others, these are diverse crimes. Some are as subtle and obscured from the eyes of onlookers as toxic dumping, but others are as violent as sexual assault. White-collar crime is different also in the backgrounds and characteristics of its perpetrators; the poor and disreputable fodder routinely encountered in police stations and in studies of street crime are seldom in evidence here.

In the United States, interest in white-collar crime dates to the Progressive era of the early twentieth century when the excesses of industrialists and political leaders were the focus of considerable attention by social critics. The early sociologist E. A. Ross was among them and highlighted what has come to be called white-collar crime. Ross (1907) noted that growing social and economic interdependence had produced a level of "mutualism" unknown to earlier generations, and the result was new and changing forms of criminal opportunity. Criminals now could victimize large numbers of citizens in a calculated yet emotionally and geographically detached fashion. Ross dubbed "criminaloids" the new breed of offenders who exploit with impunity these opportunities, and he noted how much they differ in outward appearance from the picture that comes to mind when the topic of crime is raised in conversation. Criminaloids are respectable criminals, and, Ross warned, "every year finds society more vulnerable" to them (1907:37). Likening them to "wolves," he argued that

> the villain most in need of curbing is the respectable, exemplary, trusted personage who, strategically placed at the focus of a spider-web of fiduciary relations, is able from his office-chair to pick a thousand pockets, poison a thousand sick, pollute a thousand minds, or imperil a thousand lives. It is the [criminaloid] that needs the shackle. (1907:29–30)

Ross fused scholarly objectives with a presentational style akin to muckraking, but his analysis and call received little attention. Decades passed before white-collar crime again came under critical scrutiny.

CRIMINALS OR CRIMES?

The sociologist Edwin Sutherland is credited with introducing the concept *white-collar crime* in the middle decades of the last century. In scholarly speeches and publications, Sutherland criticized social scientists for the class bias in their near-exclusive focus on crimes of the disadvantaged. He also reported results from his pioneering investigations of white-collar crime (Sutherland, 1940; 1945; 1949; 1983). For Sutherland, white-collar crime is "crime committed by a person of respectability and high social status in the course of his occupation" (Sutherland, 1983:7). Although he at times was ambiguous and inconsistent in his use of concepts, no one disputes that Sutherland regarded the respectable social status of its perpetrators as the defining characteristic of white-collar crime. In the years since he wrote, many have followed his lead in opting for a *criminal-based* definition. Fundamental to this approach is belief that the power and status of its perpetrators is the essential quality of white-collar crime.

Nothing about white-collar crime is free of controversy, however, and the way it is defined is the focus of much of it. In contrast to those who prefer criminal-based definitions, others contend that either there is no analytic advantage to be gained by highlighting offenders' privileged position or that this is misplaced. They counter with *crime-based* definitions, all of which look to formal characteristics of criminal offenses as the basis for distinguishing white-collar crime from other types. As Edelhertz (1970:3) puts it, for example, a white-collar crime is "an illegal act or series of illegal acts committed by nonphysical means and by concealment or guile, to obtain money or property, to avoid the payment or loss of money or property, or to obtain business or personal advantage." In the process of constructing crime-based definitions, the respectable status of those who commit white-collar crime disappears or loses analytic significance. Thus, Edelhertz (1970:4) makes clear his belief that "the character of white-collar crime must be found in its modus operandi and its objectives rather than in the nature of the offenders." His approach is matched by Shapiro (1990:346), who calls for "collaring the crime, not the criminal."

The democratic implications of doing so are clear if illogical. When it is defined on the basis of crime characteristics, "white-collar" crime can be "committed by a bank teller or the head of an institution. The offender can be a high government official with a conflict of interest [or] [h]e can be the destitute beneficiary of a poverty program" (Edelhertz, 1970:4). No longer is white-collar crime the province of only the remote and powerful; now the neighborhood automobile mechanic receives equal billing. Just how democratic the empirical implications of crime-based definitions of white-collar crime can be is made clear in a study carried out by investigators at Yale Law School (Weisburd et al., 1991). They began by drawing a sample of offenders from all persons who were convicted of or who pleaded guilty to any of eight statutorily defined crimes in seven U.S. District Courts in the years 1976–1978. The crimes are: securities fraud; antitrust violations; bribery; bank embezzlement; postal and wire fraud; false claims and statements; credit and lending institution fraud; and tax fraud. These offenses were designated white-collar crimes by investigators, and, by definition, individuals convicted of any of them are white-collar criminals. Subsequent analysis, however, showed that the sample included many offenders of modest financial resources; a substantial proportion were unemployed when they committed their crimes. The presence of many who obviously are not of elite background and status in samples defined on the basis of crime characteristics is one reason some have dubbed white-collar crime as "crimes of the middle classes" (Weisburd et al., 1991).

The democratic implications of crime-based definitions are evident as well in the results of a study of individuals in the United Kingdom who were convicted of selected white-collar offenses: adulteration of food, selling food from unhygienic premises, misleading descriptions of goods, and use of short weights or measures. Information about the defendants gleaned from regulatory and court records caused the investigator to remark that

> [e]xamination of the occupational or social status of [these] convicted offenders fails to expose the widespread criminality of elite groups, high status executives or large, multinational corporations, however loosely defined these terms may be. Instead, the offences of butchers, bakers, restaurateurs, porters, manual workers and small businesses are to be found equally, if not more prevalent (Croall, 1992:56).

The investigator notes as well that "[w]hite collar crime...cannot automatically be assumed to be the preserve of the rich and powerful. Employees at all levels of the occupational hierarchy have many opportunities to abuse their occupational roles, and both large and small businesses can indulge in many dangerous and deceitful practices" (Croall, 1992:56). Recall, however, that those who employ criminal-based definitions of white-collar crime generally do so with full intent of restricting its meaning to crime committed by the "rich and powerful."

Regardless of how it is defined, there is no shortage of white-collar crime. For this reason, definitional controversy may not matter much. Future historians looking backward to identify periods of widespread white-collar crime committed with apparent impunity could do worse than single out the present for closer scrutiny. A visit to the Website maintained by any state attorney general in the United States instantly confirms the high level of white-collar crime and official actions to curb it. The same eye-opening experience is produced by examining online administrative and criminal actions initiated by the U.S. Department of Justice, Federal Trade Commission, or Securities and Exchange Commission.

A more old-fashioned search for information on white-collar crime is no less revealing. To illustrate the point, we examined reports of white-collar crime in the nation's 100 largest newspapers for February 1, 2004, and February 4, 2004. One hundred forty-three news reports about white-collar crime appeared in the newspapers on these two days. Sixty-two (43.4 percent) of the stories mentioned widely publicized national or international cases. Many reported on the criminal trial of entrepreneur, business executive, and television personality Martha Stewart for lying to investigators about an illicit stock sale (*New York Times*, 2003a). Likewise, there was extensive reporting on the international mutual funds scandals that recently had come to light. September 2003 marked the beginning of investigations into this web of crime. Fund companies, it soon became apparent, used improper and criminal tactics to allow insiders or big clients to make quick profits at the expense of small and long-term investors. By early February 2004, the New York state attorney general and the U.S. Securities and Exchange Commission had brought criminal and civil actions against over half a dozen brokerage firms, fund companies, or individuals. Financial settlements were reached in other cases. On February 4, 2004, newspaper stories reported that a former executive of the Canadian Imperial Bank of Commerce was charged by state and federal authorities with larceny and fraud by helping finance illegal mutual fund trading. Officials charged that he helped others carry out improper trades from 2001 to 2003 in a trading scheme that stole more than $2 million from two mutual funds (*Washington Post*, 2004a).

Eighty-one news stories recounted incidents of white-collar crime exclusively or primarily in regional newspapers:

> A special committee was formed by the University of Colorado to investigate allegations that sex parties were used by the athletic department to lure prospective players. The investigation was launched following allegations from the district attorney and a civil lawsuit filed by one of three women who alleged they were raped during or after a 2001 party for recruits. The Colorado governor demanded answers, and the university's regents scheduled an emergency meeting to discuss the panel process and depositions taken in connection with the civil lawsuit. (*Tacoma News Tribune*, 2004a)

> Authorities in Pensacola, Florida uncovered a drug network operating out of an upscale Pensacola bar and various homes, and a prominent Pensacola couple was charged as a result of the investigation. Local prosecutors charged that cocaine was sold to influential members of the community, including a wealthy citizen who serves on the Pensacola Junior College Foundation's board of governors, two attorneys, an insurance agent, the owner of a real estate school, probation officer, teacher, dietician, restaurant manager, barkeep, chef, hair salon owner and a mental health counselor. (*Tampa Tribune*, 2004)

> A Boise, Idaho, dentist surrendered to authorities on two misdemeanor charges of sexual exploitation by a medical provider. He was accused of fondling female patients during dental work while they were heavily sedated. Boise police received at least 3 complaints about the dentist since December 1998. The charges were filed in connection with the most recent event that occurred in December 2003. (*Salt Lake Tribune*, 2004)

> On March 1, 2004, Runnemede, New Jersey appointed a new police chief. The former chief resigned a week after he was arrested at a local brothel where, authorities say, he was a regular customer. He

was charged with official misconduct and promoting prostitution.
(*Philadelphia Daily News*, 2004)

In Tacoma, Washington, a bridge builder was fined $10,000 for fail-
ing to control storm water at a construction site. Uncontrolled water
causes erosion and carries pollution downstream, potentially degrad-
ing water quality and harming aquatic life. The company was notified
of the problem four months earlier, but it failed to correct the situation as required. (*Tacoma News Tribune*, 2004b)

To judge from the number and seriousness of some of the crimes
reported by local newspapers, American citizens and, presumably, the
citizens of other nations as well live daily with large numbers of white-
collar crimes. The majority of them are mundane and do not cause
harm or extreme financial loss to large numbers of citizens.

Fraud is one of the most common forms of white-collar crime. Fraud
is committed when misrepresentation or deception are used to secure
unfair or unlawful gain. It occurs "when a person or business intentionally deceives another with promises of goods, services, or financial
benefits that do not exist, were never intended to be provided, or
were misrepresented. Typically, victims give money but never receive
what they paid for" (U.S. Department of Justice, n.d.:1). Because fraud
violates trust, its distinguishing characteristics are a stark contrast to
robbery, burglary, and other street crimes. Those who commit these
offenses must confront their victims or enter their homes or businesses,
but perpetrators of financial violence by means of fraud use staging
and talk to create the appearance of a routine transaction.

In organizational complexity and reach, fraud ranges from itinerant
vinyl siding scamsters to international banking crimes that can destabilize national economies. The number of Americans who are victimized
by fraud is large and greatly exceeds the number victimized by serious
street crime (Titus, 2000). A 1991 survey of 1,246 U.S. households
found that compared to crimes of burglary, robbery, assault, and theft,
"personal fraud . . . appears to be very common" (Titus, Heinzelmann,
and Boyle, 1995:65). Subsequently, a national survey found that
36 percent of U.S. households had experienced a fraud victimization
in the preceding twelve months (Rebovich, 1999). The Association of
Certified Fraud Examiners (2004) estimates that occupational fraud
against U.S. employers resulted in losses of $660 billion in 2004.

As with all forms of white-collar crime, many crimes of fraud are not serious, but others are enormously harmful to countless victims. There is surprisingly little systematic knowledge of those who commit it, but an increasing proportion of fraud is committed apparently by persons for whom it is a significant part of their income (e.g., Weisburd, Waring, and Chayet, 2001; Jackson, 1994; Shover, Coffey, and Sanders, 2004).

HIERARCHY AND CRIME

A substantial if undeterminable proportion of white-collar crime is committed by men and women whose lives are distinguished by some degree of *privilege*. They are privileged most importantly by a level of income that frees them from daily preoccupation with meeting basic material needs; fiscal precariousness and unceasing concern about it are largely alien to their worlds and lives. Dunk (1991:41) correctly notes the obvious, that "the necessity of paid labor and the fear of losing it dominate the lives of working-class individuals." Those who are free of this concern are beneficiaries of class inequality; they do not live in families where injury to the breadwinner can plunge all into material desperation in a matter of days. Instead, their automobiles start on command; their refrigerators and wine racks are adequately, if not amply, stocked; their homes are commodious, comfortable, and secure; and their children are well-clothed and well-fed. Material privilege is important because it shapes every aspect of life. It ensures both options at important stages of life and the leisure to evaluate them carefully.

Most who become white-collar criminals are privileged also by their location on the hierarchy of respectability. They hail from worlds where people do not do "dirty work." Dirty work is jobs or tasks that most people want carried out albeit they are undesirable to many and morally 'dirty' (Hughes, 1971a). Dirty workers hang drywall, collect and process household trash, clean the bodies and beds of nursing home residents, or guard prisoners. Dirty workers punch time clocks, and they are paid wages, which means their income is reduced by time spent away from the job. Many are required to submit to urine testing as a condition of employment, and their location while on the clock may be tracked and recorded by global positioning systems. Increasingly their use of computer facilities while at work is monitored by employers to ensure they do not "steal time" or indulge in unproductive pursuits (Snider, 2002). Many dirty workers have lost employer-provided health insurance, and other benefits have been reduced as well. The conditions of respectable employment and the recompense it yields differ conspicuously from what is commonplace in working-class worlds (Ehrenreich, 2002; Shipler, 2004).

It is characteristic of dirty work that years spent doing it gradually if imperceptibly can wear out the body or dull the senses:

> The rough days of labor by blue-collar [men and women] are written in the MRIs, CAT scans, and X rays they're forced to sit still for in pain-filled retirement – like models posing for the medical arts. Their wrecked insides tell the stories of bricks and blocks lifted, holes dug, and punishment absorbed. If your rough hands and stooped walk don't give you away, your ruined bones and tissue surely will. (Lubrano, 2004:115)

The respectability of white-collar criminals is taken for granted in large measure because they are good people and do not do dirty work. If they ever experience a feeling of being inconsequential in any larger scheme of things, it is fleeting and quickly supplanted by realization or belief that they count. Their privilege extends to the prompt, polite, and deferential response they receive from functionaries and business owners alike should they have problems that require assistance. In disputes with dirty workers or members of subordinate classes, their account of matters is given greater credence than the latter.

Material privilege also permits development of cultivated perspectives on public issues and culture generally. Their respectability and this are two reasons why when they are ensnared by the law white-collar criminals doggedly resist defining their actions and seeing themselves as criminal. The immediate response, one that is seen repeatedly in interviews with them or in their public pronouncements, is to construe arrest and criminal charges as "preposterous," "absurd," or "ridiculous." These are the reactions of persons who take for granted that no one would imagine they intentionally could do or would think about doing the acts with which they are charged. The privileged are confident their conduct and the reasons for it can be grasped adequately only through sophisticated and arcane interpretation beyond the capability of lay persons and prosecutors.

Privilege and respectability are not dichotomous variables, and it would be foolish to pretend they are. The members of any population – this is true particularly of large and demographically heterogeneous nation-states – can be arrayed on a continuum from the poorest and least reputable to the wealthiest and most respectable citizens. The expanse is extremely wide, encompassing minority single mothers with annual incomes of less than $10,000, attorneys, medical doctors with well-stocked investment accounts, and presidents of Fortune 500 corporations whose annual "compensation package" may exceed $100 million. The demographic characteristics and crimes of white-collar criminals, particularly when crime-based definitions are used, present an equally expansive range of backgrounds, occupations, and incomes. The challenge for explanations of white-collar crime is to account for variation in diverse offenders and offenses. Supporters of rational choice theory believe it does so.

FACES OF WHITE-COLLAR CRIME

It is easier to urge an interpretation of white-collar crime as choice than to demonstrate the empirical merits of this approach using systematically marshaled evidence. The obstacles to doing so are several, but none is more imposing than the shortcomings of official data on white-collar crime and criminals. Put simply, they pale in quality and comprehensiveness beside the bountiful and readily available data on street crime. The most important problem this presents is inability to measure with comprehensiveness or confidence the volume of white-collar crime. In other words, the principal dependent variable in white-collar crime research is undeterminable. The problems of examining white-collar crime do not end there (Geis and Salinger, 1998). They also extend to shortcomings in the most common research designs employed to examine white-collar crime and uncertainty about the validity of information collected by investigators.

Past research on white-collar crime includes a high proportion of case studies. Journalists and academics alike have provided detailed descriptions and post mortem analyses of some of the most arrogant, destructive, and costly white-collar crimes. Industries and organizations in which notable crimes or a pattern of criminality occurred have been examined as well. What is often obscured by attention to newsworthy white-collar crimes are the mundane individuals and crimes that comprise the lion's share of those that draw attention from regulators, police and prosecutors (Shapiro, 1983). The newspaper search alluded to earlier turned up ample evidence of these offenses and offenders.

What follows, however, are brief descriptions of five white-collar crimes and criminals that were reported to or became known to authorities in which investigation and sanctioning eventually followed: environmental crimes committed by Davis Pipe, homicides that occurred at Imperial Food Products, the crimes of Arthur Andersen LLP, sexual assaults committed by an elected public official, and fraud committed by an entrepreneur/owner of a mortgage company. The majority of cases were located close at hand; three occurred in Tennessee. The lesson here is that white-collar crime is so commonplace that most citizens can find examples of it easily without going far afield. These crimes illustrate the diversity and difficulties of uncovering and prosecuting it. Considered along with the reports from newspapers they are graphic evidence of the challenge faced by theoretical interpretations of diverse white-collar crimes.

Davis Pipe

Evans Creek traverses Sullivan County, Tennessee, and eventually discharges into the Holston River, the principal source of drinking water for Kingsport, Tennessee. Davis Pipe, an industrial plating firm, is located on the banks of Evans Creek. The company manufactures and fabricates stainless steel, alloy pipes, and fittings, but these processes generate "spent pickle liquor" (SPL), a hazardous waste that contains lead, nickel, chromium, and acids. Environmental law and regulations require that SPL be stored in holding tanks and disposed of properly. Davis Pipe used another method: it periodically pumped the toxic waste directly into Evans Creek. When large fish kills resulted, a concerned employee of the company notified the Federal Bureau of Investigation (FBI) and the Tennessee Department of Environment and Conservation (TDEC). TDEC called Davis Pipe and scheduled a routine inspection. At the same time, the FBI began surveillance downstream in Evans Creek using water monitoring devices. They also began camera surveillance from nearby hillsides and observed company employees dumping acid waste into the creek. The water monitoring devices then detected high concentrations of waste consistent with production processes at Davis Pipe. Once the illicit disposal was detected, FBI agents went onto company property and began interviewing employees. Criminal charges followed. During pretrial hearings, attorneys for Davis Pipe attempted to secure disclosure of all company employees who were interviewed by the FBI, but the U.S. Attorney successfully argued that disclosure would have a chilling effect on future investigations. Davis Pipe and two high-level managers were convicted of violating the Clean Water Act. The individuals were put on probation and paid fines while Davis Pipe paid a $400,000 fine and $1.8 million in clean-up expenses.

Imperial Food Products
On September 3, 1991, a fire swept through the Imperial Food Products chicken processing plant in Hamlet, North Carolina, trapping and killing twenty-five employees and injuring an additional forty. Workers in this poultry processing plant fried chicken nuggets, marinated partly cooked chicken breasts, and froze the processed chicken before shipping it to restaurants and other institutions. Plant equipment was aged, and maintenance personnel were kept busy repairing it. Despite a history of safety problems, employees of Imperial Food seldom filed complaints about working conditions. On the day of the fire, hydraulic fluid from a conveyor belt under repair sprayed over a gas-fired chicken fryer. A thirty-second fireball sent flames and dense toxic smoke through the plant. Employees rushed to escape from the inferno, but many were trapped inside the building. Plant owners had padlocked exit doors, ostensibly to prevent pilferage of meat by employees. After the lock on one door was broken from the outside, employees still could not exit because the door opened inward, and the doorway was so crowded with workers desperate to get out that it could not be opened. Many employees retreated to and eventually were trapped in a cooler. Fifteen employees perished there, and

subsequent photographs of its interior walls show bloody hand prints where they tried frantically and desperately to escape (Federal Emergency Management Agency, 1992; *New York Times*, 1991a). Subsequent investigation showed that nearly all the fatalities resulted from smoke inhalation.

Congressional committees later held hearings to examine the fire, its causes and consequences. The Federal Emergency Management Agency (FEMA) also studied the incident (U.S. Congress, House of Representatives, 1991a, 1991b). Official records and testimony before Congress revealed that although there were earlier fires at the Hamlet plant, safety precautions were minimal to nonexistent. A sprinkler system installed by previous operators of the plant had been damaged in an earlier fire and never repaired or replaced. Likewise, the plant did not have automatic shut-off technology, which would have stopped the flow of flammable liquids once the fire began. There was only one fire extinguisher near the chicken fryer, but it was not adequate to control the inferno that developed.

All of the Imperial employees interviewed by congressional committee staff expressed concern that if they had complained about the plant's poor conditions management would not have responded or would have retaliated against them. In testimony before the congressional committee, employees said they had received no safety training and that during the fire they could not find exit doors because they were unmarked, and the power went out. A witness said that locking the exit doors represented

> the most callous disregard for safety and health, particularly since locked fire exits are so fundamentally contrary to basic common sense safety principles. . . . [Y]ou don't need to lock a door from the outside to maintain security. For a few dollars cost, an inside push bar lock would have provided security and safety. For a few dollars cost. We all went through fire drills in our elementary and high schools. Everyone in this room is aware that you don't block egress through fire exits. (U.S. Congress, House of Representatives, 1991a:139)

Eventually, the state of North Carolina fined the company $808,150, and the plant's owner pleaded guilty to involuntary manslaughter. He was sentenced to nearly twenty years' imprisonment. As part of the plea agreement, charges against his twenty-nine-year-old son and the fifty-six-year-old plant manager were dropped (*Los Angeles Times*, 1992).

Arthur Andersen LLP

Founded in 1913, Arthur Anderson LLP was one of the largest accounting firms in the world. For decades after its founding, it was also an exemplar of ethical accounting practices and took pride in its reputation as such. At the suggestion of employees, by the 1960s, Andersen created a consulting division that worked with corporate clients to adopt and use computers and other technological developments. In time, the consulting division also began advising clients on business strategy and risk management. Next to its traditional auditing division, the consulting division grew rapidly, generated much greater income for the firm and enjoyed far more status. These changes did not come without problems:

> Along with the rise of consulting came a new focus on the bottom line. Accountants hired to audit a company's books were also expected to help persuade their clients to use the firm's consultants as well. By the 1990s, there were few firms willing to quit an account on principle.... [T]here was simply too much money at stake. Not surprisingly, accounting standards eroded, and accounting fraud mushroomed.... The pressure to generate fees was intense, and so was the pressure to hold on to clients. (McLean and Elkind, 2004:144–45)

Andersen figured in more than one high-profile corporate criminal scandal of the 1990s. When it signed off on financial statements reported by the Sunbeam Corporation that later proved to be fraudulent, the U.S. Securities and Exchange Commission (SEC) imposed financial penalties. In May 2001, Andersen agreed to a $110 million settlement with Sunbeam shareholders without accepting or denying blame (*Business Week Online*, 2001). Andersen also audited Waste Management's (WM) annual financial statements for more than two decades, and WM was regarded as one of its "crown jewel" clients. Until 1997, every chief financial officer and chief accounting officer in WM's history as a public company had previously worked as an auditor at Andersen. In 1991, Andersen assigned Robert E. Allgyer as its audit engagement partner with Waste Management, noting that he "had a 'devotion to client service' and had a 'personal style that ... fit well with the Waste Management officers" (U.S. Securities and Exchange Commission, 2001:5). In 1998, Waste Management (WM) acknowledged that it had lied about its earnings to the tune of $1.4 billion between 1993 and 1996. Throughout this period Andersen annually issued unqualified audit reports despite knowing that WM was cooking its books and hiding debt. On June 19, 2001, Andersen settled charges filed by the SEC (U.S. Securities and Exchange Commission, 2001) that it had played a part in the "misstatement" and agreed to pay a fine of $7 million. The settlement with the SEC once again came with no admission of wrongdoing by the firm or the partners associated with the case. Andersen and WM also paid more than $200 million to settle numerous shareholder lawsuits. The SEC subsequently reiterated that

> [a]n auditor's "ultimate allegiance" is to the corporation's shareholders and to the investing public, not to the Company's management or to its employment relationship with the client.... When an auditor fails to stand up to management in the face of improper accounting practices but instead issues unqualified audit reports on financial statements that it knows or is reckless in not knowing are materially misstated, the auditor betrays its allegiance to the shareholders. This conduct elevates management's interests over those of the shareholders and, when publicly revealed, injures not only the shareholders but also the investing public's confidence. (U.S. Securities and Exchange Commission, 2001:12)

By the late 1990s, Enron Corporation was one of Andersen's largest and most profitable clients; in 2000 alone, the Enron account generated $52 million, the majority of this for consulting service. David Duncan, the auditor responsible for Enron rapidly became an influential figure at Andersen. As Enron launched the series of fraudulent and criminal debt hiding structures that led to its downfall, Duncan and his employer signed off. When Andersen occasionally did object to an Enron transaction, it came under intense pressure: "There were times when [Enron managers] would ask that certain accountants who were not 'responsive' enough be moved, and Duncan complied" (McLean and Elkind, 2004:148). Later, when it appeared almost certain that Enron's transactions would face close and critical external scrutiny, attorneys at Andersen recommended that documents pertaining to its dealings with Enron be altered or shredded. An orgy of shredding ensued in which thousands of pages of material related to its dealings with Enron and its accounting work were destroyed.

A few months after Enron imploded, disclosures of similar accounting crimes occurred at WorldCom, another Andersen client and one of the world's largest supplier's of telephone and wireless services. Later events would show that WorldCom was the largest bankruptcy in U.S. history with recorded losses of some $40 billion (Callahan, 2004). Shareholder losses were much higher still. "The WorldCom debacle demolished what was left of Arthur Andersen's reputation" (Jeter, 2003:207).

After Enron's collapse, David Duncan and other executives pleaded guilty to criminal charges and agreed to cooperate with the government in exchange for a light sentence and immunity from prosecution in other cases. Andersen's criminal trial was the first to emerge from the collapse of the giant energy trader. Prosecutors said Andersen doctored or destroyed documents to thwart a federal probe of Enron's finances. Enron later issued a statement saying that "more than four years worth of audits and statements approved by Andersen 'should not be relied upon' " (*Business Week Online*, 2001:2). On June 15, 2002, Andersen was found guilty in a Houston, Texas, courtroom of destroying evidence in the Enron case. The firm promptly charged that the verdict was "wrong" and represented only a "technical violation" of law, but in October 2002, Andersen was sentenced to five years' probation and fined $500,000. In May 2005 the U.S. Supreme Court overturned the conviction. Many of Andersen's former partners are targets of lawsuits from shareholders left with near-worthless stock.

In the wake of its admitted malfeasance, Andersen's business plummeted. Commentators speculated that the Enron bankruptcy gave its clients "an excuse to flee [in hopes of avoiding] the heightened attention an Andersen audit might get in shareholder litigation or [from] fear their financial reports could draw more scrutiny from regulators if they're handled by Andersen" (*Business Week Online*, 2001:2). Andersen stopped auditing public companies after eighty-nine years in the business and cut its workforce from 28,000 to 1,000. It was a catastrophic fall for a firm that once was a trusted member of the "Big Five" accounting firms with offices throughout the world.

Judicial Sexual Assault

In 1992, a federal jury convicted David Lanier, a chancery judge and former mayor of Dyersburg, Tennessee, on seven counts of sexually assaulting women who worked in his courthouse or came before him with legal matters. Evidence suggested that Lanier had engaged in this pattern of conduct over a period of years and was referred to around the courthouse as "the Grabber" (O'Brien, 1996). One of the judge's victims, a twenty-six-year-old woman with a child custody case before him, testified that she was forced to perform oral sex on him in his chambers. Another victim, a juvenile court supervisor, said that Lanier grabbed her breasts and buttocks and pinned her to a chair. When she later confronted him about the incident, he demoted her. During the time he was committing sexual assaults in the county courthouse, the judge's brother held the office of county prosecutor. Federal officials eventually stepped in to investigate and prosecute Lanier. Prior to sentencing, the prosecutor cast Lanier as a criminal for whom "power was the aphrodisiac.... [Victims'] crying turned him on" (O'Brien, 1996:93).

Two years after he began serving his prison term, the former judge was ordered released after a federal appeals court ruled in favor of his petition. When the U.S. Supreme Court ordered the appeals court to reconsider its decision, Lanier was ordered back to prison. He chose to go on the lam, however, and was not located until two months later in Mexico, where he was living under an assumed name. When arrested, Lanier was picking up mail-order false identification papers. When returned to the United States he told the judge that his decision to flee was a "bad judgment call" (*Memphis Commercial Appeal,* 1992; *Washington Post,* 1997a). After his capture, Lanier wrote to the editor of a Memphis publication charging a "conspiracy to oust... him from his position on the bench" and also that his prosecution was "politically motivated from beginning to end." His prison sentence and fine, he claimed, violated the "Eighth Amendment [prohibition] against cruel and unusual punishment." The former judge concluded by declaring that he was innocent and had refused to "plead guilty to things I did not do" (*Memphis Flyer*, 1998:3).

Apple Tree Mortgage

As president of Apple Tree Mortgage (ATM), Shirley Harwood entered into an agreement with Union Planters Bank (UPB), a financial institution with main offices in Memphis, Tennessee. The bank would advance funds to Apple Tree to make mortgage loans to individual borrowers. Apple Tree and Shirley Harwood were to submit wire transfer requests to UPB on each loan they made, and the bank in return would wire the loan funds to a designated title company for benefit of the borrower. In 1998 and 1999, Shirley Harwood created at least eleven fraudulent real estate transactions and mortgage loans using fictitious borrowers and nonexistent addresses. The loans were supported with documents containing forged signatures and false financial, legal, and tax information. She then submitted from ATM to UPB requests for wire transfers in the name of the fictitious borrowers. When the loans were approved and funds were transferred (approximately $2 million) Shirley Harwood used domestic and foreign financial accounts to convert the fraudulently obtained proceeds for her own use.

In another case, Shirley Harwood and Dennis Sutherland, a broker employed by ATM, agreed to create false and forged documents to make it appear that a borrower had collateral that could be used to secure a loan from Credit Suisse Bank. In furtherance of their crimes, Dennis Sutherland traveled to the Kingsport, Tennessee, branch of Bank of America (BOA) and obtained BOA letterhead under false pretenses. He used a color copier to create forged letterhead and false "letters of credit" that appeared to have been issued by BOA. Dennis Sutherland forged signatures of two fictitious BOA employees and provided the false documents to Credit Suisse to convince it to lend approximately $4.5 million to the borrowers. When faxing these documents to Credit Suisse's offices in Lausanne, Switzerland, Sutherland altered the fax machine to make it appear they originated from Bank of America. Credit Suisse subsequently issued the requested funds. Dennis Sutherland also had a mobile telephone issued to him by Apple Tree Mortgage, and he and Shirley Harwood agreed that he would answer any calls placed to that phone as if he were BOA vice president "James Sullivan." Several days after the loan was generated, a loan officer at Credit Suisse became concerned that he had not received the original of one of the letters that was faxed earlier. When he was unable to contact "James Sullivan" after several attempts, the FBI was notified.

Shirley Harwood and her spouse were habitual and unlucky gamblers, and investigators documented that most of her criminal proceeds were lost in casinos. She was forced into bankruptcy and tried to hide assets in the process. Subsequently both she and Dennis Sutherland entered into plea agreements and pled guilty. Shirley Harwood was sentenced to ninety-seven months' confinement, and Dennis Sutherland was sentenced to thirty-seven months. Shirley Harwood subsequently appealed her sentence, claiming misapplication of federal sentencing guidelines in the plea agreement she consented to and signed. The appeal was denied.

LESSONS AND DISTINCTIONS

Case studies that provide the detailed investigation and understanding found in the foregoing examples are rare, but they may be indispensable for understanding white-collar crime and offenders. They are important particularly given the absence of extensive or reliable statistical data and the shortcomings of well-established research techniques as used in studies of white-collar crime. Case studies are important for analysis of white-collar crime albeit they are poorly suited for rigorous statistical testing. They can be used to generate or to cast doubt on tentative explanations. The challenge of developing credible interpretations and drawing general conclusions about white-collar crime is made difficult because it encompasses diverse types of behavior that differ on a host of variables.

Case studies, however, can open the eyes of the unaware to the nature and harmfulness of white-collar crime. The official and media attention devoted to sensational cases makes for a transparency and analytic thoroughness that is absent in less harmful if more representative crimes. What is learned from investigating high-profile cases can clarify and extend understandings that can be applied no less to the former. They also shed revealing light on the nature of oversight and media coverage of white-collar crime.

There is much about David Lanier and his conduct that is found repeatedly among white-collar criminals. What is striking particularly is the brazenness of his crimes – he assaulted victims in his judicial office – and the arrogance of his taken-for-granted belief that he would never be called to account. Like many white-collar criminals, Lanier was able to commit crime over an extended period of time before knowledge of it came to official attention. His refusal to acknowledge guilt is characteristic of white-collar criminals.

The criminal actions of managers at Davis Pipe show how unconcerned they were by oversight. They used notification of an impending state inspection as cue to speed up their toxic dumping. Employees did as they were told, which overrode any reluctance they may have had. Company managers must have operated under the assumption that employees would not turn in their bosses or notify authorities. No one imagined that of FBI investigators, water testers and other technicians would be ready or mobilized.

The catastrophe at Imperial Food Products and the attention it received brought to light a travesty of self-regulation and regulatory oversight by the state. Records maintained by North Carolina's occupational safety and health regulatory agency showed that although chicken processing is a high-hazard industry, the plant had not been inspected in eleven years (Aulette and Michalowski, 1993). The Imperial Food Products case also reveals much about the larger political-economic context of the tragedy. Other investigators (Wright, Cullen, and Blankenship, 1995) used it to examine media reporting on white-collar crimes. Their research shows that newspaper reporting changed over the months between occurrence of the fire and eventual disposition of the criminal charges. Initially it was interpreted as a regulatory failure, and only later was it labeled and reported as crime. By that time, however, reports had been reduced in size significantly and appeared in obscure locations in newspapers. Shirley Harwood and Dennis Sullivan were not sophisticated money launderers, but their criminal actions required investigators to expend considerable time and resources. Their motives are not unusual, and the conclusion to their case was predictable.

Individual and Organizational Crime

Many white-collar crimes are committed by individuals exclusively or primarily for personal benefit or objectives. The sexual assaults committed by David Lanier are examples. These are individual white-collar crimes (Clinard and Quinney, 1973). In the industrialized and postindustrialized world, however, individuals overwhelmingly are employed in and spend much of their waking hours in organizations. When they commit crime, they often do so exclusively or primarily as a means of accomplishing objectives thought important to their employer. These are organizational white-collar crimes. To talk of organizational white-collar crime is neither to reify a collectivity nor endow it with volitional properties (Cressey, 1995). Organizations act through individuals and groups. The crimes at Davis Pipe, Arthur Andersen, and Imperial Food Products are examples. The distinction between individual and organizational white-collar crime, however, does not deny that those who commit the latter also may benefit personally in some way from actions meant to assist their employers.

Corporate crime is a special case of organizational crime. It is distinguished from other forms principally by belief that the paramount importance of pure economic calculation coupled with distinctive structural and cultural features of corporations make them essentially criminogenic (Pearce, 2001). Among the first to assert this belief, Ross indicted corporations as entities that "transmit the greed of investors, but not their conscience" (1907:109).

Ordinary and Upperworld Crime

White-collar crime encompasses an immense and diverse range of offenses and offenders. The analytic approach employed in this book distinguishes crudely and arbitrarily *upperworld* and *ordinary* white-collar crime. These broad categories reflect significant differences in crime and equally significant differences in oversight and the application of penalties. Particular crimes may fall neatly into them or span the distinctions. Upperworld crimes are committed by very wealthy and respectable individuals as well as the crimes of powerful organizations, whether these be Fortune 500 corporations or state agencies. The offenders at Arthur Andersen made use of corporate respect and power garnered over generations. The deals and arrangements that led to its downfall were between some of the most powerful companies in the world, and charges were brought against executives at the highest levels. The crimes resulted from long-standing practices.

The Imperial Food Products deaths, the Davis Pipe dumping, and the crimes of David Lanier are more difficult to categorize. All represent abuse of power, but probably none of the defendants could reasonably be called "upperworld." Many people possess the status it would take to commit similar crimes. Sexual harassment occurs in many offices, and extortion or abuse by supervisors probably is not uncommon. Chaining building exits shows blatant disregard for the law, but serious violations of workplace safety standards occur routinely in places where work is dangerous and oversight remote.

Using commonsense understandings of organizational size, neither Davis Pipe nor Imperial Food Products had significant resources but neither was a large or powerful company. When crime was discovered, individuals central to criminal decision making were identified easily onsite. They were not in New York, London, or Tokyo, they could not plausibly deny participation, and the details of their criminal acts could be understood readily by a jury of ordinary citizens. Upperworld crime is complex by contrast, and it typically permits pretense of moral cleanliness and physical distance from victims.

The crimes of David Lanier and Apple Tree Mortgage are ordinary in their simplicity. The crimes of Arthur Andersen LLP illustrate some of the difficulties of identifying and prosecuting culpable individuals in high positions in large organizations. Prosecutors must consider the economic fallout that could result from bringing charges against a major corporation. The enemies they will make also merit consideration. The Andersen case shows how resolute officials can be when economic markets and investor confidence are harmed by criminal acts.

Upperworld crime is the research focus for many who investigate crimes of privilege, but the perpetrators of ordinary white-collar crime by contrast include many middle class citizens. They make up a "broad band of offending above the floor of crime usually associated with street crime with its base in an underclass, yet below, in some sense, the quintessential white-collar crime and criminals that usually receive media attention" (Weisburd et al., 1991:182). Embezzling bank tellers, tax-cheating small business owners, and corrupt county sheriffs come to mind, but ordinary white-collar crime remains a broad category. It is our hope that readers inclined by background to direct their gaze upward to crimes of the privileged and powerful will find merit in what is said about upperworld crime. Those more inclined to equate white-collar crime with "crimes of the middle class" may find value in what is said about ordinary white-collar crime, its perpetrators, and responses to it by private parties and the state.

CHAPTER TWO

Lure

Rates of white-collar crime vary temporally and spatially. Although we lack data needed to demonstrate this with precision, no one doubts what the outcome would be if adequate data were available. Why rates of crime fluctuate over time and why some geographic regions, occupations, and industries are plagued by more crime than others draws attention to the distribution of 1) criminal opportunities and 2) those predisposed or tempted to exploit them. In this chapter we explore the sources and allocation of lure, one of the twin components of criminal opportunity. Chapter 3 examines the supply of tempted individuals and predisposed organizations.

Lure is arrangements or situations that turn heads. Like tinsel to a child, it draws attention. Lure is a purse left unattended where there is heavy pedestrian traffic. It is cost-plus contracts between government and business firms. And lure is officers and representatives of Fortune 500 corporations doing business with officials of fledgling nations eager for investment and economic development. Lure need not be economic, however. It is also access to dependent and vulnerable populations, whether these be children, prisoners, the sick, the aged or economically marginal workers. Recall the Imperial Food Products fire. Because North Carolina is a right-to-work state, a high proportion of its workforce are not union members. Imperial's employees had little bargaining power with the company, and this probably contributed to the plant's unsafe working conditions. In the contemporary economy, a telling example of lure in human form is the availability of a ready supply of non-English-speaking illegal residents. In 2003, two plant managers of Tyson Foods, the world's largest processor of chicken, pleaded guilty to conspiracy to smuggle undocumented workers into the United States. The workers, who were paid $7.15 per hour, were employed at a Tyson processing plant in Shelbyville, Tennessee (*National Law Journal*, 2004).

Lure is not criminal opportunity, but in the absence of credible oversight it is. Lure does not evoke a uniform response either from individuals or organizations. Many remain blithely unaware of it – they simply do not see what is apparent to others – and most who do take notice of lure react with seeming indifference. Grandmothers come to mind. We know, however, that some who chance upon and take notice of lure turn their attention immediately to whether or not there is credible oversight. Lure makes the tempted and criminally predisposed sensitive to whether or not their actions are being monitored and how oversight might be defeated. Part of the attraction of many types of lure is the apparent ease of exploitation. In the postmillennia world this may require "not much more than the ability to read, write, and fill out forms, along with some minimum level of presentation of a respectable self" (Weisburd et al., 1991:182–83). Provision of health care services is an example. The treatment and services medical patients receive are converted by physicians and their assistants into billable hours reported on standardized forms submitted for reimbursement. Medicaid investigators regularly discover fraudulent claims; some psychiatrists bill for time spent having sex with patients (Jesilow, Pontell, and Geis, 1993). Offenders may have plans for dealing with unanticipated contingencies, but generally these are not complex. They recognize that in the unlikely event that officials put investigators on the trail, it is not difficult to stay ahead of or elude them entirely.

Changes in the forms and supply of lure have been pronounced in the half-century since World War II. These changes occurred not only in the United States but in other Western democracies as well, and while the time of onset and pace of development varies from one nation to another, what is true of the United States is true elsewhere.

TRENDS

In the century that has passed since Ross (1907) described how growing social and economic interdependence permits exploitation of

trust and crime commission at a distance from victims, these changes
gained speed and momentum. The expansion of state largesse, the
financial services revolution, and new technologies for information
sharing and financial transactions are major contributors. Expanding
private-sector provision of services once provided by government is
another. This is exemplified by private management of vulnerable and
problem populations. Last, globalization of political-economic relationships also has contributed to the growth and changing forms of
lure.

State Largesse
The decades following World War II saw the emergence or the expansion of state policies and corporate practices with enormous significance for white-collar crime. These include a fundamental shift in
the states's public welfare functions, which had the effect of expanding programs and subsidies for citizens across the income spectrum.
In constant dollars, the federal outlay for entitlement programs of
all kinds increased more than 1,900 percent between 1945 and 1995
(from $75 billion to $1.5 trillion) (U.S. Department of Health, Education, and Welfare, 1959; Social Security Administration, 1999). As
a result, by 1992, 51.7 percent of American families received some
form of federal payments. Their benefits range from social security,
Medicare, and military retirement benefits to agricultural subsidies
and student loans (Samuelson, 1995). In 2002 alone, U.S. corporations received $125 billion in government subsidies (Citizen's for Tax
Justice, 2003).

Federal health care initiatives have given pharmaceutical firms, hospitals, and doctors access to large sums of federal money. To the
surprise of few, Medicare has been designated a high-risk program
for fraud and abuse (U.S. General Accounting Office, 2000). Testimony before a Senate subcommittee in 1976 suggested that the system was "so bad that it virtually invites" crime (U.S. Congress, Senate,
1976:81). Of the $164 billion in Medicare fee-for-service payments
in 1999, an estimated $13.4 billion was paid improperly for reasons
ranging from inadvertent errors to fraud and abuse (U.S. General
Accounting Office, 2000). In addition to physician fraud, much of the
money is lost to fraud by health care facilities and nursing homes that

bill for services they do not provide. The schemes show endless variety. Revco Pharmacies, for example, was caught by the state of Ohio doctoring and resubmitting claims that previously were rejected. The firm hired personnel to assign new identification numbers to them, and the scheme came to light only after state employees discovered nonsequential and improbable numbers in claims submitted for reimbursement (Vaughan, 1983).

There is lure in the city and countryside alike. The Federal Crop Insurance Program (FCIP) is a major source of risk protection for farmers. It provides financial protection against crop losses from drought, flood, and other natural disasters. Corporate farmers and hobbyists are eligible for a variety of risk protection programs and subsidies. FCIP also protects insured farmers against both inability to plant and excessive loss of crop quality due to weather or other circumstances. In most cases, insurance covers loss of yield exceeding a deductible amount, but newer FCIP products also cover loss in yield value due to falling market prices during the insurance period. The crop insurance program is administered by private insurance companies that compensate insured farmers for losses during the crop year. Federal agencies set the terms, conditions, and costs of the insurance and subsidize the program by reinsuring participating companies. Taxpayers subsidize about half of producers' insurance premiums. The FCIP provided about $37 billion in protection and $2.8 billion in subsidies in 2001 (*Wall Street Journal*, 2003). From 1995 to 2002, the median payment for all farms was approximately $1,000 per year, but 1,290 farm operations each received in excess of $1 million. Seventy-one percent of subsidies went to 10 percent of recipients, most of which were large farms (Environmental Working Group, 2003).

There is great potential for abuse in the FCIP. In the simplest schemes, fields are insured against failure and the harvest from them is recorded as the product of another field owned by claimants or someone beholden to them. Farmers then collect indemnities for the field that "failed." While purchasers of commodities are meticulous about weights and moisture content, it is significant that crop insurance payouts often operate on the honor system and crop yield estimates (*Wall Street Journal*, 2003).

In 2003, federal inspectors general submitted testimony to Congress on areas of waste, fraud, and abuse in their agencies (U.S. Congress, House of Representatives, 2003). Criminal abuse is seen as a problem thoughout. Improper fee-for-service payments under Medicare were estimated to be $13.3 billion that year. Delaware overpaid health care providers $364,000 for medical services rendered to people who state auditors discovered were deceased (U.S. Congress, House of Representatives, 2003). In education, $300 million in Pell Grants were made to ineligible applicants because of incorrect income data; noncitizens illegally received $70 million in benefits. The U.S. Department of Defense overpaid $6.1 billion to contractors, and its purchase cards are abused to the tune of $97 million annually.

Governments from local to national use tax credits to stimulate business development, boost employment, and promote economic growth. Canada and Ireland provide tax incentives to encourage investment in films made in their countries; movie producers can receive credits equal to 15 percent of the production's total budget in Canada and 12 percent in Ireland (*Irish Times*, 1997; *Ottawa Citizen*, 2000). To qualify for tax credits movie producers must hire local directors, writers, technicians, and actors. Predictably, some producers responded by creating fictitious names for workers and claiming falsely that they were citizens. In 1998, a Canadian-based company reported a net profit of $21.8 million as it collected $21.5 million in government subsidies (*Gazette*, 2000). The same company was accused later of violating the law by substituting the names of Canadians and giving them credit for scripts written by U.S. citizens. It also refunded nearly one million dollars in unearned royalties after it falsely gave script-writing credit to the sister of its co-founder and chairman (*Ottawa Citizen*, 2000).

The National School Lunch Program (NSLP) is a federal and state reimbursement program that provides funds to local school districts for each meal served to students that meets federal requirements. All NSLP-participating school districts and schools are required to offer free and reduced-price lunches to eligible children, and each day the program provides meals and financial reimbursement for more than 26 million children nationwide. Milk is a staple in lunches provided under NSLP. Producers in the fluid milk industry have a lengthy history of submitting anticompetitive bids for providing milk to local school districts (U.S. General Accounting Office, 1992). Local school boards have neither the expertise nor procedures in place to conduct rigorous and thorough oversight of the bid process. They are easy marks. In the most recent wave of abuse, dozens of fluid milk firms in more than twenty states conspired to fix prices. In Florida alone, sixteen individuals and at least nine companies were convicted on antitrust charges (Fusaro, 1997; *Washington Post*, 1991). Price-fixing conspiracies operated for decades in some states.

The foregoing examples attest to the robust creation and expansion of state largesse in the decades after World War II. These developments occurred along with rapid growth of the domestic economy, which made available goods that either were unknown or were unattainable by most citizens just a decade earlier. Houses, automobiles, refrigerators, television sets, and a host of other commodities now were within the reach of a growing segment of the population. The disposable assets held by owners of these new commodities brought them into more diversified relationships with banks and financial institutions.

Financial Services Revolution

As workers enjoyed the benefits of an expanding economy and wage concessions gained in labor struggles, a new market emerged for insurance, credit, and investment products. To secure their material acquisitions against mishap, families purchased new comprehensive policies offered by insurance underwriters. Insurance companies competed aggressively for new policyholders. Coverage for loss of life, home, and business as well as damage to household items and vehicles became standard. Increasingly, the middle-class family now is insured against not only major hazards to life, home, and business but also loss of or damage to household items (Clarke, 1990). Figure 2.1 reports worldwide growth in the market for insurance in the years 1992–2002. The growth represents the amount paid for new policies by year in U.S. dollars for countries with more than $100 million in sales. There are several potential interpretations of these data, but the trend unmistakably is upward. This suggests continuing growth in the number of policyholders worldwide. Insurance creates lure and insurance fraud.

In addition to marketing more widely and aggressively their new products, insurance underwriters catered to customers by making

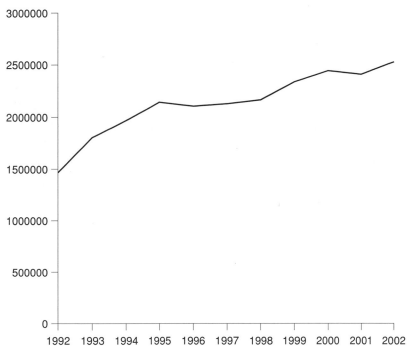

Figure 2.1. The World Insurance Market: Direct Premiums Written (in U.S. Millions), 1992–2002. *Source*: Insurance Information Institute, 2003.

claims processing less formal and time consuming. Investigation of suspected fraud was deemphasized. It is difficult to tell what the impact of these changes have been for all insurance fraud because estimates of its magnitude vary tremendously. One study, for example, put the cost of fraud to purchasers of automobile insurance at $100–$130 annually (Carroll, Abrahamse, and Vaiana, 1995).

Crime occasioned by the institution and dynamics of insurance is not entirely one sided; insurance companies have shown a capacity to turn their position to criminal advantage (Tillman, 1998). In the 1990s, they exploited loopholes in federal law and regulations governing health care coverage for workers in industries where most are uninsured. Predators created sham organizations to market health insurance, some under banners suggesting they were affiliated with trade unions or religious organizations. This exempted them from state and federal regulations. Typically, paid premiums were stolen until the plans were bankrupted. One scheme left 400,000 individuals

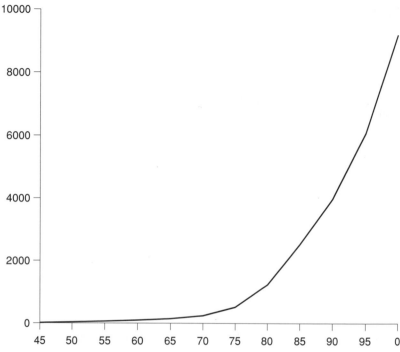

Figure 2.2. Total Consumer Credit Outstanding Per Capita (1980$), United States, 1945–2000. *Source*: U.S. Federal Reserve, 2004a; 2004b.

with $133 million in unpaid medical claims (Tillman, 1998). State officials had great difficulty combating these bogus plans, because they mirror the organization and operation of legitimate companies. Some now operate from off-shore (Tillman, 2002).

The white-collar lure produced by developments in insurance probably is exceeded several times over by the explosive growth of consumer credit. In 1980, total household liabilities for consumer credit were $350 million, and by 2004 they totaled $1.9 trillion (U.S. Federal Reserve Board, 2004a; 2004b). Fifty-million credit cards are issued annually in the United States, and members of the average household owe $7,000 in credit card debt (*Buffalo News*, 2004). On completing a baccalaureate degree, the typical graduate owes $16,000 in student loans and $2,000 in credit card debt (American Council on Education, 2001). Figure 2.2 shows changes in use of consumer credit in the United States after World War II. It shows that since 1980 the growth in consumer credit spending has been astronomical, and growing credit card fraud is the inevitable result (Levi, Bissell, and Richardson, 1991). "Credit cards produce credit fraud" (Weisburd et al., 1991:183). Even short-term changes in the availability of credit may be reflected in white-collar crime; mortgage fraud emerged as a problem in the United Kingdom in the 1980s following a rapid rise in housing prices, liberalization of lending regulations, and competition among lenders (Clarke, 1992).

American citizens began to turn away from passbooks and secure bonds in the 1970s when inflation outpaced their interest income, and an increasing number now invest. Their investments are more complex, volatile, and difficult to track than accounts traditionally provided by banks. Revisions to the *Internal Revenue Code* (IRC) created new mechanisms for deferring taxes on retirement savings. The changes to section 401 (k) of the IRC give these instruments their name. The proliferation of easy-to-use mutual funds that allow modest investors direct access to the stock market, diversification through indirect ownership, and investment advice occurred about the same time. The number of mutual fund accounts grew fourteen-fold between 1980 and 2000. The number of American stockholders has doubled, and half of all U.S. households hold at least some form of taxable stock (Investment Company Institute, 2002; Nadler, 1999). The wealthiest 10 percent of citizens hold 66 percent of securities (Azicorbe, Kennickell, and Moore, 2003; Investment Company Institute, 2003). Figure 2.3 shows the growing customer base for taxable equities in the United States for selected years from 1938 to 2002. This is a crude but not misleading indication of the growth of stock ownership. As can be seen in Figure 2.3, the trend is upward.

The rapid infusion of money into stocks along with widespread demand for speculative opportunities is a profound economic change, because eager but naive investors are lure. Just as street hustlers target those who seem out of place or confused, investment counselors and firms look to attract these "under-informed investor[s]," some of whom rely solely on their purchase recommendations (Levitt, 2002:43). Large investment firms built substantial profits from the new crop of investors. Brokerage houses that had banking relationships

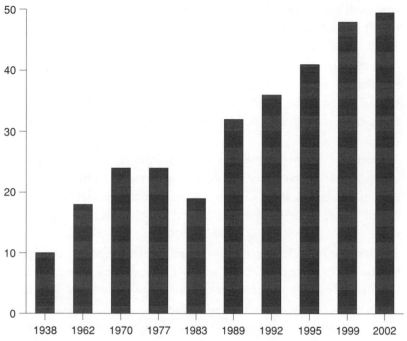

Figure 2.3. Percent of U.S. Households Invested in Taxable Equities by Year.
Note: Includes mutual funds and direct stock ownership. *Sources*: Investment
Company Institute, 1999, 2002; U.S. Federal Reserve 1962, 1970, 1977, 1983,
1989, 1992, 1995; Strunk and Cantril, 1951.

with publicly traded companies issued buy recommendations for their
corporate clients. Without admitting guilt, ten brokerage houses consented to pay $1.4 billion to settle charges of this type (Associated Press,
2003a).

Businesses now depend not only on sales of their products but also
on convincing investors of their growth potential. Firms have learned
to manipulate the price of their stock by criminal use of generally
accepted accounting practices (GAAP). This proved to be the downfall for Enron Corporation, which had promised investors growth of
25 percent annually (Eicherwald, 2005; McLean and Elkind, 2004).
These tactics generally exploit investors' tendency to rely on straightforward performance measures and mass-distributed news releases.
The line between aggressive accounting and fraud is not always easy
for outsiders to draw. The wave of corporate scandals and upperworld

crime of recent years are testimony to the financial victimization caused by fraudulent accounting practices.

Technology

Postindustrial nations have witnessed fundamental changes in communications technology and the dynamics of economic relationships (Adler, 1992; Lash and Urry, 1994). Widespread use of telecommunications and electronic financial transactions presage a depersonalized, cashless economy (Tickell, 1996). Electronic financial transfers among banks and businesses, automatic teller machines, and home banking increasingly are used around the globe. Through use of high-speed data networks, telephone lines, and satellites, funds and business accounts can be manipulated instantaneously over great distances. This development coincided with and hastened the emergence of "finance capitalism," a form of productive enterprise distinguished not by the manufacture of goods or services but instead by production of profit through the manipulation of financial accounts and derivatives trading (Calavita, Pontell, and Tillman, 1997a). Finance capitalism is the production of wealth through speculative transactions, all made possible by computer.

The computer changed everything. It made information storage, retrieval, and communication effortless, fast, and widely available in worlds where formerly they were cumbersome and time consuming. Ten percent of households in the United States owned personal computers in 1984, but this increased to half in 2000. In households with incomes of $75,000 or more, computers are as commonplace as toasters, and most also have Internet access (*Sacramento Business Journal,* 2001). Computers facilitate crime against individuals and organizations alike. Theft from organizations, for example,

> can be accomplished without breaking and entering. Records, secret information, funds and programs can be stolen. Assets can be shifted from one location to another. Large amounts can be taken in minutes, or resources can be slowly drained away over long periods. The presence of the offender is not required at the scene of the offense: electronic action can happen in the future, separated by time as well as space from the action of the individual. (Vaughan, 1983:78)

In the world of personal computers and virtual identities, individuals and organizations conduct business with remote others whose credentials and intentions cannot be determined easily. Generally, communications have become more impersonal and difficult to monitor effectively as exchanges based on face-to-face interaction yield to impersonal contact over digital networks. Parties may know one another outside of these transactions, but increasingly they do not.

Acquisition and possession of appropriate credentials is more important than ever. The process of verifying them, however, is not the easy matter it was when parties interacted personally or within geographically circumscribed and culturally shared worlds.

> When formal credentials, based upon grades, graduation, awards, and the like, become the basis for social evaluation and social status, there will be pressures to inflate the credentials, or to make them up when they do not exist. Thus, there is pressure to cheat on exams in the school system, pressure for puffery in the preparation of application forms, to make one's self out to be a little (or a lot) better than the formal record might legitimately allow. (Weisburd et al., 1991:183–84)

Online college degree institutions and programs are emblematic of what the pressures of credentialing have wrought. Pennsylvania's attorney general filed a civil lawsuit in December 2004 accusing four defendants of engaging in the fraudulent sale of bogus academic degrees. Posing as one Colby Nolan, undercover agents contacted the defendants online and purchased for $299 a baccalaureate degree in business administration from "Trinity Southern University." For an additional $99 they received a transcript that included Colby's graduation date, his student number, the courses he completed and his grades (all A's and B's). Colby Nolan is a pet cat (Attorney General, Pennsylvania, 2004).

State-funded vocational training programs are commonplace in many countries. On February 16, 2004, a regional councillor in Italy was arrested and charged with setting up fictitious job-training programs for the poor. The scams defrauded the European Union and Lombardy, Italy, out of three million euros. The accused councillor was under prior indictment for similar schemes and for providing kickbacks to officials in exchange for contracts. Two of his companies generated paperwork on fictitious program graduates by using personal information of people who had only expressed interest in job training (*ANSA Italian News*, 2004). In the United States, officials in California released results of an audit of Economic Employment Development Centers (EEDC). This corporate operator provides language training to immigrants and is paid according to its rate of employment placement. Auditors reviewed a sample of twenty-eight EEDC cases and found success was claimed fraudulently for seven (*Los Angeles Daily News*, 2004). California authorities suspected that millions of dollars were misappropriated in this and similar programs.

The escalating number of transactions between organizations also requires a high degree of trust and formalized monitoring procedures (Vaughan, 1982). Because organizations cannot afford to check for validity and accuracy all these transactions, computerized monitoring procedures typically are used to identify suspicious ones. Knowledge of how these screening processes work makes it possible for offenders to make their transactions appear routine so as not to attract attention (Sparrow, 1996). Just as rates of household burglary increased following the "miniaturization" and mass marketing of home electronic products, changing technology has created new forms of white-collar lure and made them available to a growing pool of citizens and organizations (Grabosky, Smith, and Dempsey, 2001; Weisburd, 1997). Thanks to desktop publishing, for example, official-looking documents can be produced easily and cheaply. In excess of $750 million dollars annually is lost to check counterfeiters by financial institutions (U.S. Department of the Treasury, 1999). Crimes that once were beyond the technical reach of street criminals are now within the grasp of citizens with vocational education and initiative.

Telemarketing illustrates some of the larger trends in commerce, communication, and white-collar crime. Telemarketing sales accounted for $611.7 billion in revenue in the United States in 2000, an increase of 167 percent over sales for 1995. Total annual sales from telephone marketing are expected to reach $939.5 billion in 2005 (Direct Marketing Association, 2001). The reasons for this growth are understood easily in context of the "general acceleration of everyday life, characterized by increasingly complicated personal and domestic timetables" (Taylor, 1999:45). The daily schedule no longer permits either the pace or the style of shopping that were commonplace a few decades ago, and the need to coordinate personal schedules and to economize on time drives many household activities. In the search for convenience, telemarketing sales gained in popularity, and criminals were quick to exploit it (Doocy et al., 2001; Shover, Coffey, and Sanders, 2004). There are countless variations on telemarketing fraud, but typically a consumer receives a phone call from a high-pressure salesperson soliciting funds or selling products based on untrue assertions or enticing claims. Callers offer an enormous variety of products and services, and often they use names that sound similar to bona fide charities or reputable organizations. Goods or services either are not delivered, or they are substantially inferior to what was promised (U.S. Congress, Senate, 1993).

Cyber crime threatens to become a global cottage industry (Smith, Grabosky, and Urbas, 2004). With attractive Websites, electronic bulletin boards, and online newsletters, Internet criminals attract and defraud others. An employee of a software company stole 30,000 passwords used by major financial institutions and sold them to a gang of credit thieves. The gang then used the passwords to create bogus credit accounts and plundered checking accounts to the tune of $3 million (*USA Today*, 2003). Given the variety of ways to access personal information made possible by the Internet, doubtless few were surprised by the rapid growth of identity fraud. In 2002, the Federal Trade Commission (FTC) received about 160,000 identity theft complaints, doubling the previous year's number. Auction fraud accounts for 61 percent of all complaints to the Internet Fraud Complaint Center in 2003, and the numbers show sharp and sustained increases (Internet Fraud Complaint Center, 2005). The U.S. Securities and Exchange Commission received 3,313 reports of online investment fraud from October 1, 1998, through September 30, 1999, a threefold increase from the number it received in the previous twelve months (Murray, 2000).

Legitimate business customers can be charged surreptitiously and fraudulently for unrequested products. In 2003, a class action suit against Microsoft Corporation and Best Buy, Inc. alleged that they charged customers for online services without their consent. Plaintiffs had used their debit card at a Best Buy store, but when the clerk scanned their purchases, a trial copy of software was scanned and included also. Customers mistakenly assumed it was scanned only to track inventory, but Best Buy sent their debit information to Microsoft, Inc. Microsoft activated an Internet account in the plaintiffs' name and began charging them a monthly service charge for use of the software. The plaintiff's attorney observed that "the ability of companies to charge people and actually take money from them without their knowledge is an interesting development and one that we are seeing more often, particularly through debit cards" (Cable News Network, 2003).

Telephone service providers moved quickly to exploit lure created by the computer and changes in telecommunications. Some create or alter customer contracts without their consent. Phone *cramming* is the practice by telephone service providers of adding unrequested services to phone contracts without customers' permission. Phone *slamming* is switching service providers without their knowledge. As telephone bills become more complex and confusing, consumers are less likely to detect these practices. Qwest Communications International paid $20.3 million in fines in 2003 for illegally adding customers and placing charges on thousands of bills in California. The state utilities commission reported that many violations occurred in Latino and Asian neighborhoods where language barriers facilitated the fraudulent practices (*Los Angeles Times*, 2003).

The Internet also has changed how child pornographers operate; sexual exploitation has entered a new era. A 2004 investigation begun by U.S. authorities of a Website run by Russian organized crime figures led to cooperation by law enforcement in twenty nations and the arrest of individuals around the world. More than 190 Australians including known sex offenders, childcare workers, police officers, and government officials were charged (*Melbourne Herald Sun*, 2004). Most were in possession of downloaded child pornography, but some were producing and distributing it across national borders.

Managing Vulnerable/Problem Populations
In the United States, *privatization* of government generally means contracting for services that formerly were provided by public agencies and employees. The rate at which public services are transferred to contractors fluctuates and varies considerably by service, but it has

increased in the last decade. "More and more governments have been inviting private firms to compete for contracts to provide services once restricted to public sources. This practice, also known as competitive sourcing, has been embraced as an effective policy tool for driving change in organizations, improving performance and restraining costs" (McMahon, Moore, and Segal, 2003:5). The Federal Acitivities Inventory Reform Act was passed in 1998 and requires U.S. government agencies to identify commercial activities and open them to competition from private contractors. In fiscal year 2003, agencies studied the benefits of contracting for services provided by 17,596 full-time equivalent employees and determined in eleven percent of 662 assessments that outsourcing was the appropriate route (Office of Management and Budget, 2004). Privatization has been pronounced particularly at the state level (Boardman, Laurin, and Vining, 2003).

The changing functions and declining size of the nuclear family over the past half-century is accompanied by emergence of specialized institutions that perform functions once performed at home or by the state. The living situations of elderly widows are illustrative. At the start of World War II, 18 percent of elderly women lived alone, 59 percent lived with adult children, and 3.7 percent lived in group quarters. By 1990, 62 percent lived alone, 20 percent lived with adult children, and 10 percent lived in group quarters (McGarry and Schoeni, 2000). The result is the nursing home industry. Care-giving services are provided on a contractual basis by private companies paid by the family or state. There are more than 16,000 nursing homes in the United States with 1.8 million beds and an occupancy rate exceeding 80 percent (U.S. Center for Disease Control, 2003). About 53 percent of U.S. nursing homes are for-profit operations, and nearly half are run by companies with two or more facilities (U.S. Department of Health and Human Services, 2002). Child care and the nursing-home industry are examples also of the rapid growth of new institutions that care for family members. There are more than 100,000 childcare facilities in the United States. Kindercare and other corporate preschool firms now watch more than 100,000 children daily.

Cost-cutting is key for companies that provide nursing home and child care. Their low-ranking employees are paid much less than state employees who perform comparable work. Operating procedures that enable corporate service providers to operate below cost schedules stipulated in contracts is a major form of lure. Clients processed by or held in institutions may be incapable of bringing to the public's attention reports of improper treatment or care that falls below contractual standards. Negligence is common, but complaints are easily dismissed or ignored. Seventy-three percent of nursing-home residents pay for their care with Medicaid and Medicare funds, and nursing-home managers have access to their personal information (U.S. Department of Health and Human Services, 2002). Since many patients are incapable of checking their statements, they can be billed for services, medicines, and supplies they do not receive (Sparrow, 1996).

In addition to financial fraud, conditions in the childcare and nursing-home industries open the door to criminal abuse and client neglect. In Memphis, Tennessee, a toddler left in a van outside a state-subsidized childcare center died in the heat. The state investigation that followed showed that the daycare facility received $3.5 million in state funds between 1995 and 2002, much of which was stolen. The board that was supposed to oversee facility operations never met, but board "minutes" were fabricated by one embezzler to justify expenditures. The owners of the daycare facility were convicted of twenty-nine counts of fraud, theft, money-laundering, filing false tax returns, and tax evasion (*Memphis Commercial Appeal*, 2004).

A Wisconsin nursing home and one of its administrators were prosecuted successfully for homicide by reckless conduct after a seventy-eight-year-old resident walked out into the frigid air of a Milwaukee night, trudged through deep snow, climbed a fence, collapsed, and froze to death. The incident was not discovered until the following morning, but the last entry in the patient's chart reported that he was "checked every two hours" during the night, "no problems" were encountered, and he "slept well" (Schudson, Onellion, and Hochstedler, 1984:131). In subsequent hearings and trials, evidence showed that staffing levels, supplies and care at the facility for "mentally retarded, elderly and infirm patients" had deteriorated to where they jeopardized the "health, safety and welfare of the patients" (Schudson, Onellion and Hochstedler, 1984:133). On the night when the death occurred, one nurse and two aides were responsible for three wards with more than 200 patients. Highly publicized cases of abuse and neglect are uncommon. So long as there are no dead bodies or persistent reports by investigative journalists, the public remains happily unaware of or unconcerned with crime that exploits the elderly, prisoners, the mentally challenged, and illegal immigrants.

The drive to reduce the size of government and economize on services causes officials at all levels to contract with corporations for services as diverse as public security, debt collection, and public sanitation (Christie, 2000). In 1980 there were only a few private prisons in the United States, and they housed approximately 3,000 of the nation's inmates. Twenty years later there were 150 privately operated jails and prisons (Tabarrock, 2002). There were 94,361 residents in state or federal prisons run by private companies in 2003, representing 6.5 percent of the nation's prisoners. The vast majority are housed by a few large companies (U.S. Department of Justice, 2003). Wackenhut Corrections Corporation and Corrections Corporation of America (CCA) are prominent among then. The former operates sixty-nine correctional facilities and the latter sixty-five. CCA settled a 1999 lawsuit by prisoners for $1.6 million and $756,000 in legal fees after a federal court found that its failure to classify prisoners properly had led to "mixing predators and their prey." A high rate of violence in an Ohio facility that housed out of state inmates was the result (*Washington Post*, 1999).

Companies in the corrections business compete aggressively for state contracts, and when bids can go no lower, some resort to other means of securing contracts. Bribery is not unknown. In New York state, Correctional Service Corporation (CSC) provided free chauffeur-driven limousine rides to state lawmakers. Some legislators later billed the state for thousands of dollars in travel mileage for these trips. The vice-president of CSC acknowledged later that his company provided free transportation for campaign workers and assemblymen as well. One legislator received perks estimated to be worth $2,000 per month. Seventeen of twenty-two employees of a halfway house operated by CSC worked in various election campaigns. They later said that although they did not contribute money to the campaigns, their names appeared on contributor lists. This suggests that others gave money in their names (*New York Times*, 2003b). When an investigation into these illegal campaign contributions was launched, CSC agreed to pay $300,000 in lieu of a $250,000 fine and a seven-year ban on lobbying (*New York Daily News*, 2003). Officials in other states likewise have been convicted of influencing legislators to transfer prisoners to their facilities (*Atlanta Journal Constitution*, 2003).

Globalization

Globalization designates the increasing number and complexity of political-economic relationships that cross national borders. Economic indicators make clear that it is on the march (Baca, Garbe, and Weiss, 2000; Brahmbhatt, 1998; Brooks and Del Negro, 2002; Cavaglia, Brightman, and Aked, 2000; Forbes and Chinn, 2003). Increasingly, when nations fail to curb emergent forms of white-collar crime the effects ripple throughout the world. This happens, for example, when unrestrained business and trading practices cause international catastrophes. Albania's economy was brought to its knees in 1997 by a widespread investment fraud that caused a run on banks and frustrated foreign investors trying to stabilize its economy (*Washington Post*, 1997a).

The expanding and diversifying international financial sector arguably will be the most significant source of globalization in the future. Measures of foreign direct investment (FDI) surpassed $700 billion in 2002 (United Nations, 2004). While some of the connections and contracts between capitalists throughout the world occur through face-to-face meetings and government liaisons, most occur via telephone and trading computers. Modern communications allow investors to react instantly, to partner with people they will never meet, and to exploit changing state policies and market fluctuation. Between 1982 and 1987, there was a "remarkably sudden globalization of securities markets; in the U.S., foreign securities transactions increased ten-fold" (Braithwaite and Drahos, 2000:153). In 2002, seventy foreign companies entered U.S. public markets for the first time, and the stock of 1,300 foreign companies now trade there (United Nations, 2004). Wealth in all its forms moves across borders at an unprecedented pace, and national economies are connected in the process. Transnational corporations (TNCs) are major actors in furthering political and economic globalization. Their power is increasing. Of the fifty largest economies in the world, fourteen are TNCs and thirty-six are countries (United Nations, 2004:99). Economic links between nations occur through these TNCs and governments depend on these links.

Easy access to large pools of potential victims is an obvious consequence of globalization. Around the globe they can be reached in mass electronic mailings requesting bank account numbers, for example. Brokers may fraudulently represent their investments in foreign-language press releases sent abroad. Off-shore victims may have little recourse against remote and anonymous predators.

The criminal machinations of Alan Teale are illustrative of developments in white-collar crime made possible by globalization. Teale operated insurance firms from locations offshore and specialized in selling U.S. residents bogus insurance policies (Tillman, 2002). After a long career in Europe, he emigrated to the United States and went to work for a Florida insurer that later went bankrupt. Teale then set up shop in Atlanta, Georgia, where he helped found dozens of supposedly independent insurance companies. The companies collected premiums from policyholders and shifted money through a complex chain of corporate entities. When policyholders tried to file claims, they were met with a runaround that could busy a law firm for months. Each company would blame another for failing to pay and claim that they too had been victimized. If regulators got too close to one of the companies it folded, and its proprietors set up new ones. Teale and a partner also used worthless securities to start a reinsurance company, but when regulators discovered that the company had leased the securities that comprised its claimed assets, it was shut down. His partner went to prison, and Teale eventually met his downfall as well; when an insurance scheme in Pennsylvania left $5 million in unpaid claims, he was sentenced to seventeen years' imprisonment (Tillman, 2002). He and his many partners operated on a grand scale, but there must be hundreds if not thousands like him. They are aided by the difficulties of investigating transactions across borders and by the massive stream of legitimate commerce they mimic.

Trade agreements among nations create new economic production and trading entities, and lure is created in the process. Agricultural subsidies in the European Community designed to ensure quality as well as stable production and incomes for farmers are an example. In one scheme, vineyard owners took advantage of subsidies paid for withholding surplus wine from the market. They supplemented their supposed local production with clandestine purchases made abroad and then used cellars full of this inferior product as basis for collecting payments (Clarke 1993; Passas and Nelken, 1993). Misrepresentation of quality, origin, and destination of goods can be a profitable venture. The United States, Canada, and Mexico adopted the North American Free Trade Agreement (NAFTA) in 1992. This compact significantly reduces restrictions on trade across their common borders, but in order to qualify for NAFTA treatment, goods must meet specific origin criteria. Merchandise produced in a country other than Mexico or Canada generally does not qualify for NAFTA treatment upon entry into the United States. Just as farmers and agribusinesses quickly learned how to profit criminally from European Union regulations, firms closer to home have learned how to profit criminally from NAFTA. In one investigation, a company and its principal officers pled guilty to customs fraud and marketing violations related to the undervaluation and removal of country of origin markings on medical equipment imported into the United States (*Los Angeles Times*, 1991).

As TNCs acquire interest in the affairs and economies of distant nations, largesse flows increasingly across borders, much of it is in the form of international aid. It flows, for example, from Western nations to developing countries for humanitarian reasons and economic stabilization. The United States has given about $10 billion in foreign aid annually in recent years (*World Almanac*, 2003). Two executives of the U.S. Agency for International Development defrauded the program of $700,000 (U.S. Congress, House of Representatives, 2003). Aid goes to corrupt governments and noncorrupt alike. While some nations manage aid better than others, the United States is more likely to aid corrupt governments than most (Alesina and Weder, 2002). Embarrassing if not criminal incidents sometimes result; soccer stadia paid for by international contributions were venues for public executions by the Afghan Taliban government in the 1990s. More than $20 million deposited by embassies and international aid agencies in a Bosnian bank vanished (Schaefer, 1999). Russia's Central Bank transferred $1.2 billion received from the International Monetary Fund to a shell company known as Fimaco in order to bolster balance sheets and support Boris Yeltsin's presidential election campaign

(Schaefer, 1999). As the world becomes smaller and economies link, criminal opportunities increase for ordinary and upperworld offenders alike.

LURE PRODUCTION AND ALLOCATION

Constituencies across the spectrum of wealth and respectability, make diverse demands on the state, and many are demands for lure of one kind or another. Lure production is a thoroughly political process, and inequality is a major constraint at every step. Although the supply of lure has been expanded for increasing numbers of citizens and organizations, privileged citizens and large corporations are prime beneficiaries. They demand access to tax coffers, protection from market forces, and freedom to conduct their affairs unencumbered by oversight. In return, the state routinely makes available to them an astounding array of tax incentives, subsidies, low-interest loans, and other forms of access to public funds. Superfund was created by Congress in 1980 to identify and clean up hazardous waste sites in the United States. The costs are paid by federal and state governments and by corporations responsible for decades of improper toxic waste disposal. Program implementation has been contentious, and the environmental benefits of Superfund are unclear:

> Guided by the social judgment to make polluters pay, regulators attempt to impose costs on responsible parties, who in turn resist these efforts. The resulting conflict generates substantial enforcement and litigation and delays cleanup. . . . Increased costs combined with reduced benefits compromise program efficiency. (Barnett, 1994:49)

Many parties benefit financially from Superfund, but attorneys are in the front ranks. Although they are compensated by funds set aside for cleanup, the size of their fees hinges on the degree of conflict. There are few checks on the bills they submit in any case, which caused some to call Superfund a "welfare program for lawyers" (Barnett, 1994:41).

The Canadian Scientific Research Tax Credit program was established in 1984 to stimulate scientific research and development. It was discontinued ten years later after reports that nearly half of the

$3 billion spent to that date was lost to impractical or scientifically suspect projects (*Ottawa Citizen*, 1994). In the United States, presidential decisions and congressional legislation during the 1980s made available to savings and loans institutions larger pools of money along with liberalized federal deposit insurance coverage. The savings and loan industry became attractive to aggressive entrepreneurs without knowledge of or experience in banking. A beneficiary of state policies and changes in oversight of savings and loan institutions recalls that

> I was absolutely amazed at how easy it was to suddenly own an S&L in Little Rock, especially when neither Jim or I had any expertise in running one. This pretty much summed up the attitude toward S&L ownership in the 80s. They required a ton of documentation for a person to get a loan or to wire money, or even to open a checking account, but any idiot could own and run an S&L. (McDougal and Harris, 2003:79)

The result of changes in the regulatory environment of the savings and loan industry was one of the costliest waves of public fraud in modern history (Calavita et al., 1997a).

The state is pressed increasingly to create new forms of lure, and elites insist theirs be provided without oversight. These dynamics are clear when powerful TNCs negotiate with the weak governments of impoverished nations. States offer them development and recruitment packages and promise to maintain a pro-business environment. In return, government officials may receive illegal tribute, and protection of local populations sometimes is sacrificed (Friedrichs and Friedrichs, 2002; Passas, 2000). Few dispute that TNCs get more than their share of aid or that oversight is lax. This caused one newspaper editorial commentator to remark that "[t]here is one, increasingly strict rule for broad social welfare policies, such as unemployment assistance, health insurance and tertiary education. But the rules governing incentive payments to business – what can fairly be called corporate welfare – are as loose and as easily abused as ever" (*Sydney Morning Herald*, 1999:A18).

Lure is made easier to exploit anytime powerful constituencies negotiate the terms under which they will submit to government initiatives they regard as contrary to their short-term interests. In the United

States, the federally funded Medicare program provides health care benefits to the elderly while Medicaid, which is funded by the states, provides health care to the needy. The programs were created by Congress in 1965. In encouraging them over stiff resistance from the American Medical Association, administrative and congressional leaders said little about their potential for fraud and abuse because they "feared a wholesale unwillingness on the part of disgruntled physicians to participate in the . . . programs" (Jesilow et al., 1993:44). Program advocates responded to physicians' concern that participation would encumber them with red tape with an implicit promise that doctors and their office managers would not be bothered greatly or questioned in the exercise of their professional judgments. As this chapter has shown, this is not the only area of commerce and services that has witnessed a burgeoning growth of lure without corresponding increase in credible oversight. The next chapter takes up the problem of accounting for the large and growing pool of those willing to exploit lure.

CHAPTER THREE

The Predisposed and Tempted

Criminal opportunities are arrangements or situations that offer potential for criminal reward with little apparent risk of detection or penalty (Coleman, 1987). Opportunity is in the eye of the beholder, but there is an objective and commonsense aspect to many criminal opportunities. This is why a high proportion of adults see and recognize it in similar circumstances. It is the reason we are cautioned, and we recognize wisdom in the admonition not to leave our automobile keys in the ignition switch or leave attractively wrapped gifts in plain sight while away from our cars. Regardless of how legitimate and convincing telephone callers may seem, the prudent do not give their checking account number to strangers. Widely shared understandings about situations where one is vulnerable are the reason secretaries who are harassed sexually by day do not work overtime. Criminal opportunities are found throughout the diverse spheres and routines of everyday life, but they cluster in the workplace.

The availability of lure is a key determinant of the supply of opportunities for white-collar crime, but for a high rate of crime to occur opportunities must be coupled with an ample supply of individuals and organizations who are aware of their existence and prepared to exploit them. The sources and precise nature of what distinguishes the criminally predisposed is varied, and it differs for individuals and organizations. Organizations that are *predisposed* to exploit lure are distinguished by structural, cultural, or procedural characteristics that increase the odds that their personnel will recognize and exploit lure. Tempted individuals possess qualities or experiences that make them more likely than peers who lack these distinctions to weigh exploitation of lure. Research into the lives of street criminals has shown that some go about their daily activities alert to and searching for criminal opportunities while others pay little attention to these unless they encounter something that piques their interest (Shover, 1996). The same is true of white-collar criminals (Weisburd et al., 2001).

The supply of predisposed organizations and tempted individuals varies temporally and spatially even as the pool from which it winnows grows larger. Reiss and Tonry (1993:1) point out that "[p]erhaps the most striking revolution of the twentieth century was the rapid expansion of the population of organizations." In the United States, the number grew fivefold between 1917 and 1969, and in the past three decades alone it tripled (Coleman, 1982; Internal Revenue Service, 2003). As a result, "the population of profit, not-for-profit, and governmental organizations in the United States rivals in number the population of individuals" (Reiss and Tonry, 1993:1). As for individuals, the proportion of the U.S. workforce reporting white-collar employment increased from 18 percent in 1900 to more than 60 percent in 2003 (U.S. Department of Commerce, 1975; U.S. Bureau of Labor Statistics, 2003). There appears to be no shortage of potential recruits to white-collar crime.

The backgrounds and characteristics of those who step forward to take their place in the ranks differ conspicuously from what is typical of street criminals. Indisputably, they are more advantaged by material circumstances and respectability. The full extent of their advantage is obscured substantially when crime-based definitions of white-collar crime are used, because this approach inevitably counts as white-collar criminals many of modest circumstance (Weisburd et al., 1991). Demographically, a minority are nearly indistinguishable from street offenders, and a surprisingly high proportion of those convicted of crimes of deception are unemployed when they offend (Daly, 1989).

That said, white-collar crime, regardless of how it is defined, generally is not committed by working-class citizens. Middle-class parental homes are characteristic of a substantial proportion of its perpetrators. In one sample, 15 percent came from families that had trouble providing necessities, but the same was true of 25 percent of street offenders (Benson, 2002; Forst and Rhodes, 1980). In the larger

TABLE 3.1. *Characteristics of individuals sentenced for federal street crimes and white-collar crimes, United States, 1995–2002*

Characteristic	Street offenders[a]	White-Collar offenders[b]
Race (percent African American and Hispanic)	48.5	32.3
Gender (percent male)	92.8	72.7
Education		
Less than high school	38.6	17.1
High school graduate	39.7	28.7
Some college	18.4	30.2
College graduate	2.8	19.5
Age		
Under 21	10.4	1.6
21–30	41.8	24.6
31–40	29.1	29.4
41–50	15.7	25.0
50+	7.2	20.5
Average age	31.8	44.2
Average Number of Cases Annually	2,600	8,205

[a] Includes defendants convicted of murder, manslaughter, assault, robbery, burglary, and auto theft.

[b] Includes defendants convicted of fraud, embezzlement, bribery, tax offenses, antitrust offenses, and food and drug violations.

Source: U.S. Sentencing Commission, *Sourcebook of Federal Sentencing Statistics* (1997–2004).

scheme of sophistication and seriousness, telemarketing offenders and their crimes are a long way from upperworld criminals. They enjoy a measure of privilege nonetheless. Research shows that overwhelmingly they are products of parental homes in which financial circumstances were secure if not comfortable. Information on their educational attainment also shows a level of achievement beyond what is true of street criminals; of forty-seven interviewed, eight dropped out of high school, but most graduated. Twenty-one attended college, and five held baccalaureate degrees (Shover, Coffey, and Sanders, 2004). Other research likewise shows white-collar criminals are better educated than street offenders (Benson and Moore, 1992).

Table 3.1 compares characteristics of individual white-collar criminals and street criminals sentenced in U.S. District Courts in the years 1995–2002. It confirms what has been said about differences between white-collar and street offenders. It shows that as compared with the

latter white-collar offenders are significantly older and better educated. Since these data describe *convicted offenders* they cannot be generalized to the larger population of ordinary white-collar criminals; a
high proportion of white-collar crimes go unnoticed or unreported,
and there is no way of determining whether the perpetrators of these
crimes share the characteristics of convicted offenders. Nevertheless,
confidence in the picture presented by Table 3.1 is strengthened by its
similarity to other reports (Benson and Kerley, 2001). Table 3.1 also
attests to the democratic implications of defining white-collar crime
using crime characteristics; where gender and race are concerned, differences between white-collar criminals and street criminals are surprisingly narrow.

Interestingly, Table 3.1 shows that federal courts sentenced substantially more white-collar criminals than street criminals during the
period 1995–2002. Some of this counterintuitive pattern is explained
by the fact that the category "street criminals" as employed there does
not include drug offenders, who comprise an enormous proportion
of sentenced federal defendants. Part of the reason also may lie in
strengthened federal efforts against white-collar crime in the years for
which the sentencing data are reported. Prosecutions of white-collar
defendants increased somewhat toward the close of the 1980s. Last,
there are comparatively few *federal* burglars and robbers but many
fraudsters; the former generally violate state laws while the latter's
schemes typically involve use of the mails, telephone, and Internet, all
of which are hallmarks of federal violations.

The backgrounds of upperworld offenders are another matter. They
are the most privileged of white-collar criminals, and their roots likely
are in wealth and high status. Many have elite family pedigrees and
educational credentials. They are more likely than ordinary white-
collar criminals to belong to exclusive social clubs and to move in
high circles. Probably they are older on average than ordinary white-
collar offenders and much older than street criminals. The ranks of
upperworld offenders almost certainly include very few members of
racial or ethnic minority groups.

As compared with what is known about the characteristics of individual white-collar offenders the picture of organizational defendants is
less clear. Data on 601 organizations sentenced in U.S. district courts in

1988 and 1989 show that 90.7 percent are closely held companies; only 8.2 percent are publicly traded firms. Less than 1 percent of sentenced organizations are nonprofit (U.S. Sentencing Commission, n.d.). In the United States, organizational defendants are prosecuted generally for fraud and antitrust offenses; these offenses account for 57.2 percent of the total. Environmental offenses comprise 9.3 percent. "The typical case [of convicted organizational crime] is a fraud that involves a loss of approximately $30,000" (U.S. Sentencing Commission, n.d.:3). What has been learned about organizational noncompliance from studies in both the United States and other nations suggests that smaller firms are more likely than larger ones to be singled out for investigation and prosecution (Shover, Clelland, and Lynxwiler, 1986; Grabosky and Braithwaite, 1986). This appears to be true of organizational criminals sentenced in U.S. district courts. This does not mean that they are more likely than larger ones to commit crime.

GENERATIVE WORLDS

The backgrounds of white-collar criminals are tilted conspicuously toward the middle and upper classes. Children of these worlds have little material need, yet many appear as ready recruits to white-collar crime. Products of privilege and location in the class structure where personal respect is granted routinely and rarely disputed openly, they also exploit positions of organizational power. The ease with which the products of privilege turn to crime suggests there may be qualities and pathologies in their *generative worlds* that are functional equivalents of family conflict and deprivation that figure prominently in the early lives of street criminals. Whether at home, at school, or engaged in leisure activities, social and cultural conditions of middle-class life appear to generate ample and probably increasing numbers of individuals prepared to commit white-collar crime. Hagan (1992) notes that both social power and risk taking characteristic of privileged classes may contribute to crime and delinquency in children from these worlds. Others point out as well that social class "alters a variety of life contexts and chances" from differences in economic opportunities to culture, and this can increase delinquency by privileged youth (Wright et al., 1999:178). The sources of variation in the

supply of predisposed organizations probably is explained by factors
that overlap only in part with these.

Crime and other forms of rule breaking spring from a remarkably
small number of base motives and meanings. This is obvious given
what is known, for example, about compliance with regulatory rules.
Kagan and Scholz (1984) point out that some business owners – the
authors dub them "amoral calculators" – willfully violate regulatory
requirements in a calculated fashion. "Organizational incompetents"
violate because managers and employees either do not understand
what they are required to do or else they lack the competence to comply. A third group of firms – Kagan and Scholz call them "political
citizens" – violate because of principled disagreement with the rules.
Valerie Braithwaite and her colleagues (2001) likewise find that citizens approach the requirement to comply with tax law from a variety
of "motivational postures." Many citizens and business owners comply
because either they are committed to the obligations of citizenship or
because they have no way of avoiding compliance. Taxes owed by wage
earners, for example, generally are withheld from their weekly pay by
the employer and sent to the tax collector. Among those who do not
comply with tax law, some are disengaged from the process, but others
either are openly resistive or engaged in calculated strategies aimed at
minimizing their tax obligations. May (2004) shows that compliance
with regulatory requirements is produced by both positive and negative motivations. What is true of regulatory noncompliance is no less
true of serious street crimes: motives and meanings are diverse but
finite in number.

The worlds in which meanings and justifications for crime are
acquired vary structurally and culturally. Social class is a fundamental source of variation. To speak of *class* is to highlight how material conditions of life shape perspectives and understandings of a
host of matters including crime and punishment. Class is important,
because it

> is script, map and guide. [It] tells us how to talk, how to dress, how
> to hold ourselves, how to eat, and how to socialize. It affects who
> we marry; where we live; the friends we choose; the jobs we have;
> the vacations we take; the books we read; the movies we see; the
> restaurants we pick; how we decide to buy houses, carpets, furniture,

and cars; where our kids are educated; what we tell our children at
the dinner table (conversations about the Middle East, for example,
versus the continuing sagas of the broken vacuum cleaner or the
half-wit neighbor). (Lubrano, 2004:5)

As it is used here, however, the analytic focus is the cultural components
of social class rather than its structural properties. This is class as lived
experience. Class origins and experiences account for how both crises
and opportunities are experienced, and they also help understand
how transgression is resorted to and justified.

Work, Respectability, and Cultural Capital

Decades of research shows that street offenders disproportionately hail
from poor and working-class backgrounds. One implication of this is
that the kinds of work they are familiar with and perform is unlike work
performed by those situated higher in the class structure. Much of the
work done by working-class citizens is physically hazardous or mind
numbing. Normally they work under the direct supervision of and
on schedules constructed by others. Their work neither requires nor
permits them to set production goals or to plan and complete tasks as
they see fit. This is done by superiors or by other subalterns and in any
case is thought to be none of laborers' business. Subordination is one
of the most important distinguishing characteristics of working-class
employment. Always it features bosses, schedules, and time clocks.

   Social relationships on the job have distinctive qualities where blue-
collar employees are concerned. An easy, informal egalitarianism pre-
vails in most places and circumstances, and there is remarkably little competitiveness among them. Most share a common status, and
prospects for upward mobility are limited in any case. Dunk (1991:75)
points out that in this world, a "great deal of effort is put into appearing
casual" and "this attitude and the accompanying body technique are
part of shopfloor culture." Not surprising also, in their work worlds
those who work too rapidly or maintain distance from co-workers
in hopes of being noticed by superiors are derided as "rate busters"
or "company men." "One does not want to give the impression of
being too eager or of trying too hard" (Dunk, 1991:75). Those with
a background in the working class who subsequently find themselves

in middle-class work worlds often remark by contrast on the competitiveness they encounter:

> In the factories I've worked in, if you talk down to another worker
> you can expect to be "punched out." The basic operating proce-
> dure of academia and graduate school...are based on competiti-
> ive game playing, which in working-class setting would make you an
> outcast....In my previous work environments this type of behavior
> had specific names: "brown nosing," "kissing ass," and so on....The
> modus operandi among middle-class careerists is based on competi-
> tion. (Langston, 1993:66–7)

Fortune is not generous to most who must make their way in the
working-class world, but they generally do not blame others for this.
Instead, what has been said about chemical factory workers is true for
nearly all of them:

> [T]hese workers typically believe that their position in the class struc-
> ture is of their own doing. They are factory workers because they want
> to be or, if they do not want to be, because "they missed the boat."
> They "had their chances." If they regret their position they tend to
> blame not their class origins but themselves. (Halle, 1984:169)

Many realize as well that their lack of connections or well-placed contacts limited their chances in life, but this is accepted as "the way the
world works" and not something to lament for long.

This is not to ignore substantial variation in the conditions and
rewards of working-class lives. At one end of this range are men and
women who earn high wages, who have adequate health insurance,
and who may own a home. Their work, perhaps in the highly skilled
and unionized construction trades, is challenging, allows for exercise
of some self-direction, and results in visible and enduring products that
they often point to with pride. Nevertheless, the changing labor market
characteristic of contemporary Western nations has left an increasingly large fraction of the working class in economically marginal
or desperate circumstances (Rubin, 1994). Here, for example, are
persons employed at the lowest levels of the nursing home industry;
their work often requires cleaning the beds and bodies of incontinent
residents. The nature of this work ensures that only those with few
options choose to do it, particularly at the minimum wage it pays. Few

working-class citizens do work that is exciting or newsworthy. This and their low status gives to many a sense of personal insignificance that is only strengthened by awareness that their views are not solicited and usually are not taken into account by people who count (Sennett and Cobb, 1972; Ehrenreich, 2002). Like it or not, they must come to terms with "the shame" of living near the material edge (McCourt, 1996:298). Neither they nor their opinions matter much.

Lareau (2002, 2003) and her students spent hours participating in and observing the daily lives of a sample of working-class and middle-class families. They noted that parents of poor and working-class children employ practices of child rearing Lareau (2002:747) describes as "natural growth." By this is meant that "parents viewed children's development as spontaneously unfolding, as long as they were provided with comfort, food, shelter and other basic support" (Lareau, 2002:773). Poor and working-class parents try to provide "the conditions under which children can grow but [leave] leisure activities to children themselves."

Lareau also notes that "these parents ... use directives rather than reasoning." In blue-collar households, communication is implicit; much is understood but goes unsaid, and children do not engage in conversation with adults so much as receive opinions or edicts. This is one reason many do not develop self-assurance dealing with superiors and impersonal organizations. Parental discipline in poor and working-class families runs to the immediate, painful, and quick. Corporal punishment is used more often by working-class parents than those at higher levels of the class structure (Strauss and Donnelly, 1994). Working-class children, however, develop a generalized conformism, and they generally see legal threats as legitimate and binding (Kohn, 1977).

When they run afoul of the law, men and women of working-class origins are as likely as not to blame themselves for their misfortune. If they recognize that others influenced them, they are quick to add "I got myself into the situation" or "no one twisted my arm." They consider it irrelevant that economic or labor-market conditions may have shaped their actions and the actions of others. Street criminals discourage public exploration of motives and may interpret it as weakness, deception, or whining. They did not belong to high-school forensic

or debate clubs nor did they take classes that encouraged search for
arcane meanings and complex interpretations. As adults, the conditions of their work do not facilitate or require development of these
cultural skills. Work days are filled with the need for physical action,
immediate responses, and outcomes that are judged by others either as
satisfactory or lacking. Their crimes share many of these qualities and
seem not to permit or require from investigators a complex search
for the facts and their meaning. Twenty-year-old males arrested on
the street carrying electronic equipment and a pry bar only blocks
from where residents were burglarized readily invite the interpretation
and label perpetrator. Reflecting on his younger years, the songwriter
and singer Merle Haggard rejects the possibility that his upbringing
was responsible for his later imprisonment. He concludes instead that
"leaves only me to blame" (Haggard, 1968). There are millions like
him.

As adults, the products of middle-class households generally do work
that is morally and physically cleaner than work done by those lower
in the class hierarchy. For many, employment is interesting and creative, and they are permitted considerable self-direction. Many occupy
offices, access to which is restricted by secretaries or other subalterns.
Personal assistants maintain their appointment calenders and smooth
out problems in the work day, while the inconveniences and unpleas-
antries of life beyond the office are managed by paying others to take
care of them. Middle-class adults generally do not return home at the
end of the day with mud, grease, cotton dust, or toxic chemicals on
their clothing, and they and their superiors prefer not to know very
much about those who do. Nor do they want to know how the dirty
work is going, just so long as it *is* going. This is one reason elite citizens do not show up at local police stations unaccompanied by media
representatives simply to talk with officers and to let them know how
much their work is appreciated.

Their backgrounds provide to middle-class children who later
become white-collar criminals experiences sharply different in many
ways from what is commonplace in poor and working-class households. Consider the amount of space available to family members and
accommodative patterns produced by what statisticians call a high rate
of "density." "It is one of the distinguishing marks of . . . working-class
family life that there's not enough room in the house either for the

people who live in it or the things they collect as they pursue their lives" (Rubin, 1994:17). Family members as a result must accommodate to the wishes and schedules of others in matters as mundane as the nightly bathtub queue. Middle-class homes are spacious, families are small, and space generally is close at hand for those who want to be alone. Children typically have private bedrooms. Throughout the homes of working-class families, empty space is public space, which makes for both a reduced sense of personal privacy and inability to get away easily to indulge the brain or emotions. In marked contrast to their living arrangements, middle-class homes "don't have a bed in the living room" (Bragg, 1997:98).

Other benefits of a materially secure and respectable upbringing are not nearly as apparent, but they are consequential for children reared in these circumstances. The focus here are benefits and perspectives that are acquired gradually in the routine conversations and dynamics of family life. Lareau (2002:773) describes the child-rearing practices of middle-class parents as "concerted cultivation." In contrast to working-class parents, who see the lives of their children "unfolding," middle-class parents make a "deliberate and sustained effort to stimulate children's development and to cultivate their cognitive and social skills." They attempt to foster children's talents through organized activities and extensive reasoning. Children reared in these families have little time for self-directed leisure pursuits and the benefits these bring. They are exposed to and given opportunity to engage in a range of leisure and educational activities.

Consider the implications for child development and leisure activities of having an assured and adequate income for family coffers. It makes it possible for parents to pay for the not insubstantial costs of their children's leisure and educational experiences. The leisure activities of working-class youth are played out in geographically more restricted and less expensive terrain. Their parents have neither the fiscal nor cultural resources to provide for their children the kind of support that is commonplace in middle-class households. This limits their children's participation in both school and extracurricular activities (Lareau, 2003).

Middle-class children are encouraged verbally and included in conversation with their parents and other adults. Parents often defer to them, and middle-class children witness parental juggling of family

schedules around them and their activities. Lareau suggests that this
and other aspects of middle-class child rearing produce a sense of
entitlement in middle-class children, one that may find expression
throughout life. They have little knowledge of drudgery and subordinate status save perhaps for temporary employment as youth.

Products of child rearing in which communication is predominantly
implicit, working-class citizens are attuned and pay attention to external qualities of behavior. In middle-class child rearing communication is explicit, and much of it is devoted to unraveling the intentions
behind puzzling or deviant actions. Children learn to look for and
consider what is behind untoward conduct and to pay less attention to
its formal status. The reasons for punishment or correction must be
explained defensibly. Privileged citizens are more likely to view norms
not as absolutes but as situationally applicable, and infraction, which is
seen as a product of internal dynamics that explain if not justify it, is a
matter for discussion and negotiation. It can be a protracted process.
Middle-class children learn early that arguable lack of intent mitigates
a wide array of misconduct, and they gain experience evading moral
and legal responsibility for their unpleasant actions. It is a lesson they
learn well. Many convicted white-collar criminals have little experience
as penitents.

The culture and ethos of worlds from which privileged offenders
are drawn and live is reproduced and reinforced in their employment
worlds (Kohn, 1977). Law is viewed with disdain or challenge, and
when they violate it they have little difficulty fashioning and bringing
to bear linguistic constructions that excuse or explain their actions. In
part because they generally view their circumstances as exceptional,
middle-class citizens generate, elaborate, and employ complex interpretations of their motives. Casual familiarity with the defenses of
white-collar criminals shows how imaginative they can be at disputing
criminal intent. Consider the case of William Aramony, former president of United Way of America (*New York Times*, 1995). Federal prosecutors in New York alleged that Aramony fraudulently diverted for his
own use nearly $2 million of the charity's money. The stolen funds were
used to pay for vacations, chauffeurs, luxury apartments, and exotic
vacations for the defendant and his teenage girlfriend. Other monies
were given to a friend who operated a charitable company, and large

sums were funneled into Aramony's personal accounts. His attorney unsuccessfully argued that Aramony's crimes were caused by shrinkage in the area of the brain that controls impulses and inhibitions. Those reared in poor or blue-collar circumstances likely would laugh at this notion. The jury found him guilty.

Interpretations of street crime and those who commit it invariably highlight the importance of childhood pathologies. Poverty and dysfunctional families are pointed to repeatedly as problems, because all recognize that it is in worlds close at hand that the "rewards, penalties, and rituals of daily life . . . constrain or subvert the operation of the moral sense" (Wilson, 1997:24). Three cultural components of middle-class and upper-class worlds are significant for how they shape manifestations of white-collar crime and also the numbers of citizens who choose to commit it: normatively unbridled competition, a pervasive sense of arrogance, and an ethic of entitlement. These are among the reasons why not only taverns and jails but also corporate offices can be breeding grounds for transgression.

Competition

Competitiveness is striving or vying with others for profit, prize, or position. It is a sense of rivalry. Lareau (2002; 2003) observed that middle-class children often develop and experience a sense of competitiveness with their siblings. As with their overall style of child rearing, middle-class parents believe competition is a positive experience and one they try to provide for their children (Lareau, 2003:60–1). They monitor the progress of their children regularly and precisely so they will develop skills needed to thrive in the middle- or upperclass workforce. They push them to compete and excel. In countless ways, middle-class children are sent the message that their parents and others expect them to succeed. They expect life to offer rewarding opportunities. This is less common and salient in working-class homes.

In cultures of competition individuals are driven to strive for success, whether this be fortune, fame, or respect, and they worry ceaselessly about conditions that might stand in their way. Locales and time periods vary in how powerfully and pervasively an ethos of competitiveness dominates interpersonal relationships and individual actions.

At Enron Corporation, management policies required each year that employees be evaluated on a forced curve so that 15 percent would receive performance ratings of unacceptable (Cruver, 2002). The pervasive insecurity generated in competitive environments like this provides powerful motivational pushes toward misconduct. On the basis of interviews with convicted white-collar offenders, Spencer (1965) notes that they place an exaggerated emphasis on elevating their social position and prevailing in competition with others. It can become all-consuming and trump all obligations and commitments. In competitive worlds, progress is assessed by comparison with peers, and inevitably there are winners and losers. Desire to be the former is fueled in part by fear of becoming the latter. Enron's system of "rank and yank" bred intense fear:

> Suffice it to say any [annual] ranking that plummeted you lower than your previous assessment gave many people a reason to start a course of antidepressants or switch from beer to bourbon. A reduction in your ranking status would affect your salary, your self-esteem, your standing among your peers and, worst of all, your bonus. Once wounded with an "issues" ranking, like a stricken animal in a herd, other employees would begin to shun you as you might draw lions. (Brewer, 2002:92)

A convicted telemarketer could be talking for most:

> You could be selling a $10 thousand ticket, you could be selling a $49.95 ticket. And it's the same principle, it's the same rules. It's the same game. I like to win. I like to win in all the games I play, you know. And the money is a reason to be there, and a reason to have that job. But winning is what I want to do. I want to beat everybody else in the office. (Shover, Coffey, and Hobbs, 2003:497)

Nor is he alone in describing the power of culturally competitive worlds:

> I sold the first person I ever talked to on the phone. And it was just like that first shot of heroin, you know. I'm not a heroin addict. . . . I've only done heroin a couple of times. But it was amazing. It was like, "I can't believe I just did this!" It was incredible. It was never about the money after that. . . . Yeah, it was about the money initially, but when I realized that I could do this everyday, it was no longer about the money. It was about the competition, you know. I wanted to be the

best salesman, and I want to make the most money that day. (Shover, Coffey, and Hobbs, 2003:497).

In competitive cultures, people generally evaluate personal success in terms of wealth and material possessions.

Competition need not be economic, however. Establishing or maintaining respect by peers for exceptional achievement is a priority for many, but humans compete for attention from superiors, plum assignments, and career advancement. Charles Colson, once a White House staff member, remarks that

Nixon and I understood one another – a young ambitious political kingmaker and an older pretender to the throne. We were both men of the same lower middle-class origins, men who'd known hard work all our lives, prideful men seeking that most elusive goal of all – acceptance and the respect of those who had spurned us in earlier years. (Colson, 1976:31–2)

Desire to demonstrate through competitive struggle that respect is deserved plays no small part in some white-collar crimes.

Money, however, is unsurpassed as a medium for gauging competitive success. Its decimalized metric is far superior to the disputed and nuanced ones used to measure respect.

To those of us who raced along the Wall Street treadmill of the 80s, money assumed a mystical aura. Once you achieved a modest level of success, once you knew that you had your mortgage and your car payment covered, once you had a full belly, money simply became the way you gauged your level of success, compared to those about you.... [M]oney became the points on the scoreboard. (Levine, 1991:390)

This suggests that not all who emerge as winners from competitive struggle will find relief in victory. Once achieved they know only insecurity over hanging on to what they have gained. For others, successful competition only kindles desire for more of the same:

[A]t each new level of my career, I had pushed my goals higher. When I was an associate, I wanted to be a vice president. When I became a vice president, I wanted to be a senior vice president.... When I was earning $20,000 a year, I thought, *I can make $100,000....* When I was making a $1 million, I thought *I can make $3 million.* There was always somebody one rung higher on the ladder, and I could never stop wondering: Is he really twice as good as I am? Ambition eclipsed rationality. I was unable to find fulfillment in realistic limits. . . . The hours grew longer, the numbers grew bigger, the stakes grew more critical, the fire grew ever hotter. (Levine, 1991:391)

By elevating and rewarding success above all else, competitive environments provide both characteristic understandings and justifications for misconduct (Coleman, 1987). In these worlds normative restraints are transformed into challenges to be circumvented or used to advantage. The roots of workplace competitiveness reach well into the past for many who cannot elude its undertow. The morally corrosive effects of unbridled competition are seen in a range of settings, but they are evident most glaringly where competitors are young males. In places where their numbers and influence predominate, their perspectives define the collective ethos. Patriarchal notions of masculinity and competitors of privileged background predominate in worlds that breed tempted individuals and predisposed organizations.

Arrogance

Arrogance and an air of imperiousness occasionally are seen in the conduct of street criminals; the swaggering gun-wielding figure is encountered in real life often enough to reacquaint us with this fact. But arrogance is a more likely springboard for crime in places and on the part of offenders who do not live so close to the material edge. The inhabitants of materially secure and respectable worlds are accustomed to being superordinates; they give orders, and others move to their dictates. Their views are solicited and taken seriously by people who count. They are waited on. Many of them have known success and emerged as winners from competitive struggle. All do not handle it well, however; the self-important, arrogant white-collar offender is a recurring figure in chronicles of white-collar crime. The face of arrogance is inescapable, for example, in decisions by powerful and wealthy public figures to award lucrative noncompetitive contracts to friends and associates. The chief executive officer of Enron Corporation reportedly referred to a persistent questioning accountant in a public meeting as an "asshole" (Cruver, 2002:54; Swartz, 2003:265). Such public lapses of respectability are uncommon for elite white-collar criminals; normally they do not display such inappropriate behavior. A securities fraudster recalls the sense of self-importance bordering on arrogance that he experienced before his scheme collapsed:

> [My wife] and I were becoming more and more in demand. I was successful enough that people were laughing at my stories. Even my brother-in-law invested with the kid brother who was taking the world by storm down there in Atlanta. . . .
> [M]y mother-in-law claimed I was a genius. I secretly admired her discernment. My office had to be enlarged to house a person of my intelligence, kindness, and shrinking humility. Class A personalities asked for my opinion about things. (Lawson, 1992:67)

He and others like him may come to believe that "they [don't] have to follow the rules because they made them" (Swartz, 2003:302).

Arrogance probably is less common among ordinary white-collar criminals, chiefly because many are employed in occupations that do not provide the requisite material, organizational, and dramaturgical supports. It can find expression in disdain or indifference for legal restrictions and their creators. The idea that the state reserves the right to intervene in their work environments and restrain their decision making is accepted conditionally. Further, the presumption that they should exercise due diligence and responsible concern for details expected of ordinary citizens is rejected. Asked to explain his crimes, a former corporate CEO and convicted inside trader replied:

> I think I was arrogant enough at the time to believe that I could cut corners. Not care about details that were going on and not think about consequences. [But] one of my great faults is – I refused to deal with everyday details that people have to deal with to make sure that mistakes aren't made. And I think, in that way, there may have been arrogance where I didn't have to deal with details – that these details were meant for other people, not for me. (Waksal, 2003:7)

The arrogant are accustomed to a world they can manipulate, and their days are devoted to the search for shortcuts. When caught and convicted of crime, they deny everything or characterize it as a mistake and an aberration. Belief in their personal integrity is grounded in what they have accomplished and their success in other aspects of life. They distinguish themselves from "real criminals."

Entitlement

Cultures of entitlement cause actors in a range of circumstances to believe that benefits of some kind are due them and that questioning or disruption of delivery is illegitimate. Behn and Sperduto (1979:55) point out that this ethic is not a "conscious creed that prescribes personal or political conduct [but one that] . . . applies in specific situations, as a . . . constraint on . . . behavior." Lareau (2003) observed that middle-class children question and contest authority. They dispute and refute correction routinely. The children she observed were quick to offer advice to authority figures and to make special requests. They readily passed judgment and already had a sense that their efforts and accomplishments made them special. The investigators noted also that when privileges were denied, middle-class children badgered their parents until they were provided. These children acquired and operated with a sense of entitlement.

In a ground-breaking study of fraud among medical doctors, a team of investigators from the University of California interviewed sixty Medicare/Medicaid and American Medical Association officials, forty-two physicians convicted of medical scams, and a control group of thirty-two physicians with no record of criminal conviction (Jesilow et al., 1993). They also examined the cases of 358 medical workers suspended from Medicare/Medicaid between 1977 and 1982. The investigators found that among conditions that facilitate Medicaid fraud by physicians is their belief that insensitive external forces are interfering with their just desserts. In other words, felonious physicians believe they are *entitled* to pursue wealth without external restraint. What is instructive about this finding is confirmation that an ethos of entitlement can become so pervasive among occupational practitioners or organizational managers that it becomes taken for granted, and erodes individual willingness to comply with law.

The professions do not stand alone. The owners and managers of commercial establishments believe they contribute importantly to civic life and to community welfare generally by providing employment to citizens. They often point to the wealth returned to government by taxes of one kind or another paid by them and their workforce. Many donate time and money to civic organizations and causes. Professional persons, whether physicians, attorneys, or engineers, point to their work and its visible results as evidence of their importance. It is common for them and for high-level public-sector managers to believe that their contributions to community life and the sacrifices their families make because of their work entitles them to cut corners and claim perks not available to others.

Moral hierarchy is another source of entitlement. The privileged understand that fortune or luck has placed them in positions of power and control over organizations and others. They are not brick layers, and they know it. They operate daily with understanding that their honor and respectability are a given, and they are entitled to be treated accordingly; privilege and deference is their due. Consequently, when austerity measures are called for the response may be something different. Throughout the corporate restructuring of recent decades, as employees made concessions in wages and benefits, management compensation skyrocketed. In 2000, before the house of cards and lies that was Enron collapsed, the behavior of Keneth Lay, its CEO,

> betrayed a powerful sense of personal entitlement. Long after his annual compensation ... had climbed into the millions, Lay arranged to take out large personal loans from the company. He gave Enron jobs and contracts to his relatives. And Lay and his family used Enron's fleet of corporate jets as if they owned them. On one occasion, a secretary sought to arrange a flight for an executive on Enron business only to told that members of the Lay family had reserved *three* of the company's planes. (McLean and Elkind, 2004:3–4)

As their employer spiraled to destruction, Enron's employees,

> continued taking business-related trips, staying in the best hotels and eating in the best restaurants. These were the perks that the majority of Enron employees enjoyed – and it was a fair trade for being on the road, for being away from families, and for working fourteen-hour days. We considered it part of our compensation. (Cruver, 2002:73)

Their sense of entitlement is only strengthened by the enormous amount of largesse that is made available to the privileged. This has been the case for so long and has become such an accepted part of life that it is no longer seen as discretionary.

The contrast with working-class experience and perspectives is striking. Located closer to the bottom of the class structure, working-class citizens witness ample misfortune either personally or vicariously. They are cautioned from early in life to be prepared for and to take setbacks in stride. Their calloused dreams include a healthy dose of fatalism. It is "a common condition of being poor white trash: you are always afraid that the good things in life are temporary, that someone can take them away" (Bragg, 1997:297). Lacking a sense of efficacy even, entitlement as a cultural or individual quality is the last thing encountered in their worlds (Croteau, 1995). Aware that "the only thing worse than doing without is to be given something and then have it snatched away," they want nothing so much as a time when all the bills are paid, and they can sit (Bragg, 1997:309).

CULTURAL CAPITAL AND CRIME FACILITATION

The great majority of individuals placed in a position of financial trust fulfill their fiduciary responsibilities honestly and faithfully. But some do not. What has been learned about why some persons embezzle from their employers while others do not highlights the importance of self conversations in framing prospective acts. Men and women who embezzle are able to do so in part because they define the act of stealing in a way that enables them to maintain a favorable self-concept (Cressey, 1953; Zeitz, 1981). Some define it as borrowing or as fair compensation due them for the long hours they put in without overtime pay. Others see it as something done to provide for their children or significant others that cannot be provided legitimately. Studies over more than four decades consistently show that ability to neutralize obeisance to law facilitates criminal decision making. A generation of investigators have documented and catalogued the variety of ways criminal decision makers excuse and explain their actions (Maruna and Copes, 2004). Crisis and attractive opportunities figure prominently in their explanations. Apparently there is no shortage of either in the lives of middle-class and upperworld criminals (Weisburd et al., 1991).

Their cultural capital and general conformism means that working-class citizens have available a narrow range of acceptable explanations for their crimes. This may help explain why street thieves generally refer to their activities as "stealing" or "doin' wrong." Class differences in cultural capital means that upper-class and middle-class children gain acuity with a larger and more diverse array of neutralizing justifications than those less privileged (Hazani, 1991). Computer hackers, who disproportionately are young middle-class males, engage in unending verbal and ideological disputes with state representatives over the harmfulness of their actions (Levi, 2001a; Schell, Dodge, and Moutsatsos, 2002). They claim that they act not for personal enrichment but for the betterment of all by dispersing intellectual property and encouraging innovation. Hackers minimize their crimes also by claims that they could do much greater harm if they put their minds to it. By identifying points of system vulnerability, they contend what they do is no different from what security technicians are paid to do. That they might also be compared to trespassers, prowlers, or thieves is a possibility they are unprepared to appreciate.

The linguistic and conversational skills of privileged citizens give them an advantage at construing criminal decisions as legitimate and socially acceptable actions that is denied citizens of more humble circumstance. Where the latter must resort to drugs and the influence of others to overcome the bind of law, white-collar citizens can do so easily using rhetorical devices. That they do so attests not to their belief in the moral legitimacy of law but their crucial need to see and be seen as respectable. Perspectives and skills acquired in early generative worlds and reinforced in their occupational lives facilitate this process. They make it possible for respectable citizens to weigh criminal options without adopting a criminal identity. Their verbal and rhetorical skills allow them to construe their acts "through a sanitizing ideological prism, which gives them the appearance of not being criminal" (Simon and Eitzen, 1993:300). These sanitizing ideologies include vocabularies that gloss over criminality and harm. When weighing criminal opportunity, white-collar offenders employ rhetorical and linguistic constructions that make it seem acceptable and routine. They can draw from a rich repertoire of excuses and explanations. If they admit to knowing they were on ambiguous legal ground, their acts are portrayed as unimportant. A convicted insider trader remembers that his peers referred to their questionable and illegal tactics as the "poison pill" and "shark repellant" (Levine, 1991). Savings and loans crooks referred to the practice of hiding bad loans from bank regulators as "flip-flopping"

(Calavita et al., 1998). Participants in price-fixing conspiracies talk of "price stabilization" (Geis, 1967). "Massaging data" and "creative accounting" work for others.

White-collar offenders perhaps are more successful than street offenders at getting others to empathize when they explain their misfortune; accusers are portrayed as unjust and the government as obtrusive and inefficient. Some cite the necessity of cheating in order to compete with others who cut corners. Many white-collar offenders claim they committed crime to benefit their employer, which leaves them free to argue also that gains for employers benefit many people. No few white-collar offenders draw on professional expertise to argue that overseers do not understand the requirements or realities of their work. In this way, "social controls that serve to check or inhibit deviant motivational patterns are rendered inoperative, and the individual is freed to engage in [crime] without serious damage to his self image" (Sykes and Matza, 1957:667).

BEYOND GENERATIVE WORLDS

The generative worlds of white-collar criminals do not exist in a social vacuum. Nor are they immutable and unchanging. Instead, characteristics and dynamics of the larger worlds in which indidividuals and organizations are situated constrain their perceptions and assessments. Three aspects may be critical for their effect on the readiness of the competitive, arrogant, and entitled either to move closer to or away from the breakwaters of the law: the culture of work organizations; flucuations of the business cycle and market(s) uncertainty; and the pervasiveness of belief that credible oversight is lacking. We shall defer until chapter 7 discussion of the first.

Business Cycles and Market(s) Uncertainty

Fluctuation in the business cycle has been linked repeatedly to changes in the size of the pool of white-collar offenders (Baucus, 1994; Clinard and Yeager, 1980; Simpson, 1987; Staw and Szwajkowski, 1975). Economic downturns depress both income and prospects for the future, which increases fear and competition. As larger numbers of citizens and organizations are pushed closer to insolvency, crime escalates. As is true of street addicts, growing desperation can cause respectable citizens to consider behavioral options they normally would find unacceptable. This may be true particularly for entrepreneurs and small businesses operating near the margin of insolvency. The imperatives of competition can cause them to cut corners. Because they pay a much greater price for seeds than their national competitors, for example, some local seed companies repackage unsold, out-of-date seed from previous years. This is made easier by the fact that few customers inquire what they do with surplus stock. During downturns in the business cycle, entreaties from superiors that they engage in illicit conduct may fall on receptive ears among subordinates who fear for the future. In difficult times, the arrogant and entitled may feel that what is rightfully theirs will not be unless they take preemptive action. The supply of tempted individuals may have increased significantly in the decades bounding arrival of the millenium because of increasing income inequality and "fear of falling" (Callahan, 2004). These pressures have been severe particularly for the professional and managerial segment of the middle-class (Ehrenreich, 1989).

The relationship between economic conditions and the supply of potential white-collar criminals may be curvilinear; severe upturns and downturns alike may increase the number of individuals and organizations weighing criminal options. Competitive cultures stimulate excess and crime during boom times when there is widespread belief "everyone is getting rich." Periods of sustained economic expansion increase success and breed arrogance. At these times when everyone seems to be doing well, belief that it is foolish to hold back and not engage in the games of the moment finds broad appeal. Many come to believe that to pass up any opportunity is to miss the boat. Those who choose crime may be emboldened by their assumption that a rising economic tide hides their activities and increases their chances of criminal success. Growth can also create both a sense of entitlement to the fruits of a thriving economy and belief that "now is the time to strike."

Evidence of a relationship between the state of the economy and the supply of predisposed organizational offenders comes from case studies of industries and industry sectors. In the 1961 heavy electrical equipment price-fixing cases, exaggerated stories about "white-sales" by competitors, the destructive effects of past competition, and reports that foreign competitors were "dumping" cheap electrical equipment on the U.S. market contributed to willingness to engage in price fixing (Baker and Faulkner, 1993). Structural conditions in the auto industry, which compel dealers to compete for premium cars, also spawns kickback schemes and bribery of distributors (Farberman, 1977; Leonard and Weber, 1970). This enables automobile dealers to ensure a supply of automobiles most in demand by consumers. In industries where producers can provide little product or quality differentiation, have limited access to markets and where firms depend on a few large contracts, antitrust crime increases. Fluid milk producers and the folding box industry are instrutive examples (Sonnenfeld and Lawrence, 1978). Organizations must enter and conduct business in several markets, and conditions in these markets can cause fluctuations in business uncertainty. When conditions in the credit, capital, labor, or sales markets are unsettled, firm owners and managers become less willing to rule out criminal solutions to their problems (Baucus and Near, 1991).

The number and variety of behaviors that qualify as white-collar crime is large. Links between the economy and crime may be general or specific to particular forms of it. In some cases, offenders contend that economic circumstances seemed to require criminal responses, and here the links are easy to draw. Whether or not there is a relationship between fluctuating economic conditions and the supply of offenders prepared to commit noneconomic white-collar crimes is unclear. Are executives of private security firms, for example, more inclined to tolerate mistreatment of inmates in their charge when profits are threatened? Are corporate officials more inclined to engage the services of prostitutes for their meetings or gatherings when the economy is robust? Does the economy effect illegal dispensation of narcotics by doctors?

Official Resolve and Attentiveness

Legal threats and the possibility of painful consequences resulting from infraction are key causal variables in rational-choice theory. When the state monitors criminal behavior closely and gives indication of intolerence in response to apprehended offenders rates of infraction decline. Where it appears distracted or indifferent to crime and treats with leniency the offenders it ensnares, inevitably the belief grows that the odds of paying more than minor penalty are slim. The rate of white-collar crime rises accordingly. When the U.S. Internal Revenue Service (IRS) sent clear messages in the mid-1990s that it was becoming a kinder, gentler agency, revenue collections decreased. An IRS commissioner observed:

> [T]he drawing down of enforcement has had a negative effect. People have seen others get away with things they shouldn't have been able to; they've seen the corporate scandals; they know about the unseemly behavior by too many attorneys and accountants in these clearly outrageous shelters, and some have concluded it not as important [to obey the law]. (*Washington Post*, 2004b:E3)

Official resolve and attentiveness acquire strength in broad crime-control ideologies promoted or endorsed by political leaders and in state-enforced strategies of crime control. There is evidence, for example, that antitrust crime increases during Republican presidential administrations, because offenders sense they can get away with more crime during these times. "Republican ideology and dogma is traditionally more supportive of business interests and, Republican administrations are often hostile to corporate regulation" (Simpson, 1987:951). Ensconced in their peculiar generative worlds, privileged citizens and organizations are aware of whether or not and how closely overseers are paying attention to them. They can also estimate, however imprecisely, whether resources are available for investigation and enforcement. Where official attention is hazy in focus and weak in application, arrogance increases. Where it is clear and strong, humility grows. This is because the level of state commitment to and resources invested in rule enforcement helps shape prevailing assessments of the cost likelihood and potential of punishment (Pontell, Calavita, and Tillman, 1994).

CHAPTER FOUR

Self-Restraint and Oversight

Lure becomes criminal opportunity in the absence of credible oversight. When the criminally predisposed and the momentarily tempted sense attentiveness by others, they move on. In this chapter we suggest that the changes described in chapter 2 coupled with the presence of a large population of the tempted and predisposed produced in the generative worlds sketched in chapter 3 give reason to believe that white-collar crime has increased substantially. It is impossible to estimate the magnitude and parameters of the increase, but the logic of rational-choice theory gives reason to believe it may be substantial.

Self-restraint is the first line of defense against criminal decision making by any who are attracted by lure. This is the willingness of individuals and groups to be constrained in their consideration of options not by fear of legal penalties but instead by potential self-reproach borne of a guilty conscience or concern for the opinions of others. Commitment to norms of morality and ethics, self-respect, and determination not to let down those who look to them for exemplary conduct and community standing are among the most important reasons many obey the law (Paternoster and Simpson, 1993). Lure is seen more quickly as criminal opportunity where decision makers are indifferent to the tug of conscience, reputation, or concern for family and peers. Crime-as-choice theory leads to expectation that fear of adverse publicity restrains the behavior of potential white-collar offenders. There is no doubt, for example, that owners and managers of many organizations value their good reputation and emphasize to employees the importance of operating ethically and in compliance with law. The large sums of money invested by some companies in advertising and charitable contributions leaves little doubt that for some an upstanding reputation whether earned or manufactured is a valued asset.

Few doubt as well that weak self-control is linked not only to criminal participation but to a variety of risky and deviant behaviors. Renewed interest in self-restraint in recent years was spurred by a bevy of analytically hard-nosed commentators who charge increasing failure by parents, schools, and churches to provide young people with adequate moral education. Moral education equips individuals to assess options constrained by altruism and the recognized importance of deferred gratification (Wilson, 1975; Gottfredson and Hirschi, 1990; Dilulio, 1991). It insulates individuals from concern with if not recognition of lure.

The worlds that generate white-collar offenders and the settings where they make criminal decisions are nested in larger moral contexts, and these are significant as sources of self-restraint or as crime facilitators (Vaughan, 1992). Criminal decisions are more likely in permissive cultures where infraction generally meets with indifference or indulgence from superiors and others. Some believe the growth of permissiveness has reached a critical point:

> There is trouble in River City, on Main Street, and in the Hamptons [as well as in impoverished urban communities]. And while the problems there are somewhat different in nature (e.g., prolific divorce remains more widespread than illegitimacy), they pose no less a threat to the nations's long term prospects. A free society depends ultimately on the beliefs, behavior, and standards of the average citizen. What makes our situation today different from previous periods in American history – and fundamentally more serious – is the "demoralization" of much of middle- and upper-middle-class life. The ballast that was once there isn't any longer. (Bennett et al., 1996:199)

What is known about morality in the workplace does little to allay concern. One commentator remarks:

> Leaving aside all the scandals [of recent years], the ethics at many companies remain dismal.... A large survey of corporate employees in 2000 by KPMG found that half of the respondents had observed violations of the law or company standards during the previous year, and many reported that these violations were quite serious (Callahan, 2004:283).

The 2003 National Business Ethics Survey found that 22 percent of employees reported observing unethical conduct at work in the past year. Ten percent said they experienced pressure to compromise ethical standards. A third of the respondents reported that their co-workers condone questionable ethical practices by showing respect for those who achieve success using them (Ethics Resource Center, 2003).

PRIVATE OVERSIGHT

Injured parties and nongovernmental organizations (NGOs) provide oversight of the tempted and predisposed and respond to evidence or complaints of misconduct. This may happen particularly when state agencies decline to take action. Professional societies, for example, promulgate and enforce codes of ethics and generally accepted practices. Most also have procedures for hearing complaints of improper conduct and imposing sanctions. The American Medical Association, Chicago Board of Trade, the National Basketball Association, the New York Stock Exchange, and the recently created Rules of the Public Company Accounting Oversight Board are examples of organizations that employ rule-making and enforcement procedures in oversight of members. The enforcement machinery employed by most NGOs is small and has time and energy for little more than reactive enforcement. Morrison and Wickersham (1998) show that 0.24 percent of California physicians annually are disciplined by the state's Medical Board. Of these, 34 percent lose their license to practice medicine. The same pattern of apparent leniency is found in disciplinary actions by state bar associations; the proportion of cases of alleged malpractice that are referred for investigation and possible disciplinary action is small, and the proportion that eventuate in significant sanction is very small (State Bar of California, 2003).

The norms promulgated and enforced by NGOs are shaped disproportionately by elite members of these professional and trade associations. Their content reflects elite problems and interests, and enforcement generally falls heaviest on smaller firms and least powerful individuals. Physicians disciplined for medical fraud disproportionately are minorities who were trained at foreign universities and practice in inner-city neighborhoods and small clinics (Jesilow et al., 1993). This does not mean they commit more fraud than colleagues with domestic training and more advantaged practices, but it does mean that foreign-trained, minority and inner-city physicians are under closer watch because their clientele more often receive subsidized medical care. Also, enforcement resources are concentrated in large cities, which facilitates investigation of urban clinics.

Civil Action

Private parties harmed by what they believe are criminal actions of others can pursue civil remedies individually or as a class. *Class-action* law suits usually are filed by a large number of parties who believe they have been harmed by another. They make it possible for parties who otherwise could not afford litigation to pool their resources, form a class, and pursue redress. Class-action suits originate in all areas of commercial life including building and construction products, stocks and securities, drug and medical products, and motor vehicle products. On April 19, 2004, Microsoft Corporation settled a class-action antitrust lawsuit brought by Minnesota customers who alleged that the company overcharged them for products. The settlement ended a jury trial that was expected to last several more weeks and to cost the company $1.5 billion (*Washington Post*, 2004b). Microsoft previously settled similar suits in nine states and Washington, D.C. In many class-action suits, the cost of litigation exceeds the eventual settlement or court award.

Whistleblowers

Whistleblowers are employees of legitimate organizations who divulge to outsiders knowledge or suspicions of wrongdoing in the workplace. The identity of whistleblowers becomes known, but informants generally remain anonymous. Recall that the crimes of Davis Pipe and its managers, which were described in chapter 1, came to light because of an informant. In one of the best known cases of whistleblowing, an employee of a federal contractor made available to congressional representatives and the media copies of secret Pentagon studies of the Vietnam war (Ellsberg, 2002).

In the United States, several states and the federal government provide employment protection and monetary rewards for whistle-blowers. The U.S. Whistleblower Protection Act of 1989 as amended provides they can receive a proportion of any settlement or recoveries in cases where they provided key information (Devine, 1999). This is meant to spur insiders with knowledge of wrongdoing to come forward, to report to authorities, and to do so without fear of reprisals. In 2002, crew members aboard a Danish oil tanker notified the U.S. Coast Guard of a hazardous leak. Coast Guard officers found the leak, and they also found directions from shipping company officials that the leak not be reported as required by law. The two crew members who notified the Coast Guard were awarded one-half of the criminal fine assessed in the case ($250,000) (U.S. Department of Justice, 2002b). In January 2003, the U.S. Sentencing Commission issued new sentencing guidelines meant to enhance protection of whistleblowers (Solow, 2003). Informants are private citizens who report to authorities something untoward that causes them to believe crime is occurring. They are exemplified by individuals who may chance to see the destructive environmental effects of criminal toxic dumping and report this to officials. The Association of Certified Fraud Examiners (2005) has shown that tips are the principal means by which fraud committed by or against organizations is uncovered.

Whatever potential private oversight may have for controlling white-collar crime it probably varies by whether or not the offender is an upperworld criminal. Prospects are discouraging particularly when they are directed at large corporate actors and powerful interests. They do not always sit by when attacked; many use their resources not only to bully but also to retaliate (*Wall Street Journal*, 1995). Litigation is one vehicle for doing so. SLAPP (Strategic Litigation Against Public Participation) gets its name from the fact that plaintiffs generally are experienced users of the court while defendants more likely are private citizens or groups that have resisted the former's efforts or in other ways cast them in an unfavorable public light (Canan and Pring, 1988; Pring and Canan, 1996). Typically, these lawsuits claim injury from citizen efforts to influence government or sway voters on an issue of public interest. In 1998, the television personality Oprah Winfrey was sued by Texas cattlemen over critical comments about beef she made on her show. The case was tried before a jury in Amarillo, Texas, and ended with a verdict that Ms. Winfrey's comments were protected by free-speech guarantees and did not harm the beef industry in any case. Like Oprah Winfrey, the targets of retaliatory actions usually prevail, but the financial and emotional costs of resisting SLAPP litigation can be staggering.

The powerful can retaliate in other ways as well. On March 5, 1999, a Miami, Florida, jury awarded $37 million to the family of a twelve-year-old girl who was killed in a traffic accident after Florida Power & Light Co. (FPL) turned off the electric power to a traffic light in Pinecrest, Florida. The company subsequently filed multiple requests with the trial court to set aside the verdict. Investigators hired by the company contacted the jury foreman a month later and, according to the girl's parents, offered to pay him to help determine whether the jury acted improperly in reaching its verdict. Post-trial contact with jurors is a felony and violation of Florida's ethics rules for lawyers when it is done with intent to tamper with a verdict. FPL admitted its investigators contacted the juror, but it denied doing so in hopes of overturning the jury award. It also denied offering money to the juror. It was learned subsequently that a second juror also was contacted by FPL investigators. That juror had admonished the company after the verdict was announced by turning to its lawyers in the courtroom and saying, "Shame on you." The judge in the case had warned FPL at the end of the trial not to interview jurors (*Miami Daily Business Review*, 1999).

Nearly two decades of experience with policies for encouraging whistleblowers, informants, and other private actions as mechanisms for promoting white-collar accountability leaves unanswered questions of efficacy. The toll on those who come forward can be profound, however. Whistleblowers frequently are targets of retaliatory actions by their employers or professional peers. These commonly include demotion or termination of employment; transfer to monotonous, unpleasant, or dangerous work assignments; and threats of physical harm (Glazer and Glazer, 1989). Retaliation is most likely and most severe when the reported conduct is systematic and significant, particularly if it is part of the organization's profit accumulation process (Rothschild and Miethe, 1999). The privileged generally combat the

allegations of whistleblowers by questioning their motives and character and painting them as renegades (Nichols, 1991). Faced with what
is unwelcome notoriety and the financial costs of legal representation
to resist retaliatory actions, the experience can be extremely disruptive
of life, work, and career routines. The toll on physical and emotional
health can be devastating.

Civil suits, SLAPP lawsuits, and retaliatory actions against whistleblowers are powerful reminders of the determination of the privileged
to conduct their affairs as they see fit. They stand as lessons to others
to think carefully before targeting upperworld criminals. Represented
by skilled, well-paid, and well-connected legal counsel who can draw
on a variety of technical experts to support their claims, the challenge
faced by any who oppose them is formidable. Their cultural and financial resources produce a capacity to resist, to delay, or to best oversight
efforts that is not matched by ordinary white-collar offenders.

STATE OVERSIGHT

Self-restraint and private oversight, the first lines of defense against
unethical and criminal decisions, are imperfect, and this is one reason
why the state and its oversight apparatus are on standby. If offenders
weigh the costs and benefits of crime with any care, they likely will take
account of the odds of being caught and possible sanctions. As compared with the perceived risk of committing street crimes, white-collar
crime generally is seen as safer. This probably comes from recognition that many white-collar crimes occur far from the watchful eye of
authorities, and, absent extraordinary and therefore unlikely investigation, offenders can operate with impunity. In the 2000 National
Public Survey on White Collar Crime, a national sample of adults in
the U.S. were asked to estimate the odds of being caught and punished
for the crimes of robbery and fraud. Not surprising, they see fraud as
much safer (Rebovich and Layne, 2000:18).

State oversight can take the form of direct observation by human
beings or impersonal monitoring via periodic audits, television cameras, or computer programs. The fact that an avoidable harm or form
of predation may threaten or injure others does not ensure it will be
the focus of oversight, however. The state can turn a blind eye toward

predatory or injurious behaviors, or it can choose to make them the focus of attention. It can take the lead identifying and crafting oversight, or it can wait until compelled to do so through action by citizens and organized groups. Stalking and environmental degradation are examples of harmful conduct for which the state provided little oversight until recent decades.

Criminalization is the process by which state bodies, whether legislative assemblies, appellate courts, or administrative agencies, reduce the options available to citizens and organizations in designated areas of decision making. The state criminalizes new behaviors daily, as casual perusal of the *Federal Register* attests. The products of criminalization campaigns assume an immense variety of forms, from more stringent training or licensing requirements for designated occupational specialties to new or stiffened criminal penalties. The Surface Mining Control and Reclamation Act, for example, requires that explosives employed in the mining process be prepared and detonated only by certified blasters (Shover et al., 1986). Previously explosives could be used by anyone regardless of whether or not they understood blasting or were trained to do it. The result was often dangerous and excessively destructive blasting. Regulations can be extremely narrow in focus and specific in text; regulations limit the number and size of holes in "Swiss" cheese (Skrzycki, 2003). The purpose of these restrictions and others like them is to ensure that product quality meets required standards, and the production process does not harm individuals or the environment. Like violation of criminal statutes, willful violation of regulatory requirements is grounds for criminal prosecution, although this occurs infrequently.

Decriminalization is successful reduction of restrictions or oversight, thereby permitting individuals and organizations to operate with greater latitude. Like its opposite, decriminalization occurs daily in legislative chambers, regulatory conference rooms, and appellate judicial chambers. It is no less important practically and theoretically than creation of new restrictions. Congressional easing of restrictions on investment and lending practices by savings and loan institutions in the 1980s was a noteworthy decriminalization move as was loosening of antiusury restrictions by some states (*Arkansas Democrat Gazette*, 2003; *Dallas Business Journal*, 2004). Privileged and powerful interests have been successful revising the *Internal Revenue Code* to their advantage; a substantially increased share of the tax burden has been shifted to middle-class citizens and small business firms. Sixty-three percent of U.S.-controlled corporations and 73 percent of foreign-controlled corporations with operations in the United States paid no income taxes in the years 1996–2000 (*Los Angeles Times,* 2004; U.S. General Accounting Office, 2004). Criminalization and decriminalization are conflictive processes that typically feature citizens, groups, and organizations pressing for change and others resisting these efforts. The dynamics of these contests are moral, ideological, political, and bureaucratic.

Autonomy Struggles

It is tempting to think of criminalization and decriminalization as processes with dichotomous outcomes, but the results can be substantially more complex than this. State actions imposing on citizens more restrictive requirements typically contain diverse provisions; the enabling legislation for some regulatory agencies is lengthy and may include specific and detailed requirements. Each can be the focus of dissension, political conflict and extended negotiation (Skrzycki, 2003). Some provisions impose new restrictions on those to whom they apply, but other provisions may be kinder; when powerful parties lose on one front they sometimes gain concessions and victory elsewhere. The state, for example, may provide additional lure as a calculated effort to reduce opposition to new control initiatives or to assuage powerful losers in criminalization battles. In this way what privileged interests lose in reduced autonomy they are compensated for in access to additional state largesse.

As a powerful and high-status occupational group, physicians resist restrictions on how they practice and the fees they charge. They have become more accommodating to demands for oversight in recent years as abuses have led to decreasing respect for their work. Enactment of Medicaid and Medicare in the United States was accompanied by legislative concern not to antagonize them. Legislators were

> wary of arousing new waves of antagonism from the American Medical Association by implying that physicians were other than scrupulously

honest and perfectly capable of keeping their business dealings withing the confines of what the law allowed. To have challenged this shibboleth, Congress would have risked escalating an already tense conflict into an all out war. (Jesilow et al., 1993:44)

Consequently, the statutory blueprint for Medicare and Medicaid said little about fraud or abuse and how it would be handled. There was fear that additional troublesome procedures designed to check physician honesty would be intolerable and ultimately backfire. Largesse continues to flow from Medicaid, Medicare, and similar state programs with limited accountability so they remain acceptable to physicians and hospitals.

State oversight is not assured even where there is evidence of serious harm to significant numbers of citizens. Many harmful practices do not win the kind of popular condemnation or movement strength needed for successful criminalization. When circumstances are favorable, however, there seems little doubt that public pressure to "do something" can spur state action.

The pattern in state response to scandal and catastrophe is cause for concern, however. Legislative and regulatory crackdowns generally begin with, "a high-profile event – a major bridge collapse or a ferry accident, a series of frauds, or massive corporate bankruptcies" followed by "volumes of lofty rhetoric from various politicians and officials" (Snider, 2004:3). The official response typically is weaker than promised, invariably challenged and softened by the difficulties of enforcement and prosecution. As important, once the media loses interest, the campaigns lose steam, and the long-term effects of change are eroded. Periods of lenient oversight and the political rhetoric that underpin them predictably result in new scandals that draw public ire and again lead to calls for state response. Undoubtedly, this was true of the S&L scandals in the 1980s and the massive corporate crimes of more recent years. The Sarbanes-Oxley Act of 2002 imposes new restrictions on individuals and occupations that previously operated with minimal external oversight. The Act is complex, but accountants and the responsibilities of corporate executives are major foci. It creates, for example, a Rules of the Public Company Accounting Oversight Board that, among its diverse responsibilities, is charged to:

(1) register public accounting firms; (2) establish standards for all matters relating to preparation of audit reports; (3) conduct inspections of accounting firms; and (4) enforce compliance with the act. This potentially is a significant increase of oversight. Friederichs (2004:224) suggests that one reason for passage of the act was "the firestorm of public anger over the corporate scandals of 2001–2003." Outcomes of this type in response to angry public opinion are uncommon, and they generally occur only when larger economic and political conditions do not present obstacles. Economic conditions are powerful constraints not only on the odds of success by criminalization movements but also on their emergence. It is notable that privileged citizens and organizations may have lost substantially in the corporate accounting scandals of recent years. More important, they created uncertainty in financial markets and thereby made investment decision making riskier. The cynical might see passage of the Sarbanes-Oxley Act as a preemptive strike by political elites to head off possible demands by citizens for more profound and wide-ranging action. The act adds redundancy to oversight that would not have been necessary if credible oversight had been in place.

Even at historically opportune times the struggle over new oversight goes on within the assumptions, logic, and constraints of large, privately controlled and increasingly transnational corporations (Garland, 2001). The level of and trends in corporate profits are critical determinants of the reception afforded reformers; the likelihood they will be successful increases during economic good times and decreases dramatically during recessionary periods. Timing is everything. A bill before the Oregon legislature would have given the state's Public Utility Commission (PUC) authority to impose fines on telephone service providers who engage in fraudulent practices. Other states have found this to be successful combating fraud by these firms. The Oregon PUC commissioner noted, however, that "the telephone utilities really don't want the PUC to have that authority, and they seem to have found a comfortable ear in the legislature" (Associated Press, 2003a:1). Typical of many perhaps, one legislator said "I just have a general rule that I'm not going to put additional rules on businesses because of the poor economy that we have" (Associated Press,

2003b:1). When times are good and profits are up, it is more difficult to resist new oversight on grounds of cost.

When it does take notice of and creates new oversight the state can choose from a range of options, from revocation of professional license to civil penalties and, ultimately, to criminal prosecution. Unlike robbers and cocaine users, the privileged and their representatives play an active part in crafting the laws and regulatory standards that circumscribe their conduct. The importance of accommodating and gaining acquiescence from representatives of commerce and finance is taken for granted, and the need to avoid action that could harm business confidence is a paramount concern. These are some reasons why statutes that represent weak or symbolic threats to harmful conduct may be followed by administrative bureaucracies unwilling or unable to mount serious efforts against white-collar criminals (Calavita, 1983).

Behind the conflict over specific criminalization and decriminalization efforts, the larger struggle is over autonomy, freedom from market forces, and access to state largesse. Privileged individuals and groups want always to conduct their affairs autonomously and to draw from public coffers doing so. They push to sustain or strengthen their right to be free of oversight, first on grounds they are honorable, honest, and deserving and second, with claims that opposition would be unreasonable, anticompetitive, and prohibitively costly. Trade and professional organizations invariably charge that practices dangerous or harmful to others are attributable to a few bad apples and that most individuals or firms are exemplary citizens.

Access and Outcomes
When they and their representatives are asked what is gained by favors done for and cash contributions to political leaders, the answer invariably is "access." By this is meant the opportunity to explain their position on public issues at length and in detail. The privileged have assured avenues and procedures for making their views known to political decision makers. Through social contacts, personal favors, paid lobbyists, and monetary contributions, the privileged gain the access needed to ensure their perspectives are known and taken seriously by political leaders and state managers (Lofquist, 1993). Fronted by a

phalanx of attorneys, lobbyists, publicists, and hired technical experts, they press their self-interested notions of what is reasonable oversight. They are in the battle for the long haul, they press the fight on many fronts, and their advance, which may be imperceptible, can be relentless. Large corporations convicted of crimes between 1990 and 2000 gave more than $9 million to the Republican and Democratic political parties (*Corporate Crime Reporter*, 2003). The influence process generally occurs in private settings, far from the public eye. In these venues, a style and worldview are reinforced, and employed in decision making. Elected representatives and top-level state managers share with those who are paid to influence them not only class background but also deeply ingrained regard for respectability and the good life. As a result, political decision makers generally come to see issues much as the privileged do. Little pressure may be needed to bring them to where they can appreciate the complexity of issues and the need, therefore, for caution and further study. When the influence process is exposed to the public spotlight or scandal, representatives of the privileged disavow trying to rig oversight debate and construction. Their success at defeating, stalling, or converting to their own purposes actions meant to restrict their behavioral options is the first step in a process of accumulating advantages afforded upperworld white-collar criminals (Yeager, 1992).

Talk, discussion, and persuasion are the stock in trade of the social classes that produce white-collar criminals. Products of child rearing in which discussion is employed liberally, they handle interpersonal sticking points and conflicts with courtesy and civility. Discussion and negotiation may continue over weeks or months, but they keep their eye on the objective. In the process, seemingly irreconcilable differences are resolved cordially. Adults reared in privilege who have known success in respectable pursuits are confident they can negotiate nearly anything and that deals can be worked out rationally without emotions getting in the way. Accustomed to dealing with bureaucracies and professionals, they work them deftly and they speak the language of state officials. On the final day of his administration, President Bill Clinton granted 176 petitions for executive clemency from persons convicted of federal crimes (Ruckman, 2003). Forty-eight percent (eighty-five) of the petitions were submitted and presumably written by white-collar offenders. No one familiar with the written pleadings of garden-variety criminal supplicants would find this remarkable.

Where loss or concession in criminalization contests is unavoidable, the privileged generally hold out for broad requirements to do only what is least inconvenient. Legislatures rarely provide severe penalties for white-collar crimes, and where they entrust to independent agencies the task of developing a scale of penalties the result is not appreciably different. Created by Congress in 1984, the U.S. Sentencing Commission (USSC) collects public opinion data on crime and uses them to construct and justify penalty schedules (Rossi and Berk, 1997). Its sentencing guidelines increased uniformity in sentencing by providing federal judges and prosecutors with detailed tables that prescribe the range of appropriate sentences for federal crimes. The USSC publicized widely its stiffened sentencing guidelines for white-collar crimes in the 1990s. A participant in legislative hearings that produced a call for even tougher maximum corporate fines commented later that when they were issued,

> all hell broke loose. According to news stories and my colleagues on the commission, many angry corporate leaders called the Bush White House, which alerted the Justice Department. The commission quickly backpedaled, scaling back the penalties by some 97%. The new maximum penalty was dropped to $12.6 million (it has since increased, but remains far less than the commission first had proposed). The commission also made it easier for corporations to reduce their fines even more based on a set of mitigating factors. For instance, if a corporation had an effective compliance program, it could subtract three points from its culpability score and possibly reduce its fine by more than 30%. (There are also factors that increase a culpability score.) Little wonder corporate executives are not losing sleep if it is found that they crossed the line. (Etzioni, 2002:2)

Less than a decade later, in the Sarbanes-Oxley Act, the USSC again was directed and increased penalties for designated white-collar crimes. After years of use, the status of federal sentencing guidelines is unclear, however. In January 2005, the U.S. Supreme Court ruled that they violate the Sixth Amendment to the U.S. Constitution by allowing judicial rather than jury factfinding as the basis for sentencing.

TABLE 4.1. *Sentences imposed on individuals convicted of federal white-collar crimes and street crimes, United States, 1995–2002.*

Penalty type and characteristic*	Street crimes*	White-collar crimes*
Monetary Penalties		
Average number sentenced annually with monetary penalties	1533	7550
Mean monetary penalty	$131,326	$230,935
Percent sentenced with fines	6.4	16.3
Percent sentenced with restitution	51.4	50.3
Percent sentenced with fines and restitution	3.5	6.1
Probation/Imprisonment		
Average number annually sentenced to imprisonment or probation	2,579.4	10,690.5
Percent sentenced to probation	6.5	42.7
Percent sentenced to prison	93.4	57.2
Mean sentence length (months)	79.1	10.6

*   Includes murder, manslaughter, assault, robbery, burglary, and auto theft.
** Includes larceny, fraud, embezzlement, bribery, tax offenses, antitrust offenses, and food and drug violations.
Source: U.S. Sentencing Commission, *Sourcebook of Federal Sentencing Statistics* (1997–2004).

Despite changes in criminal sentencing in recent years, penalties on the order of those routinely handed out to street offenders are given to only the most predatory and gluttonous white-collar defendants. Table 4.1 reports data on sentencing in U.S. District courts for the years 1995–2002. It shows that as compared with street criminals, white-collar offenders less often received prison sentences, and the sentences of those who did were shorter. Robbers sentenced to prison in 2002 received a median sentence of 70 months while the median prison sentence for white-collar crimes were 15 months for food and drug violations, 14 months for fraud, 12 months for tax crimes, and 6 months for antitrust crimes (U.S. Sentencing Commission, 2003).

Unlike individuals, organizational defendants cannot be incarcerated, but they can be placed on probation, fined, and ordered to make financial restitution for their crimes. Table 4.2 shows average fines imposed on convicted organizations for the years 1995–2002. In 2002, the average fine was $2.82 million. The fact that most fines are

TABLE 4.2. *Numbers of and sentences imposed on organizations convicted of federal crimes, United States, 1995–2002.*

Characteristic	1995	1996	1997	1998	1999	2000	2001	2002
Total number of organizations sentenced annually	108	155	222	213	255	304	238	252
Number of organizations with fine imposed	85	114	183	154	200	219	186	165
Mean fine imposed (million)	$0.242	$1.120	$1.475	$1.762	$6.136	$1.595	$2.154	$2.815
Median fine imposed (million)	$0.030	$0.089	$0.048	$0.064	$0.075	$0.100	$0.060	$0.096
Number of organizations with restitution imposed	35	46	70	72	83	98	78	112
Mean restitution imposed (million)	$0.232	$0.567	$0.873	$0.729	$0.601	$0.776	$4.081	$6.293
Median restitution imposed (million)	$0.028	$0.058	$0.100	$0.064	$0.100	$0.127	$0.177	$0.200

Source: U.S. Sentencing Commission, *Sourcebook of Federal Sentencing Statistics* (1995–2004).

substantially less than this suggests that a small minority of organizational defendants probably received very large fines. Etzioni (2002:2) remarks that "during the past 10 years, fines imposed on corporations have increased some, but are still relatively modest." The extremely small number of organizations sentenced is noteworthy as well.

Criminal Prosecution and Sentencing

Legislative provision of criminal penalties for injurious conduct does not ensure they will be used or that their full force will be felt by offenders. State agencies and personnel have substantial discretion in these matters; officials have at their disposal an array of options. The familiar machinery of criminal prosecution is used liberally in the war on street crime, but as a matter of course the state does not pursue white-collar crime aggressively.

Local officials with finite budget and personnel resources must use them judiciously. When they investigate suspected crimes, officials routinely encounter behaviors that can range from straightforward and easily understood acts to complex behaviors of many individuals that are extremely difficult to comprehend or reconstruct. The structures created by Enron to hide its indebtedness and create the illusion of profitability were monumentally complex and difficult to understand (Eichenwald, 2005). For the privileged this means that the advantages gained in rule making can be augmented by stingy allocation of resources needed for credible oversight. One way this is accomplished is by limiting severely the personnel and budget of investigative agencies (Pontell et al., 1994).

The level of state commitment to and resources invested in rule enforcement helps shape beliefs about the credibility of legal threats and, therefore, the attractiveness of lure. When the agencies and personnel charged with combating white-collar crime receive minimal political and fiscal support for doing their job, inevitably the belief grows among the targets of oversight that they may be able to break the law and get away with it. The environment that is created is like one in which broken windows go unrepaired. As Wilson and Kelling (1982) note, "if the first broken window ... is not repaired, then people who like breaking windows will assume that no one cares about the building and more windows will be broken." Failure by Enron

Corporation's top executives to take action against employees who profited illegally from deals a decade before it collapsed sent a signal to others that they would not be called to account for misconduct (Cruver, 2002; Eichenwald, 2005; McLean and Elkind, 2004).

Oversight of state-funded medical reimbursement programs are so lacking in credibility that one investigator calls them a "license to steal" (Sparrow, 1996), and oversight by private insurance companies may not be better; few suspicious insurance claims are reported to the police, and fewer still result in criminal prosecution (Litton, 1998). National information on insurance fraud is not available, but less than 1 percent of cases of suspected fraud reported to California's office of insurance fraud in a one-year period resulted in criminal prosecution (Tennyson, 1997). Because the practical challenges of detecting and investigating insurance fraud can be daunting, some insurance companies readily pay claims they suspect are fraudulent. Experience in Massachusetts suggests that only 2.6 percent of suspicious insurance claims contain evidence sufficient for denial (Weisberg and Derrig, 1991).

Persuasive evidence of crime and culpability is not only difficult to produce, but it also is costly. This is true particularly of crimes committed by organizations. Hierarchy and division of labor can diffuse responsibility for criminal decisions to the point that culpable individuals cannot be identified easily. The variety of reasons why decision making generally is opaque to external observation constitutes an "organizational veil" (Katz, 1980a; Wheeler and Rothman, 1982). Largely because of it, by the time prosecutors pinpoint the origins of criminal decisions time has passed, evidence has been shredded, and cover stories have been constructed.

Problems are compounded enormously when the organizations are large and powerful. This is one reason reactive enforcement must be dispensed with in favor of techniques commonly employed against geographically far-flung and hierarchical criminal organizations. Proactive enforcement can include use of undercover investigators, informants, and sting operations. Once an opening is secured, threats and inducements are used to enlist from suspects information about how crimes occurred and the identities of higher level participants. Upperworld criminals and their counsel predictably charge that these tactics

CHOOSING WHITE-COLLAR CRIME

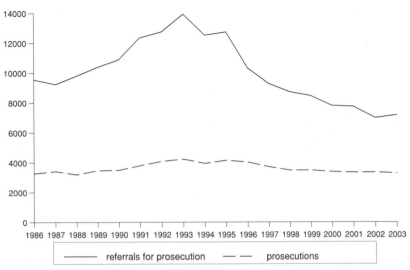

Figure 4.1. Rate of Referral for and Prosecution of Federal White-Collar Crimes, United States, 1986–2003 (Per 100 Million Persons). *Source:* Transactional Records Access Clearinghouse, 2003.

are inappropriate for and unjustified when used against respectable citizens. When guilty individuals cannot be identified or clear-cut evidence of criminal intent cannot be found, prosecutors may see no course but to file criminal charges against the organization.

Figure 4.1 shows the rate of referral to U.S. attorneys for criminal prosecution of white-collar crimes for the years 1986–2003. It shows that a sharp increase in referrals began in 1988 and continued upward for nearly seven years before beginning a decline that by 2002 brought it below the level for 1986. Increased referrals for prosecution of computer crimes accounts for part of the increase; they grew from 115 in 1992 to 853 in 2001 (Smith et al., 2004:38). Importantly, Figure 4.1 shows also that the short-term increase in referrals produced a much weaker increase in prosecutions. Recall from Table 3.1 that in the years 1995 through 2002, an average of 8,205 offenders annually were sentenced for federal white-collar crimes in the United States. Some of the steam of the modest if short-lived movement against white-collar crime has been lost due to a pro-business presidential administration and changes in investigative priorities after September 11, 2001. The Federal Bureau of Investigation (FBI), which is the primary federal agency charged to investigate white-collar crime in the United States, dramatically revamped its investigative priorities following the attacks on the World Trade Center. Investigation of white-collar crime was a loser.

When they screen cases of reported white-collar crime, prosecutors pay attention particularly to the number and extent of harm to victims and whether there was evidence of multiple offenses. Just as criminalization initiatives are easily thwarted by claims that business cannot afford additional oversight, prosecutors carefully weigh local economic conditions and interests when they screen white-collar crimes; they sometime elect not to pursue aggressively crimes committed by businesses for fear of harming employment and the local economy (Benson and Cullen, 1998). Likewise, concern for possible economic repercussions occurs on a grander scale in crimes where massive financial losses potentially could destabilize important institutions or a nation's economy (Levi, 1987; Leeson, 1996). At every level and stage of the oversight process its potential economic impacts affect the way options are weighed and the ones selected.

Before arrest and the spotlight of publicity finds them white-collar defendants sometimes manage to put aside funds to retain private counsel:

> 'ZZZZ Best Files for Bankruptcy' was the radio announcer's lead story...I was glad the July Fourth weekend had ended. Usually I enjoyed the summer holiday, but not this time. Too many things had gone wrong....I knew it wouldn't be long before the company went under. Before I resigned, I took out almost $700,000. I gave my attorney a generous retainer, hired a private investigator to work on my defense, and earmarked the balance for discreet business investments that I hoped would provide me with enough money to live on. (Minkow, 1995:181)

Jeffrey Skilling, the former CEO of Enron who played a major role in its downfall, reportedly put away $23 million to pay attorneys to defend him against criminal charges (McLean and Elkind, 2004).

Few ordinary white-collar criminals and no upperworld ones spend time in jail (Irwin, 1985). Following arrest, the latter and their attorneys remain in close contact with investigatory officials, and they plan

strategically whether and how to cooperate. In early proceedings most
are confident:

> I wasn't scared of them or their "evidence." I was confident I would
> impress them as a credible person and a powerful witness. Either they
> would believe me and drop the case, or they would conclude that they
> would lose ... if they brought it to trial. ... It made sense, logically and
> emotionally. I was ... certain of my ability as a speaker, and certain I
> could never be indicted. I was a lawyer, a former Assistant Secretary
> of State ... It was ridiculous. It was impossible. (Abrams, 1993:26)

If witnesses or defendants with upperworld backgrounds antagonize
prosecutors, it will not be for failure to show up or to pay attention to
court dates. The information some white-collar offenders can provide
gives them bargaining power with prosecutors, and fear of impending
prosecution can set off a "mad rush to the courthouse" by suspects
willing to trade information for immunity or lenient penalties (Ross,
1980). This is important for the reason that "life is deals," and this is
true of criminal justice no less than elsewhere (Kornbluth, 1992:269).
The words of a street criminal could not be more accurate:

> [Dealing] is the backbone of American justice. It doesn't matter if
> you've killed your kindly old parents, robbed the orphans' fund, or
> criminally molested an entire Sunday school class; if you have some-
> thing to deal with, you can disentangle yourself from the law without
> earning a single gray hair behind bars. ... The whole thing is mar-
> velously flexible. (MacIsaac, 1968:204–5)

Federal sentencing guidelines permit prosecutors to weigh and take
account of whether defendants provided material evidence of crime
committed by others. This can result in substantially reduced sentences. Many ordinary white-collar criminals, however, have little to
offer prosecutors in return for leniency. They generally have sufficient
resources to avoid use of public defenders, but mounting a defense
against criminal charges can easily threaten or deplete their fiscal
resources (U.S. Department of Justice, 2000a). Eventually, the great
majority of them decide to move on and put the entire experience
behind them; they plead guilty (U.S. Sentencing Commission, 2003).
   When white-collar defendants stand for sentencing matters usually
are not as bleak as the institutional setting would suggest, however.

Judges commonly use as justification for not imposing prison time defendants' suffering and the damage to reputation caused by arrest and prosecution. When sentencing Medicaid fraudsters, for example, they

> recognize that damage to a physician's reputation is a form of punishment in itself. As one Medicaid official noted, "You put [a doctor's] name on the front page of the paper as a thief, you've destroyed him." ... In this peculiar bit of folk wisdom, falls from high places are the stuff of tragedy, but the tumbles of those who had not climbed so high are assumed to be less painful – the latter are supposed to suffer less because they are accustomed to having so little. Nonetheless, judges typically refer to the loss of standing already experienced by a white-collar criminal as a basis for a light sentence. (Jesilow, Pontell, and Geis, 1993:99)

This is another reason why guilty but key participants in white-collar crimes may avoid harsh sanctions. It is the advantage of fiscal resources, respectability and privately compensated counsel. Still, much leniency in sentencing white-collar criminals comes not from judicial discretion but from sentencing guidelines (U.S. Sentencing Commission, 2003).

Many white-collar criminal defendants receive more than one form of penalty (i.e., restitution, probation, prison, fines). Research on 1,094 white-collar defendants sentenced in seven U.S. district courts during 1976–1979 found that 50 percent were sentenced to imprisonment, 80 percent received a term of probation, and 33 percent were fined. The average prison sentence was twenty-one months, and the median term was six months (Weisburd et al., 1991:131). For defendants sentenced to incarceration, 33 percent were sentenced to more than one year, but only 2.5 percent were sentenced to more than five years. They were sentenced before abolition of federal parole in 1984 and creation of federal sentencing guidelines, and in the late 1970s, offenders typically served about one-third of their sentences. The guidelines increased the proportion of their sentence served by prisoners.

Analysis of 499 investigations undertaken by the U.S. Securities and Exchange Commission (SEC) between 1948 and 1972 shows that of every 100 suspects investigated, 93 had committed securities violations that carry criminal penalties (Shapiro, 1985). Criminal action was initiated against eleven, six were indicted, five were convicted, and three received prison sentences. In other words, diversionary, administrative, and civil actions are the norm. Analysis of all federal actions initiated or completed in 1975 and 1976 against 477 of the largest U.S. manufacturing firms showed that by the time the dust had settled, 75.8 percent received no penalties, 21 percent received civil fines, and 2.4 percent received criminal penalties (Clinard and Yeager, 1980). Monetary penalties may be less than the profits gained from violation (Etzioni, 1993). The state's failure to respond decisively to massive crime in the savings and loan industry in the 1980s meant that large numbers of S&L officials managed to avoid criminal penalties entirely (Black, 2005; Calavita et al., 1997b). Rational-choice theory highlights the need for certain and severe penalties for white-collar crime, but criminal penalties are neither probable nor unusually severe.

Regulation

The bulk of output from criminalization campaigns are rules that carry minimal civil penalties for most forms of white-collar noncompliance; the body of statute law that organizations and citizens are expected to meet is small when compared with the volume of regulatory rules that confronts them. At all levels of government a host of regulatory agencies and personnel are empowered by legislative bodies to promulgate and enforce standards of safe, fair, and reasonable conduct. Established more than a century ago as the earliest federal regulatory agency, the Interstate Commerce Commission has been joined by scores of others, from the familiar U.S. Federal Trade Commission (FTC) and Environmental Protection Agency (EPA) to the less familiar Office of Surface Mining Reclamation and Enforcement (OSM). The administrative departments of state and local government generally parallel this array of federal agencies.

   Economic regulation, which predominated until the 1970s, is focused on problems of finance, market relationships, and integrity in trade, but the final decades of the last century witnessed the extension of state regulatory oversight into areas that previously were discretionary for corporate interests. The newer *social regulation* "affects the conditions under which goods and services are produced and the physical characteristics of products that are manufactured. [It] ... also extends to more industries" (Lilly and Miller, 1977:53). The heart of social regulation is protection of employee health and safety and the environment.

Business leaders charge that the need to comply with regulations and regulators harms productivity, and criticism of social regulation particularly is intense. The facts about trends in regulatory oversight and its costs are difficult to determine, but they give reason to dispute broad indictments about regulatory cost and excess. For one thing, regulators must play catch up to the growing number of business firms and the increasing complexity of business transactions. The lesson is apparent, for example, in derivatives trading, or betting whether financial performance indicators will rise or fall. Some forms of derivative trading are conducted by entering into mathematical formulae variables linked to national currencies, bonds, and stocks. It is impractical even for specialists at institutional investment firms to track these returns routinely and carefully. A retired Wall Street derivatives trader remarks that

> [o]nly a handful of derivatives salesmen know the closely guarded secrets of how derivatives are actually used, and those elite few have no reason to share secrets worth millions of dollars with me or you. Derivatives insiders won't even tell their colleagues the most valuable secrets. One reason I wanted to move to Morgan Stanley's derivatives group was that they seemed to know more of those secrets. Even for me as a derivatives salesman at First Boston, it was almost impossible to learn the details of the most profitable deals on Wall Street. Imagine how difficult it still must be for journalists and regulators, who can learn only what the derivatives insiders are willing to tell them. (Partnoy, 1997:30)

It may be all but impossible for civil servants to monitor derivatives trading and similar complex transactions. Here and elsewhere the responsibilities of regulators and the challenges they face have increased in the face of the former's decreasing numbers.

Figure 4.2 shows the number of social and economic regulatory personnel (per 100 tax-filing corporations) for the years 1975–2000. As can be seen, in 1975 there were approximately four federal regulators for every 100 corporations, but by 2000 this declined to just over two. Figure 4.2 also shows the decrease occurred for both economic and

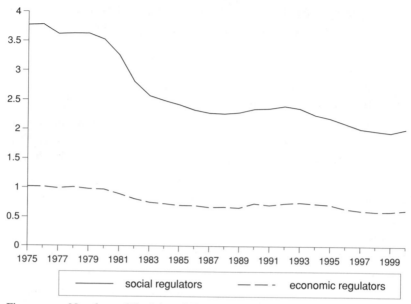

Figure 4.2. Number of Social and Economic Regulators Per 100 Tax-Filing Corporations, United States, 1975–2000. *Sources:* Dudley and Warren, 2003; Internal Revenue Service, 2003.

social regulators. Decline at the federal level occurred in part because some regulatory responsibilities have been shifted to state government, and it is unclear if there was a net increase overall in social regulators.

Doubt about whether regulatory oversight has kept pace with increasing lure is raised also by examining trends in expenditures for regulation. Figure 4.3 shows federal expenditure on regulation (per corporation) for the years 1975–2000 for both economic and social regulation. In constant dollars, the amount spent on regulation per U.S. corporation has varied over the period but declined since its high in 1975. In that year, about $3,500 per corporation was spent in the area of social regulation, a level of expenditure that would not be approached again for a quarter century. The low was in 1986 at about $2,500. Expenditures for economic regulation fluctuated between $550 and $750 over the final quarter of the last century and closed only marginally higher than the beginning. These data suggest that oversight has failed to keep up with the growing supply of lure.

Regulatory enforcement suffers from the same problems faced by police and prosecutors. Few regulatory bureaucracies approximate the

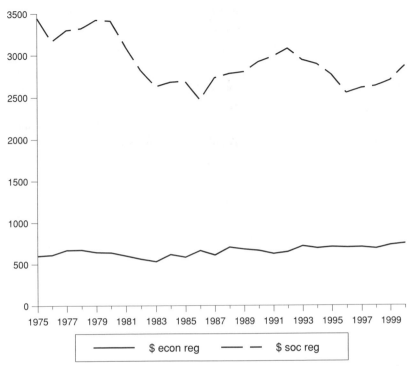

Figure 4.3. Federal Investment in Social and Economic Regulation (1996$) Per Tax-Filing Corporation, United States, 1975–2000. *Sources*: Dudley and Warren, 2003; Internal Revenue Service, 2003.

amply funded, aggressive, and credible adversaries envisioned by their creators. The SEC began an inquiry into Enron's use of debt-hiding structures and transaction only after the *Wall Street Journal* called attention to them. "Strange as it might seem, it wasn't unusual for the agency to begin a securities probe on the basis of a media report. The SEC was short staffed and overwhelmed; its staff hadn't conducted a routine review of Enron's annual financial filings since 1997" (McLean and Elkind, 2004:371). Instead of routine and detailed scrutiny of all cases oversight increasingly takes the form of computer-generated spot checks of anomalous ones (Vaughan, 1982).

Experience with regulatory enforcement suggests that agencies are prone to "capture" by the industries and firms they were created to oversee; as they interact routinely over months and years, and personnel move back and forth between them, industry supplants the public as their client. Following several well-publicized cases of drugs

that were marketed widely but subsequently proved to be riskier than
thought, the U.S. Food and Drug Administration (FDA) and the Office
of Drug Safety (ODS) have come under criticism for failure to test or
oversee use of drugs once approved for marketing. In November 2004,
for example, Merck & Company voluntarily withdrew from the market
its drug Vioxx, which was prescribed by physicians as a pain medica-
tion for arthritis patients (U.S. Food and Drug Administration, 2004).
Critics argue that because the ODS, which is responsible for recalls,
is not independent it is unlikely to recall drugs already approved by
the FDA. Drug companies recognize this and in many cases fail to follow through on studies they promise to conduct when their drugs are
approved (*Baltimore Sun*, 2004). Generally regulatory inspectors issue
many notices of violation which carry minor civil fines. Larger penalties and criminal prosecution are exceedingly uncommon. Against the
suspicion that they are prone to capture most regulatory agencies are
unable or unwilling to mount serious efforts against white-collar criminals. Although the efficacy of regulatory oversight remains unclear,
it apparently works better in some locales and industries than others. Studies of the impact of regulation on corporate environmental
performance, for example, generally support theoretically based predictions of an inverse relationship between the intensity of regulation
and compliance (Shover and Routhe, 2004). Close regulatory oversight can produce large reductions in environmental crime, and its
interaction with activist pressure, market forces, and corporate culture is particularly effective in improving environmental compliance
(Kagan, Gunningham, and Thornton, 2003).

Systematic evidence is not compiled easily, but anecdotal reports of
the effects of oversight are revealing. The federal Risk Management
Agency (RMA) has enforcement responsibility for the Federal Crop
Insurance program. In 2000, the RMA implemented a strategy to
screen for anomalous claims submitted for indemnification for crop
loss and prevented planting. Using computerized screening procedures, auditors searched for claims for prevented planting and high
losses per acre insured in counties where other farmers were successful. Six hundred producers were identified. Although in past years
these farms received large and increasing indemnities, they were sent
letters informing them that federal authorities were pursuing cases of

fraud and alerting them that they would be visited by inspectors soon to look into their reporting. In 2001 projected pay-outs to them plummeted. When opportunities for fraud are abundant and offenders have been able to exploit them with impunity, the compliance payoff from a threatening letter is impressive.

Civil Prosecution

When prosecutors cannot identify culpable individuals, collect sufficient evidence, or reasonably assume they will prevail at trial, they opt for the less onerous standard of proof required in civil proceedings. If authorities prevail, courts can impose substantial awards against individuals or organizations. The most powerful weapon in the civil arsenal of prosecutors is the Racketeer Influenced and Corrupt Organization statute (RICO). Enacted by Congress in 1970, RICO was aimed at organized crime groups, but it has been used against organizational white-collar criminals. Use of RICO has been controversial, with supporters and opponents equally aroused, and opposition has caused tighter restrictions on its use; from a high of 972 cases brought in 1991, case filings under RICO have declined. There were 743 cases in 2003, but few target large or powerful defendants (U.S. District Courts, 2003). In September 2004, U.S. prosecutors in New York began a RICO civil jury trial of the nation's largest tobacco firms, accusing them of engaging in a fifty-year conspiracy to misrepresent the addictive nature of cigarettes. Prosecutors are seeking to force the firms to disgorge $280 billion they accuse them of earning through fraud. Other objectives are forcing public disclosure of company research on smoking and a ban on marketing to children. The trial is expected to last six months (*New York Times*, 2004).

Civil litigation reports published by the SEC for the two-week period December 1, 2003, through December 15, 2003, show there were seventeen cases of alleged fraud, five cases of insider trading or market manipulation, and two cases of failure to comply with court orders stemming from previous criminal violations. This confirms what media reporting suggests: civil actions frequently disguise serious criminal conduct. Actions taken against mining companies are illustrative. Federal worker safety regulations require mines to maintain coal dust levels in mines below two milligrams/cubic meter of air. To monitor the level of coal dust, air samples are taken by filters encased in collection devices at various locations in the mine. The filters must be changed periodically, and used ones must be sent to the U.S. Mine Safety and Health Administration (MSHA). Discovery of high levels of coal dust can lead to the mine's shutdown. According to MSHA, in 1991 mine operators were vacuuming the filters or spraying them before use with a household dust-reducing product to keep them from accumulating dense layers of coal dust. MSHA received 4,710 faked samples from 847 coal mines across the United States, or 40 percent of the mines it is charged with sampling. In response, the U.S. Department of Labor imposed on 500 mining companies a total of $5 million in civil penalties for tampering with safety testing equipment (*New York Times*, 1991b).

Szockyj and Geis (2002) examined the cases of 452 persons charged by the federal government with insider trading during the 1980s. The subjects overwhelmingly were charged civilly in proceedings in which they neither admitted nor denied their guilt and thereby avoided the stigma of criminal conviction. Generally they were required to disgorge their illegally acquired gains and were fined the same amount. The investigators conclude that "[u]ndoubtedly, the difficulty of proving violations beyond a reasonable doubt, the prospect of financial recovery of losses, and the very considerable skills of the defense bar involved in handling white-collar crimes... pressed prosecutors to file civil actions" (Szockyj and Geis, 2002:284). On December 31, 2004, Minnesota's attorney general sued credit card issuer Capital One Financial Corporation, accusing it of defrauding consumers by falsely advertising low and fixed interest rates. The complaint alleged that Capital One nearly quadruples the rate it charges cardholders who trigger a "penalty" rate by paying their bill a day late or otherwise defaulting; cardholders who received an initial 4.99 percent interest rate but later defaulted saw their rate skyrocket to 19.8 percent. The lawsuit said Capital One's marketing violates state laws against false advertising, consumer fraud, and deceptive trade practices. Minnesota is seeking restitution for cardholders, civil penalties, disgorgement of profits, and an injunction barring further wrongdoing. Monetary penalties and other civil sanctions are justified for their potential deterrent effect; they should spur business owners and private citizens to be more careful in their operations, thereby reducing the odds of similar conduct in the future (Simpson, 2002).

OFF-SHORE OVERSIGHT

The control challenge presented by white-collar crime has altered fundamentally with the global economy and increasing power of transnational corporations (TNCs). Globalization of production and markets is a powerful constraint on oversight, and it has set off a vigorous debate over how nations should respond (Braithwaite and Drahos, 2000). The difficulties of controlling corporations were enormous in a world of national economies and corporate actors, but efforts to criminalize their conduct causes firms to adopt several strategies. Some threaten to locate elsewhere or to relocate if oversight is increased. Others raise the specter of lost jobs.

Leather-tanning is a case in point (Grether and Melo, 2004; Hesselberg and Knutsen, 2002). Tanning companies cannot hope to gain from innovation in product design or from other advantages of location in rich nations to the same extent that manufacturers of sophisticated medical equipment might. The technology for tanning leather is simple. The work is labor intensive, and without expensive preventive measures it dirties the environment. Employment in the tanning industry decreased by 33 percent in the decade beginning in 1985. Most of these lost jobs moved to Central and South America. Cheaper labor, and less rigorous environmental protection requirements found there presumably are attractive to tanning companies (Hesselberg and Knutsen, 2002). A similar movement has taken place in other low-tech, environmentally "dirty" industries (Grether and Melo, 2004; Levinson and Taylor, 2001). Concern that jobs are in danger contributes to public reluctance to regulate industries and firms close to home. The presence of off-shore banking centers for companies avoiding taxation and regulation suggests that lax oversight is a development tool for some nations.

The narrow interests and muscle of TNCs are wielded in a host of ways. Amid organized opposition to the import of genetically modified cotton to Indonesia, a manager at Monsanto directed an Indonesian consulting firm to make a clandestine payment of a $50,000 to an official in Indonesia's environment ministry. The payment came with a request to waive the environmental study requirement for a strain of cotton. Facing criminal and civil charges for bribery, Monsanto agreed to pay $1.5 million in fines to the Securities and Exchange Commission and the Department of Justice and to improve internal compliance measures (British Broadcasting Company, 2005).

Disunity is inconsistency in law or enforcement across jurisdictions. It exacerbates the challenge of national-level oversight. Consider the attempt to prevent antitrust crimes in the cement industry. A case can be made that U.S. regulators prevented vertical integration and informal price agreements to a much greater extent than their counterparts in competitor nations (Dumez and Jeunamaitre, 2000). European regulators saw price stabilization as efficient and beneficial to the market and had no interest in policing many of the measures used by companies to achieve it. European firms benefitted from official disinterest. This disunity led to unforeseen consequences. When a cost-efficient means of transporting cement by barge was implemented widely, these advantaged firms tapped the U.S. market and damaged U.S. concrete companies (Dumez and Jeunamaitre, 2000).

Disunity makes it easier to resist state limits on autonomy at home because companies point to nations prepared to give them freer rein. The United States has called repeatedly for a unified international front in its war on drugs (Office of National Drug Control Policy, 2003). It demands rigorous enforcement and responds with sanctions when it is not forthcoming; nations reluctant to side with or adopt U.S. measures are pressured to do so diplomatically and economically. The same determination to mount a unified front against corporate crime and to hold companies to stringent standards is lacking. The challenge and reluctance are illustrated by Bhopal. In 1984, the Union Carbide Corporation released methyl isocyanate and hydrogen cyanide gas into the atmosphere from its plant in Bhopal, India. According to the Indian government's count, the incident killed 3,329 people and seriously injured another 20,000 (Pearce and Tombs, 1998). Indian prosecutors filed criminal charges against Union Carbide, its CEO, and eight officers of its Indian subsidiary (*Los Angeles Times*, 1989). Union Carbide won a judgment in U.S. courts establishing that Indian courts had sole jurisdiction over all civil litigation resulting from the disaster. Observers speculated that company lawyers believed they would receive favorable treatment and less costly judgments from Indian courts. The case was settled for $470 million in 1989, a sum that included payments of approximately $1,000 per claimant. The settlement also stipulated that Carbide would be immune from all pending litigation and that criminal charges against officers of the company would be dropped. The Indian Supreme Court subsequently ruled that criminal charges should stand, and seventeen years after the tragedy extradition papers were served on Warren Anderson, an officer of the company and fugitive from India. The request was rejected on technical grounds. An urgent problem brought on by development of the global economy is determining which laws and regulations will be used as standards for individual and organizational behavior. Few answers are found in international law and agreements.

Increasingly, international agreements and institutions provide rules and oversight as nations struggle to control TNCs and respond to their crimes (Braithwaite and Drahos, 2000). This movement highlights a pattern of permissiveness that rational-choice theory predicts will swell the ranks of white-collar criminals. Although the signatories to international trade agreements typically pledge to adopt and enforce in their home countries elementary regulations for environmental protection, worker rights, and product safety, police and prosecutors in jurisdictions lack the budget, expertise, and other resources to pursue these cases. As oversight becomes more distant geographically, its efficacy becomes less certain, and the gap between standards and compliance grows.

In the absence of credible oversight, tax incentives, loans, trade incentives, and other lures offered by transnational agreements and governing organizations easily become criminal opportunity. By denying freedom of association to labor organizations, companies gain an advantage over competitors in nations where workers are free to organize (U.S. Department of Labor, 2004). In the face of these practices other nations generally do little more than request an end to them. NAFTA nations are expected to enforce their labor laws and also abide by the North American Agreement on Labor Cooperation. NAFTA enforcement officials are much more likely to penalize for violation of trade restriction than for other socially harmful and illegal practices (Eisner, 2000). This fuels the claims of critics that human rights and environmental protections in trade agreements are toothless.

The substance of international agreements for trade and lending are often called into question for undermining oversight. Some provisions, for example, prevent national governments from mounting criminal-ization campaigns by defining them as protectionist measures (Mayne and Le Quesnel, 1999; Sjoberg, Gill, and Williams, 2001; Wilkinson and Hughes, 2000). For example, Canada proposed regulations to prevent Phillip Morris from labeling cigarettes "light" or "mild" for fear the labels mislead consumers into thinking these cigarettes are safe. Phillip Morris claimed that the move would be a violation of NAFTA's chapter 11, which permits firms to sue signatory governments if their investment rights are violated. The company also cited WTO agreements that require nations to use the least trade restrictive means to accomplish regulatory objectives (Mokhiber and Weissman, 2002).

Global oversight develops in dozens of forms and a complex array of institutions. It relies on criminal prosecution primarily in the nations where crimes originate. Nations, however, are reluctant to grant other nations and international bodies the right to define and pursue global oversight on their soil. Thus far, international cooperation has pushed farthest in efforts to control international organized crime and war crimes. These are areas where most nations can come to agreement. "All the while, avoidable harms (often of equivalent or greater magni-tude) by transnational corporations are ignored" (Gilbert and Russell, 2002:233).

CHAPTER FIVE

Decision Making

Rational-choice theory is best seen as a "framework, a rubric or a family of theories" that serves to "organize findings, link theoretical statements and logically guide theory construction" (Hechter and Kanazawa, 1997:194). It has been applied to a host of problems and processes, including managerial decisions, interpersonal exchange, consumer purchasing, and the dynamics of economic markets. Arguably, it is the dominant theoretical paradigm in political science (Green and Shapiro, 1994; Hechter and Kanazawa, 1997; Smith, 1991). The importance of rational-choice theory as an interpretation of crime and as justification for contemporary initiatives in crime control is on firm footing.

Decision making is the heart of rational-choice theory. It is seen as a process of cognition and calculation in which actors pursue desired goals, weigh likely consequences, and select among options. This means that the structural conditions and generative worlds that lie "behind" readiness to choose crime are important primarily because they shape offenders' evaluation of potential costs and benefits. Normative confusion and ambiguity, for example, is a background variable that has been linked theoretically to increased likelihood of misconduct by organizational employees and managers (Passas, 1990; Reichman, 1993). When this theoretical relationship is cast in the logic of rational choice, rule ambiguity is significant principally for the ways it affects calculation and decision making by discrete actors. In addition to its potential payoffs for explaining and predicting variation in crime, enhanced understanding of decision making holds promise of guiding policy interventions to minimize criminal choices. Cornish and Clarke (1986:vi) construe rational-choice theory as a way of both "rearranging existing theories and data to throw new light on criminal behaviors" and as a "policy-relevant perspective on criminal behavior." In this belief, they are not alone (Felson and Clarke, 1998; Weisburd, 1997).

Beyond rudimentary statements of crime-as-choice theory is a more complex understanding developed through critique, research, and theoretical elaboration. Its core is belief that "when faced with several courses of action, people usually do what they believe is likely to have the best overall outcome" (Elster, 1989:22). It is clear also that decision makers are "fallible learners who seek to do as well as they can, given the constraints that they face" (Ostrom, 1998:9). Individuals have considerable capacity intuitively for maximizing self-interest. They recognize rational strategies in complex exchanges, for example, and move toward exchange equilibrium (Plott, 1987; Williams et al., 2000; Smith, 1986). Laboratory studies comprise a substantial part of the corpus of research, and in these controlled settings subjects calculate and make decisions with a high degree of rationality. Research shows also that many decisions of everyday life are based on imperfect knowledge and crude, subjective assessments of utility. In many situations, for example, decision makers opt for what has become convenient and routine. There is bias toward the status quo.

Decisions become increasingly rational when there is opportunity to learn from previous choices. This happens in real markets and contrived market exercises. Predictions based on rational outcomes are most accurate in large random population samples where idiosyncratic differences in decisions cancel each other (Friedman and Hechter, 1988; Hechter, 1996; Hechter and Kanazawa, 1997). Likewise, support for the theory is found when conditions make a choice apparently more appealing to wide segments of the population than it was in the past. Empirical evidence of rationality in decision making explains the relationship, between the supply of new criminal opportunities and rates of specific types of crime and between police strikes and spikes in the rate of offending. This said, unexplained variation in decision making that may derive from distinct preferences and outlooks remains a challenge and the focus of considerable interest.

BURGLARS AND BANKERS

For nearly three decades investigators have explored how street criminals estimate the costs and benefits of crime and how they make criminal decisions. A great deal is known about their daily rounds, the contexts wherein they make criminal decisions and the dynamics of the process. A variety of methodologies have been used to examine these matters, but ethnographic studies unquestionably have shed the most revealing light. Most, for example, show that thieves are rational when it comes to choosing targets that offer security and the surest returns.

In broad outline, investigators have demonstrated that street offenders generally behave consistent with predictions based on rational-choice theory. They commit crime with an eye toward maximizing reward and minimizing risk. Research makes clear, however, that burglars, armed robbers, and other street criminals are anything but careful calculating actors (Bennett and Wright, 1984; Cromwell, Olsen, and Avary, 1991; Feeney, 1986; Katz, 1988; Shover and Honaker, 1992; Wright and Decker 1994; 1997). This body of research serves as a useful starting point for anyone interested in white-collar criminal decision making whether the results are cast as accident, scandal, or mistake.

A high proportion of street offenders break the law in the context of lifestyles that make it seem there is much to gain and little to lose by doing so (Shover, 1996). Skid-row addicts facing withdrawal may see great utility in $100 while the shame of stealing or getting caught seems negligible. Street offenders usually have little more than a hunch about their chances of apprehension, and in moments of clarity, many understand that arrest probably awaits if they continue in crime. In less reflective moments, like those that precede most crimes, they conclude that they probably can get away with at least one more offense (Shover, 1996). Their decisions generally take only an instant and result from hasty, rudimentary, and imprecise calculation. Interviews with 113 men convicted of robbery or an offense related to robbery revealed, for example, that "over half . . . reported no planning at all" (Feeney and Weir, 1975:105). The criminal ambitions of most are limited to fulfilling an immediate desire.

One reason for spontaneity is that street offenders' decisions are made in the context and dynamics of street life and hustling (Shover, 1996). As the context of decision making, hustling helps explain why research on 105 active residential burglars found that they expressed a "steadfast refusal to dwell on the possibility of being apprehended" (Wright and Decker, 1994:14). Street offenders develop an ability to put out of mind risk to self and others, to focus on the potential payoffs of specific criminal acts and steel themselves to go ahead (Shover, 1996; Wright and Decker, 1994). Those who hustle continuously develop an alert opportunism that prepares them to see opportunity where others do not. They can react instantly and with little thought when they encounter something promising.

A substantial majority of street crimes occur in groups, and interpersonal dynamics constrain decision making (Reiss, 1988; Zimring, 1981; Warr, 2002). Conversation and interactional dynamics build confidence and excitement by emphasizing positive outcomes and the ability of those present to accomplish the task while downplaying the risks. Offenders call these exchanges "talking it up" or "pumping each other up" (Cromwell et al., 1991; Hochstetler and Copes, 2003). Both the substance and tone of these discussions are influenced by drugs and alcohol or the immediate need for more.

Drug use and altered states of consciousness inevitably result in crude and hasty calculation. Youth and mood also and can make salient preferences and commitments that relegate caution to the background (Cordilia, 1986; Hochstetler, 2001). Danger and excitement that are attributes of street crime repel most but attract some. Young and intoxicated offenders looking for opportunity to prove their meddle often misjudge the potential for considerable cost and meager benefit. The circumstances in which street offenders live and play complicates immensely the challenge of frightening them into compliance.

White-Collar Criminal Choice

Much less is known about white-collar offender decision making; there are far fewer offender autobiographies and ethnographic studies to draw from. Interviews of ordinary embezzlers and fraudsters show that the appeal of these crimes is rooted in troublesome situations at work or in other areas of life that lead the offender to be alert to opportunities (Cressey, 1953; Zietz, 1981). Embezzlers strongly prefer solutions that allow them to keep financial problems secret and that do not erode reputations or undermine ascribed obligations. Criminal opportunity is attractive as a means of responding to desire to assist family crises or forestalling a fall. There are many sources of crisis, but previous business reverses, trouble with employers, family difficulties, or vices and other personal shortcomings are typical. All come to represent for the individual "threats to status-seeking or status-maintaining behavior" (Cressey, 1953:75). When combined with changes in social environment the odds of crime are increased. Individuals who suffer business reversals can become socially isolated with nowhere to turn for solutions to their financial problems. Multiple conditions contribute but preference is the same for many ordinary offenders, a financial solution that postpones revelation of secretive problems or postpones painful consequence. Women who are unattached to the workforce do it to satisfy their habits or to support domineering men. They are more likely to commit fraud than embezzlement because that is the best opportunity they have. Those that are attached to the workforce are likely to be attempting to enhance family finances by crime and are likely to embezzle (Zietz, 1981). All make the best of the criminal opportunities that they have. The pressures of relatively conventional home lives and lives of unemployment can inspire desire for instantaneous payoff.

Drug abuse, gambling debts, and family problems are common contexts for erratic and criminal behavior of all sorts. A physician recalls the circumstances surrounding his decision not to file a tax return:

> At that time I was going through some bad problems with depression and drinking. I had just quit managing my day-to-day affairs and just given up on it. In 1988, . . . I figured I would be dead. I was fatalistic about it. Finally, in 1989, through the intervention of family, friends and colleagues, I got started on treatment for depression and alcohol; that was what lead to my problems. I was so depressed. I was sure that I was going to die, and I didn't care if I did. I was trying to drink myself to death. I did not care about the government and did not think about the trouble I could get in. It totally did not matter to me. I just plain didn't care. (Mason, 1999)

For most ordinary white-collar offenders, objective circumstances have changed little directly before their offense, but their receptiveness to the draw of lure increases as problems become pressing or turmoil distracts them. Confronted with mounting pressures and disruptions, compliance seems to require too much effort and individuals reach what they experience as a breaking point. They mentally let go of or loosen the commitments that previously restrained them. Those who can reconcile violating financial trust with a positive self-concept are at increased risk to commit crime. Upperworld and organizational criminal decision making is shrouded in fog, but it is likely that the problems that lead upperworld offenders to crime are less personal and pressing.

Simpson (2002) administered to eighty-four students and twelve corporate executives surveys containing vignettes of decision-making contexts and possible criminal responses. Respondents were instructed to make decisions as if they were corporate managers. The vignettes contained descriptions of managers of varying levels confronted with opportunities to fix prices, commit sales fraud, violate environmental standards, and bribe a supplier. Drawing on these data, Simpson demonstrates that individual characteristics predict "intention to offend." Risk perceptions and other characteristics are significant predictors of it. Those who saw opportunity for career advancement and thrills also were more likely to demonstrate intent. In addition, estimates of personal benefit, an ethical reasoning scale, shame, and the possibility of informal sanctions from family, friends, and business associates affected criminal intention. The threat of being fired or correction from superiors reduced it while declining sales for the company and being ordered by supervisors to commit the act increased offending intentions.

Formal sanctions in the form of criminal or civil penalties generally were not strong predictors but the combination of morality and formal threats was significant. For highly moral "good citizens," neither sanction threats nor other variables made much difference. Respondents who scored low on personal morality were another matter; they were deterred by threat. Evidence for similar interaction between moral preferences and opportunity is reported by others as well (Benson, 2002; Bussman, 2003; Weisburd et al., 2001).

Life and decisions in an organization are not easily approximated by static variables presented in vignettes. Vaughan (1996) interviewed a host of officials at the National Aeronautics and Space Administration (NASA) and examined written internal communications to understand how the decision to launch the ill-fated *Challenger* space shuttle was made and concluded that an organizational bias toward risky decisions and maintaining deadlines placed the flight at risk. NASA scientists, engineers, and managers gradually defined certain risks to flight safety as acceptable, which ultimately led officials to authorize the shuttle launch under dangerous conditions. Through daily interactions, employees incorporated assessments of acceptable risks that were common in the organization into how they evaluated choices. Both her use of retrospective interview data and her focus on a mishap that was neither criminal nor deviant, however, means that Vaughan's interpretation cannot be generalized to criminal decisions in the absence of additional research. The ineluctable shortcoming of this research is the failure to examine *criminal* decision making. Nevertheless, her conclusions about bounded rationality differ little from what is known about decision making by burglars and robbers (Shover and Honaker, 1992). Use of culturally shared, subjective preferences in decision making increases the appeal of a risky or immoral choice.

Many white-collar criminal decisions are responses to "contemporaneous circumstances in offenders' lives" that allow them temporarily to ignore or discount potential legal consequences (Benson, 2002:165). This is true of organizational crimes and others. These proximate circumstances come in many forms and do not affect all equally. Nagging bosses, diminishing company profits, and misused expense accounts for which bills must be paid can cause decision makers to fix upon and seize crime as solution. For a great many offenders, vague recognition of criminal opportunity comes into a sharper focus as events encapsulate options and perceptions.

Weisburd and colleagues (2001) found that offenders with the least serious and extensive prior criminal records apparently were not looking for criminal opportunity beforehand. Rather, it presented itself or was made known to them by others. These low-frequency offenders responded to personal crises in their lives by seizing and exploiting

opportunity (Weisburd et al., 2001). Repeat offenders (48 percent of
the total) are more attuned to and consistently on the look out for
criminal opportunity. Street offenders are no different.

WHITE-COLLAR CRIME AND CONTEXT

The way offenders become aware of and weigh opportunity varies by
history and circumstance. Evidence is amassing that some preferences
and outlooks that increase the appeal of crime, for example, form early
in life. With differing abilities to calculate accurately and varied ends
in mind, offenders consider the costs and rewards of offending versus
the repercussions of deciding not to for their own lives and in context.
Individual and contextual variation constrain how options are assessed
and decisions are made in both background and foreground. Choices,
moreover, occur in sequences and change as circumstances develop.
Moral reservations and internal inhibitions are subject to situational
suspension or inattention. The lenses through which offenders see
criminal opportunity and make decisions are colored by the social
contexts where crime occurs.

The context for many criminal decisions are those in which white-
collar offenders labor. Many white-collar workers devote more time
and thought to work and career than to anything else and they are
sensitive to cues and messages they receive at work. Their criminal
decisions, especially in the upper ranks, are likely to be complex and
to take into account many variables and circumstances (Geis and
Salinger, 1998; Jamieson, 1994). The structure and history of the
industries where employees operate are important contextual determinants. Organizational actors often have a keen grasp of market and
organizational forces that constrain their behavior. Their preferences,
commitments, and utilities are adjusted to suit their industrial and
organizational location and what is demanded of them. A risk-averse
decision maker would not remain employed at the trading desks of
some stock firms long. A salesman in an industry where bid-rigging is
prevalent may take some time to discover from peers and superiors
that price stability and predictability in the industry override benefits
of the firm's short-term returns. Once the advantages are understood
bid-rigging might result. Internal compliance specialists can be taught

that promotion depends on identifying misconduct and finding ways to hide it from outsiders (Katz, 1980a). Salespersons get the message when their quotas go up despite regular memos from company lawyers that the practices that led to previous sales are on unsteady legal ground. Long-term employment in an industry or organization can familiarize employees with potential criminal solutions to problems the inexperienced will only discover with time. In some industries, illegal opportunities and how to exploit them guiltlessly is part of the collective ethos.

There is reason to believe that crime is rife in the pharmaceutical industry. Clinard and Yeager (1980) found that pharmaceutical companies had three times as many serious and moderately serious violations as other firms. Braithwaite (1984:5) argued that they have a "worse record of international bribery and corruption than any other industry." He based this assertion mainly on voluntary disclosures to the U.S. Securities and Exchange Commission (SEC), which learned from a program to encourage it that more than 400 U.S. companies made questionable or illegal payments to foreign officials. Pharmaceutical companies were responsible for 14 percent of the total (Braithwaite, 1984:31; Department of Justice, 2002a). Payments meant to grease the wheels of commerce are made by drug companies to health inspectors and a host of other officials. Some companies have large slush funds on hand to make bribes. These can be hidden by deceptive bookkeeping. Executives readily admit in interviews that some forms of bribery are common in the industry and part of doing business abroad (Braithwaite, 1984). The men and women Braithwaite interviewed had little difficulty justifying bribery. Many executives believe that companies or individuals who take a hard line against some types of it are at a disadvantage in environments where corruption is ordinary. They assert that heavily regulated environments contribute to the crime and that any who would compete must consider it (Braithwaite, 1984). Environmental constraints in the pharmaceutical industry probably are overstated by interviewed executives, but a glance reveals that criminal procedures are routine and widely practiced. Evidence of routinized crimes in product testing, bookkeeping, criminal negligence, deceptive advertising, and corruption can be found in government documents and hearings. Congressional hearings were held, for example, on overcharges for Medicare drug reimbursements in 2001 (U.S. Congress, 2001).

Until recently, Medicare reimbursement to clinics and physicians for drugs was based on wholesale prices submitted by pharmaceutical companies to an industrywide data base. Some companies inflated reported prices to benefit their customers at the expense of government. Audits of health care providers' catalog prices as compared to government billed prices revealed that Medicare was overcharged for drugs by more than $1 billion in 2000. The manufacturer of the chemotherapy drug Vincasar sold it to health care providers for $7.50 but then reported the price to Medicare as $740. Medicare reimbursed the provider $640 for the drug. The poor sick patient covered the remaining reported cost with a co-pay. The dangers were more than financial. Large spreads in prices promote use of drugs that are not efficacious. The tremendous profits from some procedures and drugs contributes to high rates of medically unnecessary treatment. Settlement agreements by drug firms with Medicare related to abusive price reporting in the late 1990s totaled $1.66 billion (Taxpayers Against Fraud, 2003). Unchecked, crime becomes part of the industrial context and more of it follows.

Organizational Properties
Organizational properties and dynamics are significant and autonomous constraints on the genesis and development of crime (Needleman and Needleman, 1979; Jamieson, 1994). This is the principal rationale for distinguishing organizational and individual white-collar crime. Executive pay structures may increase some crimes. Seventy-one business firms convicted of accounting violations were matched with others that did not have criminal convictions (Troy, Smith, and Gordon, 2003). The CEOs of violator firms on average held stock options that were three times their salaries, while the CEOs of nonviolator firms held options equivalent to their salaries. This suggests that provision of excessive stock options may contribute to organizational accounting offenses. There are likely to be many such structural variables that cause particular misdeeds in particular types of organizations, but there also are variables known to have effects on crime in diverse organizations.

Performance pressure and the presence of criminogenic cultural conditions have been linked repeatedly to increased likelihood that criminal choices will be made. Performance pressure is anxiety or fear induced in individuals or organizational units by the perceived need to maintain or improve performance standards. This can be the need to increase profit margins or to improve a university athletic team's won-loss record, but in all cases it stems from belief that performance has not measured up in the eyes of peers or superiors. This is often coupled with fear that "time is running out." Performance pressure is communicated in countless ways, and it can cause employees to be less concerned with legalities (Baucus, 1994; Needleman and Needleman, 1979). An engineer urged to write a misleading test report on a faulty aircraft brake reported that eventually his superior told him to "write the goddamn thing and shut up about it" (Vandivier, 2001:150).

Research in Australian nursing homes showed that for-profit homes are significantly more likely than nonprofit ones to break the law and deliver substandard care (Jenkins and Braithwaite, 1993). Apparently, top-down pressure to meet the bottom line creates an incentive to cut corners in patient treatment, leave necessary maintenance unfinished, and look the other way in the face of dangerous working conditions. Performance pressure and cultures often translate into crime because of the rewards of employment and commitment to organizations it engenders. Under pressure to offend, resigning from the organization almost always is an option, but it may not seem that way.

Organizational properties and dynamics from differential power and authority to tendentious goal displacement can be sources of variation in the strength and efficacy of normative constraints on employees. Organizational arrangements or conditions can function to refract obligation and responsibility for misconduct and thereby blur or distort moral and legal boundaries. Also, where there are obvious and long-standing patterns of criminal conduct by organizational personnel, the proclivities and pathologies of participants fail as explanation, and the causes instead must be sought in organizational conditions.

Organizational influences often are exerted and experienced in subunits of an organization. Dictates and demands from above are assumed to be authoratative in organizations, but people look to those around them for help in interpreting signals and deciding what to do in daily decisions. The line between what the organization demands and what workmates expect often is difficult to draw. Mature adults will walk away from friends that are pushing them in undesirable directions when they are not at work; it may not be as easy where livelihoods are on the line. Regular and structured meetings make gradual adjustments to moral codes and prodding resistant offenders more likely than it is in casual relationships. Regular contact and formal ties between white-collar co-offenders build allegiance, particularly when a secret is shared that places everyone at risk.

Criminal decisions in organizations sometimes are the result of careful and routine problem solving. People are sent home with problems and decisions to ponder and they reassemble at regularly scheduled intervals to assess developments and adjust strategies. Decision making occurs in many minds incrementally, over time, and only eventually by consensus. Not all organizational crimes are so, but in some there is a complex division of labor and a formal procedure for reaching a decision. Criminal ideas may be passed between relevant players and across organizational subunits. Participants may bounce them off workmates, submit them to superiors or bring them to a vote. In a high-profile corporate price-fixing conspiracy of the 1990s, conspirators believed and decided that rigging markets was to their corporate advantage (Eichenwald, 2000; Simpson and Piquero, 2001a). The decision was not made, however, until agreement could be reached and details arranged. The meetings resembled those for licit but secretive deals. Early conversations were held in private rooms over drinks. Participants were vague and cautious. They avoided words like "agreement" that were too precise and that could be used against them in court. Other meetings that were thought to be safe because all were insiders and surveillance was highly unlikely were casual. In many, the purpose was overt. Visual aids sometimes were used to help arrange prices. Participants in the illegal projects were informed of progress in negotiating terms of agreements at each stage, but they concerted ignorance and maintained plausible deniability where convenient. Complex and carefully managed decision making is part of the white-collar world. A Wall Street trader recalls that his idea was sparked by escalating investment losses. Despite the urgency, a plan was developed by considering past actions, presenting solutions and ideas to peers, and then checking with superiors to make sure the decision was feasible and approved.

> If the books could be juggled once, they could be juggled again, as Bernstein suggested. I asked Joey-O, a former accountant, to work on the problem. I lay awake nights considering approaches. I twisted my trading position into pretzel shapes in my mind, looking for recourse. Eventually, I cobbled together an idea. . . . We would conduct a series of forward trades, the net impact of which would be zero. It would remove $20 billion in assets from the books and records of the firm. I went to Cerullo and Bernstein with this suggestion. They approved of the idea. (Jett, 1999:201)

The savings and loan industry in the United States experienced massive criminal behavior by thrift managers in the 1980s. Estimates of the total monetary cost of S&L failures range upward to $500 billion. Between 1988 and 1992, 1,098 criminal prosecutions were brought by U.S. attorneys in major S&L cases (Calavita et al., 1997a:157). The S&L failures resulted from "collective embezzlement." Crimes were committed by those in control of organizational resources (Black, 2005). In many, the organization became "a vehicle for committing crime against itself" (Calavita et al., 1997a). Officers of multiple organizations gradually formed relationships with each other and with helpful hands that minimized complexity and routinized criminal decision making.

"Land flips" were a common type of fraud committed by S&L officers (Calavita, Pontell, and Tillman, 1997b). Typically, S&L insiders, land developers, and appraisers conspired to inflate the value of a parcel of land. An appraiser recruited because of a reputation for inflating prices would value it in exchange for being contracted on future deals. The bankers then would pass the land around in sales from investor to investor raising its supposed value at each increment. Eventually, someone would go to a bank and borrow against the value of the land often for a proposed development project. The project would fail and the loan would be defaulted. In some cases, the defaulted loans were hidden from bank inspectors by selling them continuously between institutions. Some participants were close to politicians, which helped forestall regulatory action. The criminal designs of each participant merged and evolved to become a highly rational and self-perpetuating organizational system. Schemes continued despite replacement of individual participants.

Investigators documented the structure and effectiveness of collusion in the heavy electrical equipment price-fixing conspiracies of the 1950s using court depositions (Faulkner et al., 2003). The character of 144 meetings in the 1954–1959 period attended by 43 executives and managers were coded. Findings showed that companies respond to the strain of competitive prices and economic backlog with arranged prices most effectively when they achieve consensus at illegal meetings and when meetings come off smoothly (Faulkner et al., 2003). Usually executives left the work to middle managers, but they personally attended meetings when there were problems and authority was needed to come to agreement. Lure could be accessed only through standing relationships and organizational support. While the electrical conspiracy is a case of one, it provides rare insight into the mechanics of criminal decision-making in powerful organizations. In this case, it is much like how legal decisions are handled. Participants shared understandings of which decisions should be passed up the line, which should be checked with peers or experts, and when individuals or units could act independently. The decision-making process was managed to efficiently and safely accomplish objectives and to protect high-ranking participants.

When a web of conspirators has a mutual understanding of how everything should work, the trepidation and uncertainty characteristic of many crimes is avoided. Decision making is routinized, divided, and designed both to hide criminal intent and to ensure that uninformed or scrupulous outsiders do not throw a cog in the wheels. No party need discuss or admit what is going on explicitly; business can be conducted smoothly and as if it was legitimate.

Much of the distinctiveness of white-collar crime derives from the fact that it often occurs in organizational and industrial environments. Multiple people, subunits and tasks contribute to goals, perceptions and values at work and these influences shift constantly as new situations arise (Simpson, Piquero, and Paternoster, 2000). Performance pressure and criminogenic cultural conditions coupled with bureaucratic and hierarchical arrangements shape motivations, preferences, and decision-making dynamics. Offenders consider the risk posed by their individual role, the personal consequences, and the consequences for the organization. Standing arrangements and support sometimes ease the crimes. These complexities are indicators of the rationality of organizational crimes. Organizations are predictable environments where logic and planning pay.

Doing Deals

Deals are business transactions with negotiable terms. Deals are cultivated through social contacts and financial investments. "The social factors that bind managers to one another, whether in conflict or harmony, are the chief source of deals" (Jackall, 1988:198). The way deals typically are done in an organization and the industry where it is located are significant determinants of organizational structure and norms (Eccles and Crane, 1988). Likewise, the formal arrangement of deals can make the decision to commit crime seem small. For example, the privileged information gained by key positions in institutional networks and constant jockeying for position among corporate brokers makes them attentive to opportunities found in insider trades (Reichman, 1993). The structure of deals in an industry or organization play a significant part in the distribution of criminal opportunity.

The process of deal making and communication during it also has characteristics that potentially make criminal opportunity attractive. An important part of committing crime is the process of "anaesthetizing the conscience" with rhetorical and linguistic devices, and these devices may be shared among members of an organization or profession (Geis and Salinger, 1998:87). Conversations that precede crime often contain excuses, frustrations, reasons why crime should be done or indications that it is normal procedure. Deals are promising settings for talk that obscures moral components of decisions and that insulates participants from consideration of adverse consequences. They are competitive.

Deals have a contrived, artificial quality that allows participants to suspend reservations against aggressively seeking advantages that affect transactions in other spheres. Deal making is viewed by insiders as a game in which players manipulate others to desired ends (Hirsch, 1986; Partnoy, 1997:50). Game metaphors capture the maneuvers and manipulations found in many deals without raising unpleasant and morally unsettling connotations. Interests that are at odds characterize the most mutually beneficial business arrangements. Those who enter a deal have consented to complete, and recognizing this allows competitors to be manipulative or deceptive while maintaining a favorable view of themselves. The ethical barriers against crime are thinned in the process of deal making. In some business cultures and transactions, prevarications are common and viewed as expressions of optimism and salesmanship.

Interaction between insiders is as important for understanding deals as interaction with outside partners or victims. It is well known that presentation of alternatives as well as their substance affects decisions (Kuehberger, 1996; Tversky and Kahneman, 1981). Presentation is a substantial part of the artfulness of deals. In attending to the positives and glossing over problems, inertia builds and qualms recede. Criminal statutes can be framed as negotiable technicalities or unrealistic ideals, rather than as inflexible standards that prevent harm. Reasons that crime is necessary in an industry or organization can be recited in a timely manner to make sure that potential participants are in agreement and to convince the reluctant. Reservations can be argued and countered. The result is that the law's ability to influence a decision is diminished. A *Wall Street Journal* reporter who wrote stories and provided them in advance to a high-placed trader so that they could profit illegally recalls the interaction that obscured his ethical and professional obligations:

> I respected the *Journal* and my profession . . . and would not have agreed to any arrangement that required me to misinform in any way the editors or readers of my columns.
> 'Oh yeah!' he said enthusiastically. 'That's right. You just keep doing what you're doing. The only difference is you tell me what the column's about. I won't bother you about your business and you won't bother me about mine.'
> Another thing is I probably would be better off not knowing how much money you're making. I know that sound's funny but in a way I think it might make my job harder if I knew we'd make a ton of money. . . . '
> 'You write the columns and I'll make the trades. No one gets hurt, no one knows. Then, when we've got a few million bucks stashed away, I'll start my own firm and you'll come work for me. Deal?' (Winans, 1986:149).

As different as the context is from that of the street offender, this description shows that white-collar offenders also "talk it up" in their approach to crime.

Negotiation creates socially isolated and internally focused interactions. In competitive environments, deal makers tightly budget the time and attention they devote to transactions. The collapsed time perspective and inward, task-centered focus that results potentially lead to disregard of risk to participants and to outgroups (Janis, 1982; t'Hart, 1991). In their efforts to prioritize negotiating points participants may be dismissive of remote stakeholders or ignore matters that do not seem relevant to business. Negotiations also "forge commitments" so that when a deal is sealed "a commitment is made [and] the negotiators discontinue concerning themselves about what is to be done" (Couch, 1989:105). "Reciprocal attentiveness," or inward focus, only adds to "temporary bondedness" between participants and commitment to a shared pursuit (Couch, 1989:49). The window of opportunity to turn back can seem brief. If a deal is made overtly or implicitly to participate in a conspiracy, considerable effort, costs, and embarrassment might result from a change of heart.

Context is an unexamined exogenous variable in rational-choice theory. It is understood, however, that some choices are self-defeating and improbable when situations are unfavorable. Most decision makers are capable of scanning their wider environments and what others are doing to gain an intuitive grasp of appropriate responses. Context "structurally suggests" and influences choice through "preference shaping" (Dowding, 1991; Dunleavy, 1991). It causes decision makers to focus on some preferences to the exclusion of others. Contextual qualities do not rigidly determine action, but they influence what individuals and organizational decision makers see and how they weigh options. Context also shapes actors' stance toward legal norms. It may combine with the degree to which "they intrinsically value obeying the law" to affect assessment of criminal opportunity (Cooter, 2000a:1577). Chapter 3 described class and cultural conditions that conduce to distinctive middle-class perspectives on norms and external restrictions. These may remain dormant or be fueled by present company and context. Industrial and organizational environments can stimulate thoughts of crime and make it easier to commit as can the close at hand. Interactions can increase the salience of, or prime, cognitive templates by arranging and directing passing thoughts about a problem. Context heightens the connection of thinking and behavior (Bouffard, 2002; Maio et al., 2003).

THREAT AND CHOICE

Both street criminals and white-collar criminals calculate before committing crime; both choose to break the law. Investigators of white-collar crime generally have ignored research on decision making by other types of offenders and the similarities to decision making by white-collar offenders. Evidence is not compelling or voluminous, but it suggests, for example, that street offenders and white-collar offenders weigh the potential payoffs from crime more heavily than the estimated risks (Shover and Honaker, 1992; Simpson and Koper, 1992). They focus on immediate reward and shortcuts to goals and may fail to see moral implications that affect others (Gottfredson and Hirschi, 1990; Simpson and Piquerro, 2001b). Individual propensity shapes what they weigh and choose (Tibbets and Gibson, 2002:18). Many operate in environments where they "carry on as if nothing were wrong when they continually face evidence that something [is] wrong" (Vaughan, 1998:32). In the presence of like-minded companions, they can put out of mind how the larger public would judge their action and thereby blunt the deterrent effect of legal threats. In their efforts to cope with immediate crisis and daily hassles, these become remote and ill-considered contingencies (Vandivier, 2001; Warr, 2002). Rational-choice theory accommodates this contextual and individual variation. Weisburd and associates (2001:150) remark that:

> one implication of our emphasis on crisis and opportunity is that crimes committed by people in our sample often involve decision-making processes that are, within their context and in the understanding of the offender, reasoned. In this sense, the offenders we study appear to follow a rational model of offending.

White-collar crime is committed because some people estimate the payoff as greater than the risks or consequences of being caught. Seen in this way, it is sound crime-control policy to escalate the perceived risks of it while increasing legitimate opportunities and perceived payoff from noncriminal conduct. The key lies in using public policy to constrain individual decision making so that those who consider crime do not find it to be a profitable option. Cost-efficient ways that the state could improve reward for noncriminal conduct among those who might otherwise consider white-collar crime are difficult to imagine. It is unfathomable to think that reward and additional largesse could increase compliance by upperworld offenders. Citizens would not be pleased with the tax burden for this purpose at any rate. The natural consequences of much white-collar offending are mild by comparison to other criminal acts and its inherent dangers do not elicit panic, nausea or other unpleasant sensations. For these reasons, the criminal law may hold the greatest promise for intruding on decision making and introducing corrective thoughts into the calculus of organizational and individual offenders.

A prominent research design for investigating deterrence of white-collar crime is to examine the subsequent, short-term effect of increased sanctions or criminal prosecutions on a specific type of offending. Block, Nold, and Sidak (1981) investigated antitrust laws and bread pricing by bakeries. When firms were charged with price fixing and faced with the possibility of civil suits, the price of their bread fell. Since then, many places or industries where the state increased enforcement have been investigated; the change in behavior of the sanctioned companies or of all firms of the sanctioned type is measured in these quasi-experiments. For example, inspections and penalties for workplace safety violations reduce injuries in sanctioned firms (Mendelhoff and Gray, 2005). The jury is still out on whether the accumulated findings provide support for deterrence (Simpson, 2002). Independent and dependent variables are very different from study to study. Various controls are utilized and findings are mixed. The state's general capacity to influence both street crime and white-collar crime is difficult to demonstrate empirically using short-term correlations between specific enforcement and crime.

Nevertheless, variation in threatened aversive consequences is a fundamental explanatory variable in the theory of crime as choice (Shover and Bryant, 1993; Cohen and Simpson, 1997). Given the proven capacity for rational responses to markets, it is not a large leap to the conclusion that threatened and actual consequences can reduce rates of some types of crime. The threat of arrest for domestic violence is more effective for men with jobs than for the unemployed (Berk et al., 1992; Pate and Hamilton, 1992). White-collar offenders also should be more responsive to changes in punishment than street offenders. They may be more aware of the level of intolerance expressed in the message of changing enforcement and it may mean more to them. Should the state decide to send a message into the boardrooms and cubicles of formal organizations that it is serious about a particular crime, or crime generally, the stretch is shorter than it is to the backseat of a car occupied by impoverished and drug addicted youth. A harshly worded letter to executives can get attention and a series of arrests and jail sentences clarifies the point. Street offenders receive no trade newsletters and when one of theirs has been imprisoned it is not relevant or shocking. Some in their ranks may pay heed, however, when they read one of the billboards that says, "you + illegal gun = federal prison," or "a gun crime gets you five" that appear in many U.S. cities today. The message gets across more clearly when all know from local gossip and nightly news that it is true. Such a serious reminder well-placed can turn conversations and throw cold water on criminal plans. Those drafting ethical guidelines and administering educational programs in corporations could take a lesson.

Research on target hardening and situational crime prevention shows that few street offenders will choose to offend when the odds of being caught near certainty, where success requires creativity or significant effort, and where returns will be insignificant. Accounting firms that inflate earnings estimates to meet quarterly objectives, grocery clerks who ring employee discounts for friends, and street-corner drug dealers share a potential for significant painful consequences and are alike in this: many either ignore or view as unlikely these contingencies. Few clear-headed offenders with anything appreciable to lose would commit crime if they thought criminal prosecution or long-term imprisonment were likely consequences. Most are aware that their acts have the potential for criminal penalties if things go badly, but that is not the outcome they expect. They hope to avoid penalties by hiding their intent and responsibility. Like street offenders, most white-collar offenders do not pin their hopes on the number of months prescribed by the sentencing tables for convicted felons but on avoiding

entirely this penalty. Both groups look at the risks of detection opti-
mistically. Yet, the lives and generative worlds of street offender are
different in many respects.

Street offenders continue in crime because they avoid honest evaluation of dismal prospects or reach a point where they do not care.
White-collar offenders' positive thinking can result from the calculation that punishing their acts is a low priority for the state. Confidence
among white-collar offenders can be the result of accurate evaluation
as well as predisposition with roots in their backgrounds. The paucity
of research on white-collar criminal decision making limits what can
be concluded about the generality of the decision-making process.
Such differences as there are, however, are explicable in the logic of
rational-choice theory. These provide little justification for assuming
that deterrent measures or crime-control strategies now aimed at other
crime would be less effective in white-collar worlds.

CHAPTER SIX

Criminal Careers and Career Criminals

The ascendance of rational-choice theory as justification for a new approach to crime control occurred together with growing interest in *criminal careers.* This concept now figures prominently in public-policy debates over what should be done about crime. The principal reason is obvious: some offenders have only a brief fling with crime while others commit it repeatedly and may endure repeated convictions and imprisonment. Dubbed "career criminals," these persistent offenders have captured the attention of elite academics and political leaders alike (Piquero, Farrington, and Blumstein, 2003). Research on criminal careers and career criminals, which has focused most intensely on street offenders, shows indisputably that the great majority eventually desist from their earlier patterns.

The notion that offenders have "careers" in crime is beguiling but potentially misleading. Borrowed from the world and analysis of legitimate occupations, the career concept is an analytic tool that should not be construed literally. Proportionately few white-collar criminals may see or approach crime as an occupation, and even among these persistent criminals there probably are not the formalized career lines and well-defined career progression markers that are common in legitimate employment (Luckenbill and Best, 1981).

There is immense variation in the patterning and duration of individual criminal careers. Self-report research in which individuals are asked to indicate the number of crimes of various kinds they committed during a specified period of time provide some of the strongest evidence of this. Autobiographical descriptions and analyses also confirm career variation. Analysis of official arrest records, however, provides the most persuasive evidence (Shover, 1996). The paucity of offender autobiographies and self-report studies of white-collar criminals, however, means that arrest records provide the only evidence of variation in their criminal careers. It cannot be estimated precisely, but no one disputes it exists. Studies of narrow offender categories, for example, leave no doubt; data collected from fraudulent telemarketers show that while the majority do not have previous criminal records a sizeable minority do (Doocy et al., 2001; Shover, Coffey, and Hobbs, 2003). Upperworld white-collar offenders by contrast rarely have prior arrests and convictions.

It is also clear that some organizations have lengthy records of transgression while others have exemplary records of compliance with laws and regulations. Sutherland (1983) tabulated the adverse decisions of courts and administrative commissions against seventy of the largest U.S. manufacturing, mining, and mercantile corporations over their entire life span. There were 980 adverse decisions total, although only 16 percent (158) were criminal convictions. Sixty percent of the seventy firms had been convicted in criminal courts and had an average of four convictions each. Clinard and Yeager (1980) later analyzed administrative, civil, and criminal actions initiated or completed during 1975 and 1976 by 25 federal agencies against 582 of the largest publicly owned corporations in the United States. Like Sutherland, they employed a broad definition of crime that included not only criminal acts but also administrative violations and adverse civil decisions. Of the 582 firms, 60.1 percent were targets of at least one federal action during the two-year period. They averaged 4.4 actions each. Of the 477 manufacturing firms in the sample, 38 accounted for 52 percent of all violations, or an average of 23.5 violations each. Simply put, these studies suggest that a minority of business firms may be career criminals.

Criminal careers begin at first arrest and end when offenders cease committing crime or in death. Questions about the patterning of criminal careers and why they change are important for reasons of theory and public policy alike. Research into these questions builds on a logic and repertoire of concepts borrowed from analysis of the human life course (Laub, 2001; Benson, 2002). Investigators explore offending over time and the life events, social psychological changes, and

choices that shape it (Farrington, 1997). The focus is how changes
in life circumstances coupled with cognitive changes and adaptations
alternately turn individuals toward or away from continued criminal
participation. The underlying assumptions of most research into criminal participation over the life course is reconciled easily with rational-
choice theory (Shover and Thompson, 1992). Much remains to be
learned about career patterns in white-collar crime, however, and this
is true particularly of upperworld and organizational offenders.

There may be few organizational white-collar criminals as indifferent to legal threat and public welfare as Royal Caribbean Cruises. On
July 22, 1999, it pleaded guilty in six U.S. District Courts to dumping oil and hazardous chemicals from nine ships in coastal waters
around the United States. Royal Caribbean also admitted that it continued to dump criminally for a month after it was convicted earlier on
similar charges and had promised to stop. The firm dumped oil and
toxic solvents or toxic chemicals in New York Harbor, in Miami, in the
Virgin Islands, in Los Angeles, and in the Alaskan Inside Passage. Royal
Caribbean cruise ships used secret bypass pipes to dump waste oil and
toxic materials overboard, often at night. By dumping the substances
criminally, the company saved tens of thousands of dollars per ship per
year on oil filters and the dockside disposal of toxic substances. Ship
engineers were given bonuses for minimizing expenses, and personnel
falsified log books that they referred to by a Norwegian word meaning
"fairy tale book." Royal Caribbean pleaded guilty to twenty-one counts
of polluting and lying about it as representative of many more criminal
acts (*Boston Globe*, 1999; *Los Angeles Times*, 1999; *New York Times*, 1999).

CAREER BEGINNINGS

Age of onset is one of the strongest predictors of criminal career
length; the earlier offenders begin committing crime, the longer they
persist. A substantial proportion of persons who commit street crime
begin doing so and accumulating arrests in adolescence. White-collar
criminals do not. The lure that attracts white-collar criminals generally does not become accessible until legitimate professional and
organizational careers are established, and this may require extended

employment and years. In the Yale Law School study, the age of onset for offenders with only one offense on their record is thirty-five, while for those with more than one offense it is twenty-four (Weisburd et al., 1991). Another study found that the age of onset for white-collar criminals was forty-one for first offenders and twenty-seven for those with prior arrests (Benson, 2002).

White-collar offenders are advantaged, and their generative worlds differ profoundly as well. There is less abuse and criminality in their backgrounds; street offenders are nearly three times more likely to have a convicted offender in their immediate family while growing up, and 18 percent were abused or neglected as children as compared to 6 percent of white-collar offenders (Benson, 2002). The former are twice as likely to have performed poorly in school (Benson and Kerley, 2001). While many ordinary white-collar offenders have chronic problems with alcohol or drugs, their numbers proportionately are fewer than is true of street criminals. Weisburd and colleagues (2001:9–10) point out that while the run of them "have little in common with the powerful and wealthy individuals who are often conjured up as images of the typical white-collar offender," it is noteworthy also that "they differ at least as sharply from the lower-class criminals that are generally thought of when scholars or lay people discuss the crime problem." In sum, "one searches in vain for early precursors or early hints of trouble in the life history of the typical white-collar offender. For most, . . . [t]heir crimes do not appear . . . to be deeply rooted in a troubled social background" (Benson and Kerley, 2001:133).

When do they begin, and what distinguishes the onset of criminality by organizations? The absence of research into these matters is striking. Location in criminogenic industries or locales, weak oversight, and performance pressure may be critical. This probably explains why crime is more likely in faltering enterprises (Jenkins and Braithwaite, 1993). As Geis and Salinger (1998:94) put it, "it is a bit surprising that no research of which we are aware has spanned the life history of one or, better yet, a number of organizations and the relationships between aspects of its existence and troubles with the law." The odds of having "trouble with the law" are nearly impossible to estimate, but many organizations and privileged individuals do.

How they experience and respond to it presumably affects the odds of renewed criminal involvement and arrest.

CLASS AND PUNISHMENT

More than three decades ago, a team of researchers at Stanford University explored psychological reactions to the experience of imprisonment. The key component of the research was a simulated prison operated by the investigators in the basement of a university lecture hall. They first advertised for students, who received $15 per day for taking part in the study. Seventy males volunteered, and two dozen eventually were selected to participate. Half were arbitrarily designated "guards" and the others "prisoners." As one of the investigators explained:

> These were the roles they were to play in our simulated prison. The guards were made aware of the potential seriousness and danger of the situation and their own vulnerability. They made up their own formal rules for maintaining law, order and respect, and were generally free to improvise new ones during their eight-hour, three-man shifts. The prisoners were unexpectedly picked up at their homes by a city policeman in a squad car, searched, handcuffed, fingerprinted, booked at the Palo Alto station house, and taken blindfolded to our jail. There they were stripped, deloused, put into a uniform, given a number and put into a cell...where they expected to live for the next two weeks. (Zimbardo, 1972:6)

All activities taking place in the mock prison were observed and video taped. Participants also were tested and interviewed at various points during the study.

Guards quickly developed exaggerated roles of the kind found in real prisons, becoming high-handed and tyrannical in the process. Inmates became docile and showed signs of extreme emotional stress. Three prisoners had to be released in the first four days because of "acute situational traumatic reactions," ranging from hysterical crying and confused thinking to severe depression. Others begged to end their participation early. These and other reactions by "guards" and "prisoners" caused the investigators to terminate the study after only six days.

The participants in the Stanford research primarily were young, privileged university students (Zimbardo, 1972). Just as they found confinement to be extremely unpleasant, men from white-collar backgrounds who chance to spend any appreciable time in real confinement generally find it demeaning and difficult. The penalty of imprisonment is limited principally to street criminals, however, and one of the more noteworthy aspects of their adaptation to it is a high level of taken-for-granted compliance (Irwin, 1985). They rarely dispute the state's formal right to punish them, and they readily admit to extensive previous offending. Reflecting on many years spent in juvenile and adult institutions, an alcoholic former thief and heroin addict could be speaking for most criminals from working-class backgrounds who, like him, chance to end up in prison:

> [N]obody's done anything to me that I haven't gone clean out of my way to ask for. And I've never complained about being picked on, really. I've never had complaints about parole officers or police. I never have felt that, because I've always known that each time that I got here I worked hard to get here. I truly worked harder than other people to get myself put in this goddam place, you see, and I think the way that I did my time also indicated my willingness to accept the punishment as my lot. (Delorme, 1994:153)

Tacit acceptance of personal responsibility for their crimes is one of the most important reasons why criminal processing generally proceeds in a routine if not monotonous fashion and also why American jails and prisons generally are calm places. Active, open resistance to institutional personnel and regimens is as rare as emotional responses were commonplace in the "Stanford County Jail." Street criminals respond to incarceration in ways that reflect their cultural backgrounds and disadvantaged location in moral hierarchies. Their lives and experiences cause them to see as legitimate and to accept as proper an unambiguous link between crime and punishment. "If you can't do time, don't do crime" and "If you wanna' play, you gotta' pay" are aphorisms often heard in the prison world. Both attest to the tie between crime and punishment that is accepted by prisoners from disadvantaged and subordinate backgrounds. They are *prepared* from childhood to submit to criminal justice authority and simply "take it."

White-collar criminals experience punishment and define their plight differently.

Respectability and Reality Shock

Their initial exposure to the machinery of criminal justice will be memorable for most white-collar criminals although it may begin with a better orchestrated and less public arrest than most street criminals know; they are permitted to surrender voluntarily to authorities, and handcuffs are placed discreetly for those arrested or transported publicly. Save for the rarest of cases, upperworld criminals will never see the inside of a jail beyond what is needed to book and fingerprint them. A higher but still negligible proportion of ordinary white-collar criminals may spend a day or two in jail. For them, arrest on *felony* charges sends their lives careening "off on an angle [they] could have never imagined," and they "are plunged through the floor into the pit" of shame and disrepute (Braly, 1976:242).

Contributing to fear and shame is inexperience being treated impersonally; from childhood many are treated as if they are special and encouraged to see themselves as such. Few have experience standing in line at the unemployment office or applying for public assistance, and they know next to nothing of aggressive police tactics. They are strangers to what underclass citizens encounter and grudgingly must adapt to throughout life. The parents of white-collar criminals equip them with the verbal skills, confidence and sense of entitlement that results in challenge to institutional leaders, but the criminal justice apparatus is unlike and less yielding than any institution they will ever confront. Few are prepared for the treatment they receive at the hands of its functionaries:

> As a lawyer, I'd often been in the high-ceilinged, austerely elegant courtrooms, the warmly furnished judges 'chambers, the handsome lawyers' libraries, lined with neat rows of books and portraits of judicial greats – where the eloquent arguments are made over abstract legal principles. [But] [f]or the first time I was inside the drab quarters of the army of marshals, clerks, and investigators who enforce the law – where the law touches lives. (Colson, 1976:101)

> Inside the small plain-walled probation office, . . . I began to feel the reality of what it was to be a convicted felon. Here a clerk would

write up my report just as he did each day for street criminals, rapists, car thieves and narcotics dealers. . . . I would now be in the hands of GS-7 probation clerks, marshals, prison guards. The loss of control of my body and life was a sensation I had not fully understood before. (Colson, 1976:233)

Contacts with their fellow travelers through the world of criminal justice are a major source of unease; when good people encounter the disadvantaged and disreputable on the latter's ground and in close quarters, their discomfort is palpable. For the first time in their lives, they are processed and surrounded by those who do the dirty and low-paying work of the world. Jail brings them into close contact with men who are openly flatulent, whose fingers are indelibly stained from years of cigarette smoking, who seem incapable of omitting "fuck" from conversation or whose bodies show unusual scars or tattoos. Recalling his experience, a white-collar criminal noted that "[t]he fellow in the bed next to mine had pornographic tattoos all over his body, 'Love' and 'Hate' tattooed on the fingers of his hand, and a red and purple likeness of the devil that curled from his muscle on his left arm down to a point on the back of his hand. He wore mirrored sunglasses at all times" (Lawson, 1992:149). Those with past experience in the military or other hierarchical, mass-processing organizations fare better than white-collar offenders who lack these experiences. Even they express bemusement at the day-to-day dynamics of criminal justice (Timilty, 1997).

Likely most ordinary white-collar defendants will be surrounded by minority citizens for the first time in their lives. This is unsettling. In recounting the experience of one white-collar offender, Nathan McCall describes what is common for any who chance to spend time in large, urban, and aged county jails:

> He sat on his bunk and looked around, bewildered. I could tell by the tortured expression on his fleshy face that this was his worst nightmare. For him, the world had turned upside down and inside out; Black people were in the majority, and they ran things; white people were in the minority. . . . Clearly, he had never dreamed he'd spend a minute passing through our world. . . . Whites in general caught hell in jail. . . . White junkies, whose drug dealings had often taken them to inner-city spots, did well because they'd grown comfortable

around blacks. But that was less the case with those sheltered, smug
whites. . . . They wore their racial fears and prejudices on their sleeves.
(McCall, 1994:155–56)

White-collar offenders find intimidating both the bravado and postur-
ing of incarcerated young, underclass men. The unpredictable physical conflict that takes place within the jail is less gentlemanly than
anything they have known previously.

Post hoc descriptions of these encounters with subordinate classes
and perceived inferiors are uncommon, but their sanctimonious tone
is not: "I realized over and over, the longer I was there, that I had
absolutely nothing in common with anyone else in the jail. All the
conversation – the entire atmosphere – was filled with vulgarity, filth,
despair" (Laite, 1972:111). Classism and racism are disguised but thinly
in these accounts (Harris, 1986). "Unclean" is how they and their
families will feel after close contact with jail and the courts:

> I couldn't . . . adjust to the language. . . . Everybody swore. It was vile
> and filthy. I was horrified by the whole experience. It seemed like
> another age. It's so Dickensian. It really is unreasonable, the whole
> thing. Most of all I hated being locked up. It was not only that it
> showed that I had lost my freedom, it was because the inactivity gave
> me time to think and all I could think about was my kids. It is ghastly,
> filthy. There is rubbish lying about. Cells are inches thick in cigarette
> ash. And to top it all you are thrown in with all sorts of people.
> (Breed, 1979:52)

Processing by the agents and apparatus of criminal justice has a profound leveling effect on its human material.

Few white-collar criminals who are sentenced to confinement will
leave the courtroom, return to jail, and remain there until bureaucratic
routine or convenience conveys them to prison; most are permitted
to self-report. Rarely is their destination a traditional wall-enclosed
penitentiary; Leavenworth is not for them. More likely it will be a
small camplike facility. The inmate population will be a curious mix
of others like them and older, institutionally experienced offenders
who have settled down and learned to do time smoothly. Once there,
some white-collar criminals may find that their cultural capital helps

them secure favorable work assignments. Ability to type may prove to be as important in this regard as any other quality or skill they possess. Interactional deference from staff or inmates, however, is rarely shown because of free-world accomplishment and rank. Academic credentials are as likely to elicit derision as respect, and self-segregation from others, who they see as "real criminals," is common. They may be big talkers in the free world, but in prison white-collar criminals quickly learn the value of keeping quiet. Their fear of the unknown and uncontrollable soon gives way to a condescending distaste for the institution, its routines, and many of its staff. Many white-collar criminals adapt to confinement by becoming exemplary rule-abiding inmates and by not antagonizing custodial staff (Benson and Cullen, 1988). They find, befriend and limit their social contacts to others like themselves.

Anger, shame, and embarrassment are common reactions to criminal conviction by white-collar offenders, but a strikingly high proportion of them are unrepentant and unwilling to accept responsibility for their crimes (Benson, 1990). Many protest their innocence to the end, insisting, for example, that what they did caused no harm and hardly merited prosecutors' attention (Benson, 1985; Jesilow et al., 1993). They view the criminal process as entirely inappropriate for people like themselves.

AFTER PUNISHMENT

Recidivism, or return to criminal participation following a period of abstinence, is a key aspect of criminal careers. When investigators examine recidivism they typically monitor arrest records for offenders who received a criminal sentence to determine how many are rearrested in a specified period of time. A three-year follow-up of fraud offenders released from federal prisons in the United States – white-collar crime often is *federal* crime – during the years 1986–1997 found that 15.8 percent were later returned to prison either for new crimes or parole violation (U.S. Department of Justice, 2000b). Analysis of the arrest histories of 6,062 U.S. citizens sentenced in federal courts in fiscal year 1992 shows that 16.9 percent of defendants convicted of fraud were rearrested at least once in a two-year follow-up period (U.S. Sentencing Commission, 2004). Information on recidivism by offenders incarcerated for other types of white-collar crime is not reported.

Recall the Yale Law School study of 1,094 convicted white-collar offenders from seven federal judicial districts in the United States (Weisburd et al., 1991). Information collected from their presentence investigation reports (PSIs) indicates that 21 percent had one or more prior felony convictions, and 13 percent had a prior misdemeanor conviction. Fifteen percent of sample members had at least one prior term of incarceration. The Association of Certified Fraud Examiners (2005:36) determined that 12 percent of 363 perpetrators of occupational fraud whose previous criminal histories were known to its members who responded to a survey had previous criminal convictions. Benson and Moore (1992) examined PSIs on 2,462 white-collar offenders sentenced in eight U.S. district courts in the years 1973–1978 and found similar patterns of arrests and recidivism. Members of the sample averaged 1.79 prior arrests each, but 12 percent had been arrested four or more times previously (Benson and Kerley, 2001).

Investigators who carried out the Yale Law School study later examined their subjects' arrest histories for the eight-year period following their earlier conviction (Weisburd et al., 2001). Fourteen percent of the original sample were deceased, and the records of others had been destroyed, so the research team secured arrest records for only 70 percent of the sample. They counted as recidivists not only those who were convicted of new crimes but also those who were rearrested, regardless of whether or not a new conviction followed. Analysis shows that 33 percent of sample members who were sentenced to imprisonment following their earlier conviction subsequently were arrested or convicted of new crimes (Weisburd et al., 2001:Table 5.7). Compare this with the rate of recidivism over a much shorter follow-up period for men and women incarcerated for street crimes; of 272,111 offenders released from prison in fifteen states in 1994, 67.5 percent were rearrested within three years (U.S. Department of Justice, 2002b). [The comparable figure, after three years, for the Yale sample is 15 percent, less than one-fourth the rate for street offenders (Weisburd et al., 2001:Table 5.7).] Members of the Yale sample who were sentenced to imprisonment failed more often than those who were not imprisoned, but this is not surprising; offenders who receive more severe penalties almost certainly differ from others in ways that makes them more likely to recidivate. It is difficult statistically to control for these differences, however. There probably are multiple reasons why some white-collar criminals continue on a criminal path and build lengthy criminal careers while others return to a more compliant line are less apparent. Qualities of their generative worlds may play a part in persistent criminal offending, but they do not tell the entire story.

Recidivism rates for white-collar criminals are significantly lower than comparable rates for street criminals largely because known risk factors for recidivism are less common in their ranks. Their delayed start in crime presumably is one of the most important of these. Age at release also is a predictor of recidivism among street offenders; as age increases the odds of recidivism decrease. Rewarding employment and attachment to conventional others also lowers the odds of recidivism; the desire to avoid disappointing or embarrassing others apparently is a key variable associated with postconviction success (Burnett, 1992; Shover, 1996). Odds of recidivism also change according to criminal records; the number of previous arrests and the nature of previous crimes predict it. On all these counts white-collar criminals are advantaged and rearrest for them will take longer on average than for street offenders. It may take years. This is less common among street criminals (Petersilia, 2003).

In the Yale Law School study, females, married offenders, and those who did not have records of drug use had longer times to recidivism. Those with more arrests failed sooner (Weisburd et al., 2001). There is nothing here that contrasts sharply with statistical findings about street-offender recidivism.

There are other reasons as well why low recidivism rates for white-collar criminals do not surprise. Their victims often are unaware they have been victimized, which means any new crimes they commit are less likely to be reported. When new crimes committed by them do come to the attention of officials, they are less likely to result in arrest or punitive responses. Probation and parole officers generally do not cast white-collar offenders among their dangerous and unpredictable clients who must be monitored closely lest they foul up (McCleary, 1992). They are unlikely to search for signs that they have returned to crime in urine or erratic behavior, and evidence that they have done so generally is not found in their pockets or glove boxes during traffic stops. Nor do their prior criminal convictions make convicted white-collar criminals part of the "usual suspects" who are picked up and questioned when the police investigate well-publicized crimes. These are reasons also why white-collar criminals who do recidivate generally remain in the community longer than street criminals before rearrest or parole violation (Weisburd et al., 2001).

Upperworld offenders are rarely imprisoned, and for them the chances of being caught and imprisoned twice are negligible. Their crimes may be products of ongoing conspiracies that extend over months or years and result in many discrete criminal acts. Few of the crimes they commit require physical dexterity and nerve of the kind needed to rob and assault, and they may be carried out by subalterns or hirelings in any case. To hide their crimes and evade punishment upperworld offenders can draw upon supportive networks and relationships accumulated over years of privilege and organizational power. Upperworld crime is profitable and rewarding far beyond what is characteristic of ordinary white-collar criminals, and recidivism rates for these offenders may exceed comparable rates for street criminals. Rational-choice theory supports the expectation that offenders who meet with criminal success while avoiding punishment are unlikely to terminate transgression soon or voluntarily.

Stigma and Reintegration
The formal penalties of criminal conviction have an objective and intuitively comprehensible quality; fines, probation, and imprisonment are not contingencies that require lengthy definition or explanation for most citizens. Financial penalties and months spent in confinement also can be calculated in precise metrics of dollars and days. To their sum, however, must be added the collateral and informal consequences of criminal conviction. The state and private organizations impose on the convicted a diverse list of restrictions on employment, citizenship, leisure activities, and other conditions of life (Uggen,

Manza, and Behrens, 2004). Some professions and occupations drum out convicted felons; attorneys, for example, routinely are disbarred. The list of these collateral consequences of conviction has grown substantially in recent decades (Petersilia, 2003). The informal penalties of criminal conviction are not grasped or measured as easily as the formal ones (Maruna and Immarigeon, 2004).

Respectability and the opinions of others hold enormously important meaning for many tempted to commit white-collar crime. They have good reason to care what others think; most have farther to fall than street offenders. Loss in self-esteem, reputation, and social standing do not lend themselves to precise assessment. These informal penalties of conviction potentially may drive some deep into despair and social isolation. They may also have beneficial effects, however, particularly if they humble the arrogant, and cause them to reassess their past conduct and make them think differently about lure they encounter in the future. Despite their recognized importance, however, the effects of informal sanctions and costs as a factor in recidivism for white-collar offenders is unclear. In the Yale Law School study, estimates of the informal costs of criminal conviction had little effect on recidivism (Weisburd et al., 2001).

White-collar offenders invest in conventional social networks, and they reap the benefits of these when accused, convicted, and punished. As compared with street offenders they are four times more likely to be involved in social or community groups and far less likely to have friends who engage in or promote criminal behavior (Benson and Kerley, 2001). Twelve percent of street offenders own homes, but this is true of more than half of white-collar offenders (Benson and Kerley, 2001). A higher proportion of white-collar criminals have stable home lives and are free of addictions (Breed, 1979). They may suffer from loss of trust, but their employment skills do not degrade significantly while they are out of circulation. Evidence suggests that first contact with the criminal justice system, particularly when it occurs early in life, has a profound deleterious effect on subsequent income (Kerley, Benson, Lee, and Cullen, 2004). For white-collar criminals, as noted previously, this generally occurs some ten years later than it does for street criminals, which gives reason to believe that arrest and conviction may have minimal impact on their subsequent income (Weisburd et al., 2001). Since many have invested time and resources in education, credentials, and networking, they have advantages beyond employment and the pay packet.

From supportive social ties and employment skills to family relationships, convicted white-collar criminals can draw on resources to soften the impact of criminal conviction and hasten return to normal circumstances. Little guilt accompanies many of their criminal acts; profiting from inside information is one thing, embezzling from employers is something else, and sexual exploitation of children is another thing entirely. Revocation of one's trading license by the Securities and Exchange Commission does not make family and friends forsake the offender in the same way that extorting sex from subordinates likely would. Little damage is done to reputation. A tax code violator interviewed by Benson (1982) describes the tepid informal consequences of his crime:

> I think most people in filing a false income tax return [know that if] you are caught – if it happens to me – its an entirely different situation from being convicted of a rape. I never felt any [stigma] from family, from neighbors, from friends, from relatives, from poison pen letters. Nothing. There has been absolutely no [stigma]. Most people treat you exactly as if it didn't happen. They don't go out of their way to be solicitous, and they don't go out of their way to harm you. Some want no involvement, but never is anybody negative.... This has been my situation.... The first thing they give you is condolences and after that it's like it never happened.

Many but not all white-collar criminals manage to avoid both the interpersonal opprobrium that comes with the label criminal and self-reproach born of realization that they have committed crime.

Like individuals, organizations may suffer reputationally from criminal conviction. Fisse and Braithwaite (1983) examined seventeen cases of corporate crime by large companies where significant publicity resulted. The publicity was costly to companies in earnings and sales and, in a minority of cases, reduced stock price. Adverse publicity tends to be a brief and less severe problem for large corporations. They recover quickly. Fisse and Braithwaite (1983:243) conclude that long-term "financial impacts of any significance" are unlikely. Balanced against this finding is the experience of Arthur Andersen LLP, whose crimes and punishment were sketched briefly in chapter 1. Andersen's accounting business plummeted after the collapse of Enron corporation, and it came under the spotlight of federal agencies. It was widely believed that business firms shied away from using Andersen as their accountant from fear their financial reports could draw close scrutiny from regulators.

Paradoxically, some of the most damaging white-collar crimes result in comparably minor informal costs to offenders while less serious crimes produce substantial reputational and career fallout (Benson, 1984). Officers of investment firms whose crimes victimize many and cause great financial loss may secure similar employment after conviction, but employees caught stealing probably will lose their position. Antitrust offenders do not suffer greatly, but unskilled and public-sector employees generally pay a stiffer and longer lasting price (Anechiarico and Jacobs, 1996). Positions and career investments in public service are difficult to recover after conviction.

This inequity may be due in part to the greater resources available to upperworld criminals and also to the fact that their offenses may be organizational in nature. This facilitates and lends credibility to the claim that higher ups or circumstances beyond their control caused them to offend. Schwartz and Skolnick (1964) found that doctors sued for malpractice suffered minimal loss as a result of the action, and some said that their practices improved; colleagues sent them more business after hearing of their difficulties. Location in a community of sympathizers can hasten recovery from adverse state action.

Loss of occupational status is not permanent for most white-collar offenders (Benson, 1984). Through resources and resilience they manage to recover a significant measure of what was lost following conviction. Yale Law School investigators note that

> we were struck by the relative infrequency in which our defendants, their families, or probation officers noted suffering as a result of legal proceedings. This suggests to us that ... concern [for] the special impact of legal involvement [criminal conviction] may be overstated. At best, it applies to only some white-collar defendants, and often not those highest up the hierarchies of offense and offender. (Weisburd et al., 1991:192)

The investigator used information from federal district courts in California was linked with records of unemployment compensation to examine the effects of length of confinement on subsequent employment and earnings. There were large effects of imprisonment on the earnings of white-collar offenders, primarily because of their precipitous drop in income following arrest and conviction. Most, however, began to recover quickly, and in five years they were earning 70 percent of what others of comparable age and employment experience are paid (Kling, 2002). Their income suffers in the short term, but they eventually return to work and a middle-class life. Few end up on public assistance rolls or collect scrap-metal to get by. Convicted criminals from less privileged backgrounds are not so fortunate.

Desistance

Desistance is the label applied to the statistical relationship between aging and participation in serious crime; as age increases the odds of recidivism decrease. When applied to individuals the break with crime is not always clean cut and final. Desistance frequently is gradual, drawn out over years, and interrupted by occasional relapse, at least in the short run. Ethnographic and statistical studies have laid bare the nature and dynamics of offenders' lives following incarceration. Successful desistance varies by their readiness to learn from past mistakes. In many cases it is preceded by growing belief that continued criminal participation is not worth the cost (Glaser, 1964; Shover, 1985; Shover and Thompson, 1992; Maruna, 2001). Desistance is linked also to indicators of settled and personally rewarding lives as measured by gainful employment and satisfying marriage, for example (Shover, 1996; Laub and Sampson, 2003).

The desistance concept admittedly is presumptive, particularly when applied to white-collar criminals. Less is known about their postconviction experiences, in part because research into these matters presents significant challenges. Given the fact that white-collar offenders are more successful than street criminals delaying or avoiding arrest, the problems of measuring desistance by them are difficult to surmount. Weisburd and colleagues (2001:36), for example, point out that "we cannot be certain, except in the case of death, that the final recorded event on an offender's criminal history is actually the last crime for which he or she will ever be arrested." Whereas many street offenders desist from serious crime by age thirty, the average age at last offense for individuals in the Yale Law School study was forty-three (Weisburd et al., 2001).

Not surprising, organizational desistance is the least studied and understood process in white-collar crime scholarship. It seems likely, however, that career change only follows significant contingencies. Change in top leadership coupled with unambiguous messages that misconduct will not be tolerated may be required if organizational career criminals are to reverse patterns of transgression that have persisted for years.

DETERRENCE AND MORAL DECLARATION

Political leaders and policy advocates are united in belief that sanctioning by the criminal justice apparatus is an important contingency that shapes subsequent criminal career trajectories. As they see it, a bit of punishment surely reduces the odds that apprehended offenders will choose to commit crime again. It does so in large part because punishment nurtures development of a more precise metric and calculus of pain (Shover, 1996). By contributing to this rationalization of decision making, punishment replaces what sometimes is an emotion-laden and impulsive process with a more informed and prudent one. To the extent they learn their lesson offenders are less likely to repeat past mistakes. This is *specific* deterrence, or the effect of punishment on those who experience it. In the short term the fact that most who do so generally recoil is reason to believe its specific deterrent effect is considerable.

In the Yale study imprisonment neither increased nor decreased significantly the odds of recidivism when compared with fines or probation. The investigators note that this is true regardless of "whether we examine the likelihood, timing, frequency, or type of recidivism" (Weisburd et al., 2001:113). Beyond this report, however, there is remarkably little evidence on specific deterrence of white-collar crime. It is noteworthy, however, that evidence does not "support the opposite argument that...imprisonment sanctions will backfire and lead to more serious future offending" (Weisburd et al., 2001:113). Put differently, the hardening effect of incarceration that is found in studies of street criminals is not found here. This means that policy makers need not fear that a crackdown on white-collar criminals may backfire and create increasing numbers of career criminals.

Apart from their specific deterrent effect, threat and punishment are also meant to send a message to the wider population of citizens who have not been punished. In contrast to specific deterrence, general deterrence is the effect of punishment on this group (Andenaes, 1966). Apart from the specific deterrent effect of imprisonment is this crime prevention effect on citizens and organizations who witness from afar the fate of apprehended and punished offenders. Punishment may have limited specific deterrent effect on offenders but have a substantial overall crime-reduction effect nonetheless. As a public-policy matter, a unit of punishment may generate greater benefits against white-collar crime than the same unit employed against street crime. Since proportionately few white-collar criminals are caught and punished, there is little reason to believe that the general deterrent effect for them is high, but there is remarkably little evidence one way or the other (Simpson, 2002).

More important than narrow and technocratic issues of deterrence is the possible declarative payoff from punishment. The criminal law is a politically refracted expression of collective sensibilities, but it also shapes public opinion and moral evaluations. It helps define the boundaries of what is shameful and intolerable; when the law forbids an act, and its agents consistently act on that forbiddance, the public construes it as both wrong and serious. There is reason to belive that the members of a community eventually will develop from the way the state monitors and sanctions violations a shared sense of the egregiousness of the punished conduct. Regardless of whether or not legal threats deter, failure to enforce or repeal them may convey the impression that the designated conduct is not morally wrong (Walker and Argyle, 1964). The moral messages communicated by law and punishment are important particularly for citizens and organizations located near moral margins:

> It is neither the intention nor the purpose of the criminal law to express the optimal standard of conduct, or to delineate a code

of correct living. Unhappily, however, for many people the line of demarcation between criminal and non-criminal behavior becomes the definition of right and wrong. As long as conduct is not unlawful, or as long as unlawful conduct is not threatened with prosecution, many accept such action as proper, and sometimes even laudatory. (Wallace, 1986:2)

Aside from the anger and embarrassment it may cause, punishment generally fails to instill in convicted white-collar criminals acceptance of the immorality of their conduct. In the wake of the enormous harm caused by upperworld crime, failure to communicate unambiguous messages about the immorality of their conduct makes it easy for transgressors to argue "they did nothing wrong" (McLean and Elkind, 2004).

CHAPTER SEVEN

Beyond the Law?

No one who deigns to consider the problem of white-collar crime can avoid concluding that it exacts a staggering toll on individuals, organizations, and, possibly, social institutions. Its costs dwarf comparable losses to street crime, and the gap almost certainly is growing. Increasingly, victimization and harm cross international borders (Levi, 2001b). These are sufficient reasons to focus greater attention on white-collar crime and responses to it, albeit these do not appear to be high priorities currently. The reasons are many, but they include neglect if not unconcern from on high.

In the United States, the Bureau of Justice Statistics annually issues a torrent of descriptive research on robbers, burglars, drug offenders, and other street criminals. It publishes next to nothing on white-collar crime. The infrequent exceptions to this long-standing pattern are of little use in any case, primarily because of the overly broad definition of white-collar crime used for analysis (U.S. Department of Justice, 1986; 1987; 2000b). For all intents and purposes, the agencies of the U.S. Department of Justice that compile and publish statistical information on crime have chosen to ignore white-collar crime and its victims. This is one reason it can require painstaking work to put together useful statistical data on white-collar crime (Geis and Salinger, 1998; Szockyj and Geis, 2002). Compiling time-series data over more than a few decades, for example, is challenging and labor intensive. It is impossible in addition to know whether the results provide a representative picture of any larger population of theoretical or policy significance (Geis and Salinger, 1998).

Hughes (1971b) described how statistical reporting categories used in the *German Statistical Yearbook* changed after the 1933 ascension of National Socialism. He noted that earlier editions of the *Yearbook* did not organize or report data on racial groupings whereas subsequent editions did. Pre-Nazi editions, moreover, were presented in the dry and dispassionate language of statisticians while subsequent editions occasionally sounded a celebratory tone in reporting the accomplishments of the National Socialist state. The larger implication and lesson is that arid and disinterested statistical presentations nevertheless reflect the biases of the powerful; what they see as important finds expression, and what they see as threatening or impudent is ignored. White-collar crime is not a priority for most public agencies and departments that fund research on crime and offenders. Citizens interested in white-collar crime are not routinely presented a "crime clock" of the kind that opens the *Uniform Crime Reports.* Failure by the United States to develop and maintain statistics on white-collar crime or to assign high priority to it undoubtedly reflects the biases of political elites, elected officials, and high-level state managers alike.

The problems faced by victims of street crime are one of the principal reasons many states enacted crime victims' bill of rights in the years after 1980. These legislative initiatives generally ignore the victims of white-collar crime, however. Issued in 1982, the final report of the President's Task Force on Victims of Crime makes no mention of white-collar crime or them. Reasons for this may include the possibility that unrecoverable losses to white-collar crime are borne disproportionately by middle and lower income citizens; the former pay the economic fare while the latter pay heavily in physical injuries and diminished quality of life. Similarly, mid-size and small businesses probably are hit harder by white-collar crime than larger corporations who can pass along to consumers the economic costs of victimization.

The 1982 President's Task Force report noted that victims of street crime who come to criminal justice officials expecting protection and remedy often find something very different:

> They discover . . . that they [are] treated as appendages of a system appallingly out of balance. They learn that somewhere along the way

the system has lost track of the simple truth that it is supposed to be fair and to protect those who obey the law while punishing those who break it. Somewhere along the way, the system began to serve lawyers and judges and defendants, treating the victim with institutionalized disinterest. (1982:vi)

Without question, victims of street crime are not alone in receiving from officialdom a less than satisfactory response to their complaints (Geis, 1975). Citizens victimized by an appliance repairman, which arguably does not merit the appellation "white-collar" crime, "repeatedly expressed their indignation at being cheated and their frustration at being unable to get satisfaction from the offender, or from anyplace else" (Vaughan and Carlo, 1975:158). A study of fraud that victimized many elderly citizens points to the "callous indifference that the system demonstrates toward those whom it is particularly charged with assisting" (Geis, 1976:14). Like victims of street crimes,

> [m]any ... feel their needs have extremely low priority and that, at best, they are tolerated and then often with ill humor. Their role, they say, seems much like that of the expectant father in the hospital at delivery time: necessary for things to have gotten underway in the past but at the moment rather superfluous and mildly bothersome. ... [T]he offender, at least, is regarded by criminal justice functionaries as a doer, an antagonist, someone to be wary of, ... The victim, on the other hand, is part of the background scenery. (Geis, 1976:15)

Interviews with forty-two individuals who filed complaints with the consumer fraud bureau of the office of the Illinois Attorney General revealed that "dissatisfaction with and even hostility toward the Bureau were widespread." It was seen as "too slow, unaggressive, biased, disorganized and 'bureaucratic'" (Steele, 1975:1179).

Shover, Fox, and Mills (1994) interviewed forty investors in a finance company that was forced into bankruptcy because of crimes committed by top management. There was considerable variation in the impact of victimization caused by differences in victims' financial loss and age. Older investors who lost large sums of money suffered the greatest psychological losses, because they could see no way of recouping their depleted financial resources before retirement or death. Similar findings are reported by Shichor, Sechrest, and Doocy (2001), who identified some 8,516 victims of an investment scheme that involved gas and oil leases, mostly sold through telemarketing. They examined demographic and income data on victims that were on file in the California Department of Corporations and also received 152 completed mail surveys from a sample of 281 victims. Victims were "notably critical of the manner in which the authorities had dealt with [the crimes], and they called for severe penalties for the perpetrators." Twenty-one women who were defrauded and lost funds in the scam were "crushed" by their loss (Sechrest, Shichor, Doocy, and Geis, 1998:75). Clearly, problems caused by white-collar crime victimization do not end once the incident is reported to authorities. Victimization by white-collar crime effects many victims in ways similar to the impact of street crime (Ganzini et al., 1990; Spalek, 1999). Like their street-crime counterparts, victims who file complaints and seek redress often must negotiate a maze of agencies and institutions, most of uncertain jurisdiction and commitment. Those who wait for repayment inevitably are disappointed, and if they get financial redress it typically will be much less than their loss (Shover et al., 1994). Reporting white-collar crime and seeing one's complaint through to resolution can be frustrating, exhausting, and disillusioning. "Just as the criminal-justice system has been termed a 'nonsystem,' the approach taken by the criminal-justice system to white collar crime containment might be considered a 'nonapproach'" (Edelhertz, 1970:78). Victims who manage by whatever route to contact a victim-assistance office generally get a sympathetic hearing and some assistance but little relief.

CONFRONTING WHITE-COLLAR CRIME

The pioneering examinations of white-collar crime by E. A. Ross and Edwin Sutherland in the first half of the previous century were not undertaken solely for academic reasons. Both hoped to alert a seemingly unaware or unconcerned world to the challenge posed by forms of criminal predation that were not the object of effective control. In calling attention to its socially destructive consequences Ross assumed that once citizens were made aware of the new forms of crime their moral assessments of it would change. Better focused and more effective crime control would result, but not until public opinion was "rationalized" and "modernized." Only then would it become a "flaming sword guarding the sacred interests of society" (Ross, 1907:viii). Ross and Sutherland were unsparing in criticism of respectable criminals and the limp response to them by elected representatives and crime-control bureaucracies (Geis and Goff, 1983). In the decades that have passed since they called for greater attention and more effective responses to white-collar crime, only the uninformed would suggest. Their hopes have been realized.

The challenge of white-collar crime waxes and wanes in public consciousness, among academics, and on the agenda of public officials. A generation ago, for example, the disclosure of a range of criminal activities referred to broadly as the "Watergate scandals" marked the beginning of one of the best-known periods of attention and interest (Katz, 1980b). As Watergate receded in public memory, new life was breathed into the movement in the 1990s when the U.S. Sentencing Commission increased penalties for white-collar offenses, and the U.S. Department of Justice launched more vigorous actions against white-collar offenders. Materials presented in chapter 4 show that while federal prosecutors received significantly larger numbers of referrals during a period of seven years, prosecutions increased modestly. The size of monetary fines imposed on convicted organizations increased. For both the number of organizations convicted and the severity of fines there is evidence of some increase over previous years. Still, an average of only 218 organizations annually were sentenced in U.S. district courts. On average, 6,115 individual white-collar offenders were sentenced to imprisonment during 1995–2002 and received prison terms averaging 10.6 months. Both in numbers and sentence length, these represent increases over earlier years, albeit they are not large.

Federal agencies, however, did not move in unison during the years 1985–1995 when increased investigative and prosecutorial interest in white-collar crime was apparent; prosecutors were given additional resources and became more aggressive, but on the regulatory front the number of regulators per 100 tax filing corporations declined consistently from 1975 to 2000. Whatever was happening in the U.S. Department of Justice, federal regulators stood fast.

The small numbers of offenders on which the more severe penalties were imposed and the apparent inconsistency in oversight during the 1990s suggest that the modest campaign against white-collar crime likely failed to achieve significant impact. When coupled with the fact that the certainty of punishment is known to be a more effective general deterrent than the severity of sanctions. This conclusion seems all the more plausible. In any case, the period of more intense focus on white-collar crime has yielded to new priorities; events of September 11, 2001, likely administered the coup de grace.

The aborted increasing law enforcement interest in white-collar crime is unimpressive particularly when compared to contemporaneous measures against street criminals (Garland, 2001; Petersilia, 2003). There is little need to detail the mountain of evidence for the "war" on street crime and illicit drugs mounted in the United States post 1973, but unquestionably it includes:

1. After more than a decade without executions the death penalty was resurrected by many states and the federal government. It is used liberally in some states.
2. The proportion of the American adult population that is incarcerated, on probation, or under postrelease correctional supervision on any given day has increased continuously for thirty-four years. This historically unprecedented trend shows no sign of reversal.
3. Under the rubric of "three strikes and you're out," habitual offender laws reappeared and have been employed liberally in some states. As important, the existence of and danger posed by atavistic "super predators" and career criminals has been etched into public consciousness.
4. For the nation overall, the average length of time served by imprisoned offenders increased substantially.
5. The overall size of the crime-control apparatus and total budgetary expenditures for street-crime control increased enormously.
6. The size of the private crime-control industry increased significantly. Privatization has made into growth industries both security provision and the care and supervision of offenders.
7. Police are more proactive in identifying and monitoring those who might commit crime.
8. The message has been communicated far and wide that there can be no safe haven for illicit drugs and crime no matter how trivial its appearance.

Adoption of these measures and the underlying way of thinking about transgression is meant to ensure that any who choose street crime will meet with frustration and regret. They show what can be done when crime control is taken seriously: rates of street crime have declined or leveled off. The promise of rational-choice theory has been realized in the war against street crime. Permissiveness has been rejected in favor of crime control with a vengeance.

The same cannot be said about responses to white-collar crime. As van den Haag observes, "our judicial system seems more designed to blunt the deterrent force of punishment in the rare cases in which it is imposed and to protect defendants' rights than to protect society from crime. It certainly works that way" (1975:166). For contrast consider a legislative response from advocates of capital punishment when officials in some states grew frustrated by their inability to execute offenders as rapidly or as frequently as they wished. Statutes were enacted limiting the appellate rights of death row prisoners; they are permitted only a few months to raise any and all appellate issues before the door is closed to further appeals. White-collar criminals may rival death row prisoners in their search for appellate relief, but the limitation of appellate rights has not been applied to them.

Assessed against the prescriptive picture of credible oversight provided by rational-choice theory and examples from the war against street crime, the state has been reluctant to mount or may be incapable of mounting effective campaigns against white-collar predation. The reasons are prosaic, but they include the fact that intellectual controversy over white-collar crime has not abated and likely will not. This ensures that interpretations stressing the moral and legal culpability of white-collar criminals are matched by others that mitigate accountability or deflect moral condemnation. The state's noncredible response to white-collar crime is weakened further by fundamental biases and shortcomings in its approach.

Divergent Analytic Approaches

The fact that white-collar crime can and should be examined through the same theoretical lens used to study street crime belies the fact that few areas of criminological investigation and public policy are plagued with the intractable controversies that envelop this one. White-collar crime is the principal focus of research for proportionately few academics, and the obligatory one or two chapters on the subject in most criminology textbooks is as close to it as many instructors or investigators ever get. Theoretical and empirical investigations of white-collar crime are marginal to and largely unaffected by core developments in academic criminology. Situational crime prevention and restorative justice exemplify important developments in theory and practice in recent years, but white-collar crime receives little attention from either. There may be good reason for this. Fundamental to principles of restorative justice, for example, is the assumption that offenders must acknowledge and confront the harm they do before restorative dynamics can begin. But it is nearly impossible to picture corporate executives sitting down in victim-offender mediation conferences with hundreds or thousands of victims to confront the destructive consequences of their crimes. Some 20,000 Enron employees lost about $2 billion in 2001, but there is no chance Ken Lay, Jeffrey Skilling, or Andy Fastow ever will face their former subordinates to explain their greed and criminality. Criminals who destroy this many lives may send attorneys, but they most certainly will be indisposed on the day when victims meet as equals with those who exploited them.

Persuasion to Virtue

A movement to cooperative oversight of white-collar misconduct gained momentum in the years before the millennium. It began with agreement on the priority of avoiding the excesses of traditional approaches to regulatory oversight that rely on notions of deterrence (Bardach and Kagan, 1982; Braithwaite, 1983). Programs of *responsive regulation* legitimize and make available to officials a range of options when responding to compliance problems (Grabosky, 2001; Gunningham and Grabosky, 1998). Responsive regulation is "responsive to industry structure in that different structures will be conducive to different degrees and forms of regulation" and "attuned to the differing motivations of regulated actors" (Ayres and Braithwaite, 1992:4). Regulators are counseled to be knowledgeable about and take into account the larger contexts and individual meanings of noncompliance. Under the new regimes, overseers will get to know something about citizens, industries, and organizations and the problems they generally encounter complying with regulatory rules. Emphasis is placed on educating firms about rules and assisting them in efforts to comply. Principles of responsive regulation assign great value to the use of positive incentives and rewards for compliance while programs that rely principally on threats and the mechanical imposition of penalties are deemphasized (Grabosky, 2001).

Under programs of responsive regulation, state agencies have reduced responsibility for direct enforcement but increased responsibility for monitoring self-regulation. The fundamental assumption is that a substantial proportion of firms will self-regulate with minimal external monitoring so long as they are treated fairly by regulatory officials and are met with understanding and assistance should they encounter problems doing so (Tyler, 1990; Makkai and Braithwaite, 1996). Individuals and business firms that are inclined to comply will be strengthened in this posture by officials who treat them as trustworthy if confused or misguided citizens. Through cooperation with the state, the organizational veil can be dropped and information can be shared. Organizations can better identify and reel in rogue units. Responsive regulation also highlights the importance of involving private parties in the compliance assurance process. Industrial trade groups, professional organizations and neighborhood groups can be employed to increase the odds of compliance and ensure that regulation is not seen as a simple two-party oppositional process between state regulators and targeted business firms. The promised payoff is reduced resentment and resistance and a net increase in compliance.

Those of a more resistive bent may be nudged toward compliance through a judicious mixture of appeal to conscience, education and threat. For citizens and businesses that fail to comply despite appeals and cooperative actions, officials escalate their response in proportional fashion; as the seriousness of infractions and the willfulness they represent increases, the state adopts less conciliatory responses. Lurking in the background is the "benign big gun." This is the threat of criminal prosecution or suspension of license. It is used not only as a last resort but also as a way of keeping faith with those who comply willingly that they are not fools for doing so. They will not be harmed by competing with individuals and business firms who economize by the savings of noncompliance. The long-term payoffs of responsive regulation are more efficient and effective use of criminal prosecution, a higher overall level of compliance, and increased trust in government generally.

Unquestionably, cooperative strategies have a place in programs to maintain acceptable levels of general deterrence, but there is little conflict between principles of responsive regulation and the call for more certain and severe action against white-collar criminals, may be disagreement over priorities. A key component of the theoretical armament of responsive regulation is the need for and willingness to employ harsh penalties where appropriate. This is another way of saying that the omelet of responsive regulation requires both a willingness and capacity to "break a few eggs."

The apparent shortcomings of responsive regulation are worrisome, however. They begin with awareness that regulation takes place in a world of structured inequality and power that is not altered by cooperative approaches (Snider, 1993). When they sit down with regulators or other state officials to discuss compliance, the privileged do so from a position of strength while agency personnel may work under severe resource and political constraints. There is fear also that companies may take advantage of cooperative and lenient state officials; regulators with a mandate to cooperate with business perhaps are too easily controlled or captured (Pearce and Tombs, 1990; Snider, 1993). Nor is it clear that resource constraints on enforcement would be reduced under schemes of responsive regulation. Programs for voluntary compliance may require more of companies but they do not reduce necessarily the work required of regulators, investigators, and prosecutors. Crime fighters still must ferret out the secretive and criminal dealings of companies that fail to comply. This is costly. Whatever the eventual fate of responsive regulation, there is no doubt its appearance signals continuing disagreement over how best to treat white-collar criminals.

To judge from the contents of textbooks and other published works on white-collar crime, a substantial majority of academic investigators conceptualize and examine it in ways little different from the way they approach street crime. This begins with unflinching application of the label *crime* to harmful acts committed by privileged and respectable citizens. The focus for most is upperworld white-collar crime, and they generally opt for theoretical explanations with a decidedly critical edge. Some locate the causes of white-collar crime in the dynamics and culture of overarching production systems, but their analyses are laced with references to power, conflict and cultural domination.

The light cast on white-collar wrongdoing by others is softer, less critical, and more exculpatory as well. Crime-based definitions are preferred. This means that upperworld crime is but one part of a larger picture of predation; the crimes of Fortune 500 corporations are lumped together with crime by neighborhood appliance repair shops (Vaughan and Carlo, 1975). Use of crime-based definitions of white-collar crime thus enables use of a broad definitional net. Without distinguishing them, it lumps CEOs and rip-and-run roofers into the same analytic puzzle.

Preference for crime-based approaches to white-collar crime, moreover, is coupled with reluctance to label as crime the felonious acts of privileged citizens and powerful organizations (Vaughan, 1983; Szwajkowski, 1986; Baucus and Near, 1991). Felonies instead are lumped together with deviance, "mistakes," "dubious behavior," "unlawful behavior," and "illegal behavior" (Bromily and Marcus, 1989; Vaughan, 1999). Criminal acts are lost sight of or mislabeled in the process, which ignores the important lesson stated so clearly and succinctly by Shaprio (1983:306) that acts "not proscribed by the criminal law are not 'crime.'" Thus the probative value of investigations of noncriminal decisions cannot be accepted uncritically for application to crime (Baucus and Dworkin, 1991; Vaughan, 1996; Messerschmidt, 1995). In the eyes of political leaders, *crime* is meant to be and is unique. It may be risky behavior but, unlike other risky behaviors, the state can fine, incarcerate, or execute those who choose it. The drive for abstract concepts can mitigate the moral and legal responsibility of decision makers for acts whose precise nature is obscured.

Some political leaders and academics dwell on the victims of white-collar crime, but others ignore them entirely. For the former, the diverse costs of white-collar crime is reason enough for examining and subjecting it to more rigorous oversight. For the latter, the victims of white-collar crime are not a matter of concern. The result is an analysis cut off from the harm and the seriousness of the problem. Street-crime victims are described in tones of great seriousness, and their suffering has been used to justify sweeping reforms in the way offenders are handled (Elias, 1986; Dubber, 2002). There has been nothing comparable for victims of white-collar crime. Adoption and use of the concept *organizational culture* illustrates the complex dynamics and mixed if not skewed messages from scholarship on white-collar crime.

Organizational Culture

Emergence of the world economic system has resulted in ever larger numbers of firms conducting business and competing internationally. As they do so and work to overcome local economic barriers, the concept *organizational culture* has gained an analytic foothold (Shover and Hochstetler, 2001). As explanation for a host of corporate behaviors, it has captured the attention and allegiance of investigators as few others. The excesses and eventual downfall of Enron, for example, is attributed in large part to a culture described as one of "excess," "what's in it for me," "corrosive," and "kill-or-be-killed" (McLean and Elkind, 2004:122, 267, 300, 332). Initial explication of the notion of organizational culture is more than fifty years old (Jacques, 1951), but it did not attract attention until nearly three decades later. The animus for interest in organizational culture is belief that it is a "social force that controls patterns of organizational behavior by shaping members' cognitions and perceptions of meanings and realities" (Ott, 1989:69). Others suggest that it has "a powerful influence throughout an organization; it effects practically everything – from who gets promoted and what decisions are made, to how employees dress and what sports they play" (Deal and Kennedy, 1982:4). Those concerned with crime and misdeeds generally agree that it can "legitimate retreat from active ethical reflection on specific issues" (Alvesson, 2000:139).

Organizational culture is invoked also to make sense of organizational crime. Sonnenfeld and Lawrence (1978) indict the "culture of the business" as an important cause of differential participation in price-fixing behavior by firms in the folding-box industry during the 1970s. They point specifically to "anticompetitive norms" and suggest that price fixing became a "way of life" in guilty firms (1978:149). On the basis of interviews with retired corporate managers, Clinard (1983:65) reported that "[a]bout two-thirds... felt that

some corporations do have a generally ethical or unethical culture."
Similar interpretations for organizational crime are disseminated
widely by the mass media. *Newsweek* magazine suggests that "sexual
abuse is difficult to root out [of the U.S. Navy] because it is...so
embedded in the [organization's] day-to-day culture" (1996:70).
Indictment of culture is echoed by newspaper editors (e.g., *Los Angeles
Times*, 1997) and popular business journals as well. A writer in *Management Review* suggests that when corporate ethical violations occur,
frequently the "culprit is culture" (Frederick, 1988). In this overcon-
strained conception of upperworld actors, culture, however, is viewed
not as a context in which volitional actors make decisions but instead
as a contemplative straitjacket.

Despite the remarkably high level of consensus on the significance
of cultural variation as explanation for organizational crime, investigations of this relationship suffer from fundamental and persistent
shortcomings (Shover and Hochstetler, 2001). These include post hoc
interpretations of atypical incidents and enigmatic findings and failure
to explore the effects of hierarchy as a constraint on culture. Investigators begin by identifying highly successful or in other ways interesting
organizations and then work backward to identify cultural variables
that presumably are responsible. The danger of tautological reasoning
is obvious. Investigators invoke cultural variation post hoc to explain
enigmatic findings without measuring it (Barnett, 1986; Clinard and
Yeager, 1980; Baucus and Near, 1991).

Organizational culture takes shape in a world of calculated inequality, but research generally ignores how it is shaped by hierarchy; upper-
level managers and the ways they inevitably transmit biases and preferences to subordinates receive scant attention. Impersonal forces or
dynamics instead are singled out for causal attribution. Decision makers are lost sight of entirely or said to be incapable of making rational choices because of the refracted nature of morality and personal
responsibility in organizational environments. This flies in the face
of evidence that the stance toward ethical conduct and compliance
with law taken by top management may be a critical determinant of
organizational culture.

After the first decade of research into the nature and significance of
organizational culture, an observer charged that "[c]ulture research

remains an unpaid promissory note in the field of organizational behavior ... [and] we are still in the earliest phases of understanding ... [its] role in organizations" (Rousseau, 1990:186). Although "scholars have assigned great importance to culture as a cause of organizational crime and misconduct" (Vaughan, 1996:406), matters have changed little. Cultural explanations for organizational white-collar crime remain largely supposition.

Context and Constraints

It is tempting to imagine that theory development and policy making are wholly logical and cerebral processes, but experience suggests otherwise; they do not take place in a vacuum. Where the social sciences and policy making are concerned, contextual conditions shape concept development and the reception afforded potentially competing ideas. Putting aside the matter of their logical properties and empirical adequacy, what explains the appeal of cultural explanations for organizational white-collar crime? And what does this suggest about prospects for mounting successful campaigns against it?

The years since the resurrection of cultural explanations for organizational decisions making phenomena have seen dramatic change in American public universities that contribute to their appeal. As the proportionate share of their financial support garnered from state revenues levels off or declines, universities increasingly are strapped for resources. As never before, they look to profit financially from their operations and from pursuit of knowledge. The operating assumptions and ethic of the marketplace have taken firm root, and corporate support and funding have become more important. Reflecting these changes, procedures for faculty evaluation have become more formalized and numerically based, and increasing attention is paid to success acquiring external monies.

Potentially beneficent patrons are most likely to be drawn to and to find merit in work that takes seriously their perspectives and agendas. This is the appeal of organizational culture; it can be employed as explanation or as mitigating circumstance. It can be used to deflect responsibility for failure and misconduct while leaving organizational managers free to accept praise and financial bonuses when things go well. To the extent that organizational pathologies can be attributed to an amorphous or inertial culture, management is absolved of responsibility. As circumstances require, it can be sketched as ally or obstacle. When their efforts to reshape culture are successful, management can claim credit. Skeptics "might question whether . . . [it is] anything more than an ideology cultivated by management for the purpose of control and legitimation of activities" (Smirich, 1983:346).

This does not deny that variation in organizational culture may prove to be an important source of crime, but adequate explanation must demonstrate how it constrains decision making by specific agents. Thus far, its conceptual imprecision means that cultural explanations serve as a moral insulator between actors and organizational conditions; accountability is displaced to an invisible abstraction that cannot be fired or jailed. As they are employed today, cultural explanations of organizational crime function alternately as a weapon for critics of growing corporate power or as an apologia for upperworld predators.

Acknowledgment and analysis of organizational crime is conspicuously absent from the research agenda of most academics, and this is true particularly in business schools. The reasons are unclear, but it may be that faculty preoccupation with organizational misconduct signals the wrong priorities in the new corporate climate of higher education. Theoretical work and lines of inquiry that offend well-heeled external interests are risky. The principal strength of the concept organizational culture and one reason for its appeal may be its flexibility for application in diverse settings for a host of purposes and constituencies. Research into organizational culture potentially is a client-appealing and safe avenue for gaining the funding needed to survive or succeed in the corporate university. Salaries, moreover, can be supplemented substantially by competing successfully as consultants to corporate interests. This presupposes not that university faculty knowingly opt for analytic approaches that resonate with the biases of corporate interests, only that the attractiveness of inoffensive explanations unwittingly increase in the changing academy. In this way business application shapes intellectual work "into a serviceable instrument to promote the self-interested purposes of . . . corporate clients" (Frederick, 1995:82). The cacophony of interpretive approaches to white-collar crimes also leaves those who commit them free to argue their acts are merely mistakes for which they are not responsible in any case.

THE STATE AND CRIMES OF PRIVILEGE

Ross and Sutherland were products of an era in U.S. history and a location in the social structure that imbued citizens generally with a view of government as responsive to popular will. Few today are as sanguine as they ponder prospects for curbing crimes of privilege through resolute state action. Concern begins with fear that endemic dynamics of the state in the contemporary economy may limit or render ineffective its responses to white-collar crime. Technology and globalization have made it possible to conduct complex commercial transactions almost instantaneously. Old barriers of time and distance have been obliterated. As a result, state control "is increasingly bypassed by global flows of capital, goods, services, technology, communication and information" (Castells, 2004:303). As seen in policing international drug trafficking and money laundering the variety, scale, and complexity of cross border transactions are significant barriers to credible oversight (Guehenno, 1995). The technical and administrative capacity to regulate international trade is within reach of only a few nations. Maintaining levels of oversight comparable to what they once held over transactions and production within their borders may be unlikely if not unattainable in a global economy. Politically and legally defined territories have less influence in some residents' daily lives than in the past (Tillman, 2002).

Diminution of national borders is even greater for those who are aware of and able to shape global opportunities internationally. Corporate executives, who choose where to locate their facilities, demand lure and weak oversight. This dynamic is played out across the globe as they negotiate with political leaders for low taxes, low cost government services, free infrastructure, and limited restrictions on their autonomy. In return they promise jobs.

Domestic industries and business firms do not take lightly the recruitment of foreign companies with promises of largesse and a pro-business environment that is not available to them. Nor are they willing to accept easily that their operations should be regulated and taxed more stringently than companies that keep parts of their operations abroad. As the links between national economies strengthen and expand, so does competition among them and, "because capital is at once mobile and in short supply, the desire to attract foreign capital makes it difficult to control a nation's capital" (Guehenno, 1995:10). What once was commonplace but largely confined to intranational dynamics is reproduced on a grander scale around the globe. Trade ministers and NAFTA negotiators are not alone in making decisions that balance protection of constituents with unpleasant economic realities. This is the case increasingly where states confront economic power.

Contemporary interpretations of the state emphasize its function as a political-economic steering mechanism that operates with some autonomy. The state and regulatory process are relatively free from public campaigns and pressures and, in most cases, they service business interests without disruption, impermissible levels of corruption, or controversy. One reason is that state managers see the benefits of bargaining and cooperation with powerful constituencies for smooth administrative operations. They often work within narrow confines of detailed and limited budgets. To be considered legitimate and reasonable by businesses requires minimal conflict and resistance at every step (Offe, 1985). They are aware that resistance from industry would hamstring their efforts and undermine post investment in amicable working relationships. Political leaders and state managers understandably protect interests and agencies close to home (Block, 1977; 1981). Sutherland (1949:249) pointed out that when state agents fail to criminalize or punish illegal business activities often it is because, "cultural homogeneity, close personal relationships, and power relationships protect against critical definitions by government."

Economic cycles and political dynamics are major constraints on criminalization and oversight as well. In boom times state managers are free to respond to political pressures to limit the autonomy of privileged interests. During periods of prosperity corporations and business leaders likewise are willing to make concessions and are disinclined to put up stiff resistance to incremental increases in regulatory standards. The state responds rapidly to scandals that diminish confidence in the economy. Quick enactment of Sarbanes-Oxley can be read this way. When the faith of investors is shaken by fear that unscrupulous business is placing investments at risk, corrective measures are required. State managers always must be wary, however, about implying that they will pursue corporate malfeasance aggressively or pursue interventionist strategies. State managers see the march of globalization. Many companies have teams in place looking far and wide for the most advantageous environment, and state managers are aware of the real threat of business relocation.

The dynamics of the contemporary state raise troubling questions about its willingness and capacity to oversee increasingly transnational businesses (Strange, 1996; Streeck and Schmitter, 1991). Like nation-states, moreover, new forms of international governance derive much of their power from the services they provide to economic interests (Castells, 2004). This is seen when wealthy states and the supranational institutions they create work to keep channels of trade unimpeded. In the process, social justice, regulation, higher wages for workers, and environmental protection are moved to the background. Crime-as-choice theory points the way to effective control of white-collar crime, but there may be considerable and potentially costly resistance. It remains to be seen if a movement against white-collar crime can generate popular support, intensity, and international cooperation that yield payoffs comparable to what have been achieved where street crime is the policy focus.

PROSPECTS FOR CREDIBLE OVERSIGHT

The materials and analysis presented in the foregoing chapters give reason to believe that we are witnessing a rising tide of white-collar crime in Western nations. Reasons for the increase include new forms and an expanded supply of lure, noncredible oversight, and uncertain punishment for those who commit white-collar crime. In a word, there are unmistakable signs of permissiveness at a time when increased certainty of punishment is needed. A move to rectify this problem carries few risks:

> If we try to make the penalties for crime swifter and more certain, and it should turn out that deterrence does not work, then we have merely increased the risks facing persons who are guilty of crimes in any event. If we fail to increase the certainty and swiftness of penalties, and it should turn out that deterrence does work, then we have needlessly

increased the risk of being victimized for many innocent persons. (Wilson, 1983:84)

In stark contrast to street criminals, whose ability and willingness to calculate carefully before choosing to commit crime is reduced by the presence of other young males, the influence of psychoactive drugs, and the importance of gaining or maintaining interpersonal respect, white-collar workers generally live and work in worlds structured to promote, to monitor, and to reward prudent and deliberate decision making. As important, their orderly and comfortable lives are constructed painstakingly in a calculated fashion. From an early age, respectable if not always well-paying career options and unambiguous pathways to achieving these have been apparent to most. Throughout most of their lives, they can see the relationship between the law-abiding or virtuous behavior of yesterday and the payoffs of today. The metrics they employ are clear-cut, unidimensional, and calibrated precisely, often in monetary units. Their bourgeois world is wrapped in the rationality of accountants. A trader who enriched himself using inside information points out that deciding to commit crime was little different from his work: "I weighed the risks, just as I would analyze any other potential investment, and I concluded that the benefits outweighed what I perceived to be the minuscule chances of getting caught" (Levine, 1991:74).

Punishment affects behavior by influencing perceptions of sanction risk. Both personal and vicarious experience with it reduces the odds of offending (Piquero and Pogarsky, 2002; Stafford and Warr, 1993). Successful evasion of punishment increases offending (Homey and Marshall, 1992; Lochner, 2003; Piquero and Pogarsky, 2002). Respectability and the opinion of good people hold enormously important meaning for those tempted to commit white-collar crime. They can visualize and estimate the losses in reputation and wealth that would follow from public revelation of misconduct. If white-collar criminals need any reminder, the risks of crime are brought home by media coverage when someone like them falls from grace. The transgressions and humiliation of men and women who "ought to know better" are newsworthy stuff. Witness coverage of the Martha Stewart case (*New York Times*, 2003a). Because white-collar criminals are more rational than their street criminal cousins. They have every reason to respond to threat with renewed caution and self-restraint. As Geis (1999:156) notes:

> People in high places are much more sensitive to the loss of prestige associated with being a guest of the government in a state or federal prison. Therefore, to the extent that they are likely to be treated in this manner (as evidenced by the fact that others like them are so treated) they are more likely than street offenders to arrange their behaviors in accord with the requirements of the criminal law.

Few conclusions can be stated confidently about deterrence of organizational crime. There seems little doubt, however, that formal sanction threats serve an educative purpose and "may be necessary to control the behavior of some and serve as *reminders* to the rest" (Simpson, 2002:152). Law backed by credible enforcement can educate firms and individuals about consequences they had not considered. It can focus attention or inspire recognition of harm in actions they considered harmless or insignificant. It also can coordinate behavior because competitors assume that rivals are abiding by pronouncements when all know that failure to do so will have costs for reputations. These are reasons why reputational cost can shift preferences and internalize legal codes of conduct. By influencing people's beliefs about what others will do legal proscriptions play a crucial role in determining the outcome (Cooter, 2000:79). Compliance assurance managers in 233 firms in several industries were queried about responses by their employers to severe legal penalties for corporate environmental violations. Ninety percent could identify enforcement actions taken against other firms in their industry, and 42 percent identified "signal cases" they interpreted as evidence that regulatory officials were sending unequivocal messages about the meaning and application of rules. Sixty-three percent reported taking explicit compliance action in response to enforcement aimed at other firms. The investigators conclude that enforcement and signal cases serve as reminders of the value and importance of compliance (Thornton, Gunningham, and Kagan, 2005). By using the criminal law in this way a nation "reaffirm[s] the moral order of society and remind[s] people of what constitutes right conduct, in hopes that this reaffirmation and reminder will help people...teach each other about virtue" (Wilson and Herrnstein, 1985:528).

Enhancing Organizational Self-Restraint

Doubtless corporate officers and their agents are more capable of preventing and detecting crime than inexperienced, ill-equipped outsiders. Witness what they accomplish improving internal, employee oversight when they put their minds to it. State-of-the-art security systems used by retailers notify corporate headquarters when store managers hundreds of miles away are overusing their employee discounts, and internal security teams will soon be dispatched to examine video tape and talk with employees. One-way mirrors, lights that blink as items are scanned, and cameras in grocery stores combined with certain prosecution help assure management that cashiers will not discount cigarette prices to friends. There is no doubt organizations can be constructed and operated in ways that make noncompliance with the law both difficult and infrequent. Corporate executives point to this as reason for resisting external oversight; everything, they assure, is under control (Pearce, 2001).

Corporate governance is used increasingly to describe a range of programs and processes put in place by corporate firms to increase ethical conduct and accountability in their day-to-day operations. To the extent that compliance with law is a valued goal, managers can create place processes to promote it and to insulate their firms from contrary pressures. Failure to do so can be seen as an "organizational defect" (Finney and Lesieur, 1982). Many business firms promulgate codes of ethics or establish internal compliance programs as a sign of commitment to ethical conduct. Federal sentencing guidelines, moreover, permit them to count the latter as mitigating factor when they run afoul of the law (Geis and Salinger, 1998). When they operate effectively, internal compliance units are the organizational equivalent of conscience; they serve as a potential source of self-restraint on unethical and criminal decision making. The effectiveness of these programs and units remains unclear, however. Organizational codes of ethics, for example, generally emphasize the importance of treating the organizational employer ethically, but they are conspicuously silent about employees' obligation to obey the law (Mathews, 1987). The codes of ethics of 119 corporations examined by Cressey and Moore (1983:53) suggest that "top executives...only weakly shared the concern for social responsibility so often voiced by business leaders in the mid-1970s when most of the codes were written."

Key components of successful internal control systems include unambiguous lines of authority and responsibility for compliance, autonomous internal inspection units, and clear evidence of top management's commitment to and participation (Braithwaite, 1985). This is because the upper echelons of organizations set the moral tone of the workplace, and other employees play by the rules they establish (Clinard, 1983; Hambrick and Mason, 1984). Examination of corporate safety performance in addition shows that the presence of safety officers is substantially less important than their location on the organizational chart and whether or not resources are allocated for compliance assurance (Erickson, 1994). Research on the implementation of affirmative action legislation makes the same point. Braithwaite (1993) shows that human resource departments are central in enforcing policies on quality of work and workplace flexibility for women. She notes that "where companies [are] committed to human resource management, both procedural compliance and accommodating practices [tend] to be high" (Braithwaite, 1993:327). Furthermore,

> [c]ompanies that do not place value on human resource management or personnel functions are . . . the companies that are most likely to be doing the absolute minimum; that is assigning responsibility to someone in the company, writing out a policy statement, submitting a report containing some numbers of dubious worth and forgetting all about it for another year. (Braithwaite, 1993:350)

Information on 508 cases of occupational fraud investigated by certified fraud examiners shows that organizations with internal audits or internal fraud examination departments overall sustained less costly victimization than organizations that lack these features (Association of Certified Fraud Examiners, 2005). Although tips from employees or customers were more effective than internal audits in detecting fraud, the latter were somewhat more effective than external audits in this regard. In addition to the need for greater intra-organizational knowledge and publicity about internal control mechanisms, the critical but often missing ingredient is unambiguous commitment from the top.

Sonnenfeld and Lawrence (1978) interviewed a sample of executives in the forest products industry about their experience with management methods to control illegal behavior. They conclude that "one of the consistent and early points that came up was the example set for the company by the behavior of top management" (Sonnenfeld and Lawrence, 1978:152). The same findings are reported by Clinard (1983) based on interviews with sixty-four retired middle-management executives who formerly were employed by Fortune 500 corporations. "Signaling behaviors" by upper management are particularly important (Baumhart, 1961; Brenner and Molander, 1977, Clinard, 1983; Hambrick and Mason, 1984; Sonnenfeld and Lawrence, 1978). When management communicates unequivocal messages to colleagues and employees about the importance of compliance, the message is not lost (Braithwaite, 1985). The value and priority they assign to compliance with the law can permeate the organization and affects the outcome of countless decisions by subordinates. A corporate manager explains that "[w]hat is right in the corporation is not what is right in a man's home or church. *What is right in the corporation is what the guy above you wants from you.* That's what morality is in the corporation" (Jackall, 1988:108). Despite questions about the effectiveness of codes of ethics, the late twentieth century saw their adoption by major corporations around the world (Wood and Rimmer, 2003). Uncertainty about them importance as constraint on decision making persists, but their potential remains unchallenged. Callahan (2004:282 suggests that questions about their effectiveness will not change "until companies [develop] the means to integrate ethical values into daily routines." The principal obstacle is that "many business leaders just don't buy the idea that more integrity means high profits" (Callahan, 2004:284).

It is difficult to assess the potential gains and losses of punishment for offenders. There is reason to suppose, however, that white-collar offenders may be positioned ideally for learning the lessons of imprisonment. Prison is painful for them in ways that differ from the pains of the typical street offender (Braithwaite, 1989). Their ties to conventional work trajectories are not as fragile and few serve sentences so long that it destroys all they have achieved. Their resources aid them in navigating the difficulties of reintegration and postrelease supervision. The point of punishment is not to destroy lives by taking so much that little can be achieved afterward. That can be justified for only the most devastating crimes and unscrupulous offenders. But we are far from reaching that point when it comes to how the fight against white-collar crime now is waged. There is reason to believe that many white-collar offenders could be humbled and turned from crime by experiencing more certain and marginally more severe punishment. Imprisonment should be used more often in the battle against white-collar predators. If nothing else, it shocks and forces them to confront the fact that many people take their crime seriously. Those who choose to offend deserve to be punished and to have their prospects diminished by it. More would be turned away from crime if the unpleasantness and degradation of the most severe forms of punishment were communicated credibly throughout the ranks of privileged citizens.

In calling for greater use of harsher sanctions, gratuitous pain is not the object. Larger numbers of punished white-collar offenders are key, not draconian increases in severity. Whether or not the contemporary state is up to the challenge posed by increasing white-collar crime is uncertain, but a strong effort will be needed to stem the tide. Lure is changing and increasing, and awareness of it grows as well. The state meanwhile sends morally limpid and permissive signals about its willingness to fight white-collar crime, and globalization makes oversight by nation states increasingly difficult. International initiatives fighting white-collar crime are piecemeal and in their infancy.

The importance of a citizenry mobilized to insist upon greater oversight cannot be exagerrated. They must press for more credible and effective controls on white-collar crime. Kagan and colleagues (2003) show that oversight works best when it is coupled with active citizen participation and the presence of stakeholders who pressure firms to comply. In the absence of this it seems unlikely that they will be forthcoming. This is an area of public policy where increased attention and investment is almost sure to yield worthwhile results. The war on street crime has exacerbated inequities in the treatment of offenders to the point that many citizens now see that there are two systems of justice in the United States. It is easy to point to the lack of significant movement against white-collar crime. The lessons from rational-choice theory make it sobering to imagine the long-term consequences if this continues.

References

Abrams, Elliot. 1993. *Undue Process: A Story of How Political Differences Turned into Crime.* New York: The Free Press.

Adler, Paul S. 1992. *Technology and the Future of Work.* New York: Oxford University Press.

Alesina, Alberta, and Beatrice Weder. 2002. "Do corrupt governments receive less foreign aid?" *American Economic Review* 92:1126–37.

Alveson, Mats. 2002. *Understanding Organizational Culture.* London: Sage.

American Council on Education. 2001. "Student borrowing in the 1990s." *ACE Issue Brief*, November.

Andenaes, Johannes. 1966. "The general preventive effects of punishment." *University of Pennsylvania Law Review* 114:949–83.

Anechiarico, Frank, and James B. Jacobs. 1996. *Pursuit of Absolute Integrity.* Chicago: University of Chicago Press.

ANSA Italian News (Milan). 2004. "Councillor accused of fraud in phantom training course probe." February 16, page 1A.

Arkansas Democrat Gazette. 2003. "Ross plans bill to target usury limit: New Fed policy clouds state law." January 25, page 1A.

Associated Press. 2003a. "Ten brokerage firms to pay $1.4 B in fraud settlement." April 29, *Business News*, page 1.

Associated Press. 2003b. "Bills on slamming and cramming die in House." March 17, *Business News*, page 1.

Association of Certified Fraud Examiners. 2004. *Report to the Nation on Occupational Fraud and Abuse.* Austin, TX: Association of Certified Fraud Examiners.

Atlanta Journal Constitution. 2003. "Ex-prison chief indicted: Whitworth accused of corruption." July 26, page 1A.

Attorney General, Pennsylvania. 2004. "AG names defendants in e-mail scheme to sell bogus academic degrees." Harrisburg: Office of Attorney General, December 8.

Aulette, Judy Root, and Raymond J. Michalowski. 1993. "Fire in Hamlet: A case study of a state-corporate crime." Pp. 171–206 in *Political Crime in Contemporary America: A Critical Approach*, edited by Kenneth D. Tunnell. New York: Garland.

Ayres, Ian, and John Braithwaite. 1992. *Responsive Regulation*. Cambridge: Cambridge University Press.

Azicorbe, Anna M., Arthur B. Kennickell, and Kevin B. Moore. 2003. "Recent changes in US family finances: Evidence from the 1998 and 2001 surveys of consumer finances." *The Federal Reserve Bulletin*, January. Washington, DC: U.S. Federal Reserve Board.

Baca, Sean P., Brian L. Garbe, and Richard A. Weiss. 2000. "The rise of sector effects in major equity markets." *Financial Analysts Journal* September:35–40.

Baker, Wayne E., and Robert R. Faulkner. 1993. "The social organization of conspiracy: Illegal networks in the heavy electrical equipment industry." *American Sociological Review* 58:837–60.

Baltimore Sun. 2004. "FDA critics propose key changes for drug safety: Independent review board, cutting financial ties urged." November 28, page A1.

Bardach, Eugene, and Robert A. Kagan. 1982. *Going by the Book: The Problem of Regulatory Unreasonableness*. Philadelphia: Temple University Press.

Barlow, Hugh. 1993. "From fiddle factors to networks of collusion: Charting the waters of small business crime." *Crime, Law and Social Change* 20:319–37.

Barnett, Harold C. 1986. "Industry culture and industry economy: Correlates of tax noncompliance in Sweden." *Criminology* 24:553–74.
    1994. *Toxic Debts and the Superfund Dilemma*. Chapel Hill: University of North Carolina Press.

Baucus, Melissa S. 1994. "Pressure, opportunity and predisposition: A multivariate model of corporate illegality." *Journal of Management* 20:699–721.

Baucus, Melissa S., and T. M. Dworkin. 1991. "What is corporate crime? It is not illegal corporate behavior." *Law and Policy* 13:231–44.

Baucus, Melissa S., and Janet P. Near. 1991. "Can illegal corporate behavior be predicted? An event history analysis." *Academy of Management Journal* 34:9–36.

Baumhart, Raymond C. 1961. "How ethical are businessmen?" *Harvard Business Review*, July–August:6–17.

Behn, Robert D., and Kim Sperduto. 1979. "Medical schools and the 'entitlement ethic.'" *Public Interest* 57:48–68.

Bennett, Trevor, and Richard Wright. 1984. *Burglars on Burglary*. Hampshire, UK: Gower.

Bennett, William J. 1992. *The De-valuing of America*. New York: Summit.

Bennett, William J., John Dilulio Jr., and John P. Walters. 1996. *Body Count: Moral Poverty and How to Win America's War Against Crime and Drugs.* New York: Simon and Schuster.

Benson, Michael L. 1982. *Unpublished Qualitative Interviews of White-Collar Offenders.* Courtesy of Michael L. Benson, University of Cincinnati.

———. 1984. "Fall from grace: Loss of occupational status as a consequence of conviction for a white-collar crime." *Criminology* 22:573–95.

———. 1985. "Denying the guilty mind: Accounting for involvement in a white-collar crime." *Criminology* 23:589–99.

———. 1990. "Emotions and adjudication: Status degradation among white-collar criminals." *Justice Quarterly* 7:515–28.

———. 2002. *Crime and the Life Course: An Introduction.* Los Angeles: Roxbury.

Benson, Michael L., and Francis T. Cullen. 1988. "The special sensitivity of white-collar offenders to prison: A critique and research agenda." *Journal of Criminal Justice* 16:207–15.

———. 1998. *Combating Corporate Crime: Local Prosecutors at Work.* Boston: Northeastern University Press.

Benson, Michael L., and Kent R. Kerley. 2001. "Life-course theory and white-collar crime." Pp. 121–36 in *Contemporary Issues in Crime and Criminal Justice: Essays in Honor of Gilbert Geis,* edited by Henry N. Pontell and David Shichor. Upper Saddle River, NJ: Prentice Hall.

Benson, Michael L., and Elizabeth Moore. 1992. "Are white-collar and common criminals the same?" *Journal of Research in Crime and Delinquency* 29:251–72.

Berk, Richard A., Alec Campbell, Ruth Klap, and Bruce Western. 1992. "A Bayesian analysis of the Colorado Springs Spouse Abuse Experiment." *Journal of Criminal Law and Criminology* 83:170–200.

Black, William K. 2005. *The Best Way to Rob a Bank is to Own One: How Corporate Executives and Politicians Looted the S&L Industry.* Austin: University of Texas Press.

Block, Fred. 1977. "The ruling class does not rule: Notes on the Marxist theory of the state." *Socialist Revolution* 33 (May–June):6–28.

———. 1981. "Beyond relative autonomy: State managers as historical subjects." *New Political Science* 2:33–49.

Block, Michael Kent, Frederick Carl Nold, and Joseph Gregory Sidak. 1981. "The deterrent effects of antitrust enforcement." *Journal of Political Economy* 89:429–45.

Boardman, Anthony E., Claude Laurin, and Aidan R. Vining. 2003. "Privatization in North America." Pp. 129–160 in *International Handbook on Privatization,* edited by David Parker and David Saal. Cheltenham, UK: Edward Elgar.

Boston Globe. 1998. "People's play: Hide-and-seek with tax ruble." October 5, page A2.

1999. "Cruise line fined in pollution case: Royal Caribbean to pay $18m." July 22, page 1.

Bouffard, Jeffrey A. 2002. "The influence of emotion on rational decision making in sexual aggression." *Journal of Criminal Justice* 30:121–34.

Bragg, Rick. 1997. *All Over But the Shoutin'.* New York: Random House.

Brahmbhatt, Milan. 1998. "Measuring global integration: A review of the literature and recent evidence." World Bank Paper. www1.worldbank.org/economicpolicy/globalizatization/documents/measuring.pdf.

Braithwaite, John. 1983. "Enforced self-regulation: A new strategy for corporate crime control." *Michigan Law Review* 80:1466–1507.

——— 1984. *Corporate Crime in the Pharmaceutical Industry.* London: Routledge and Kagan.

——— 1985. *To Punish or Persuade.* Albany: State University of New York Press.

——— 1989. *Crime, Shame and Reintegration.* Cambridge: Cambridge University Press.

Braithwaite, John, and Peter Drahos. 2000. *Global Business Regulation.* Cambridge: Cambridge University Press.

Braithwaite, John, and Gilbert Geis. 1982. "On theory and action for corporate crime control." Pp. 189–210 in *On White-Collar Crime,* edited by Gilbert Geis. Lexington, MA: D.C. Heath.

Braithwaite, John, and Toni Makkai. 1991. "Testing an expected utility model of corporate deterrence." *Law & Society Review* 25:7–39.

Braithwaite, Valerie. 1993. "The Australian government's affirmative action legislation: Achieving social change through resource management." *Law and Policy* 15:327–54.

Braithwaite, Valerie, Monika Reinhart, Malcolm Mearns, and Rachelle Graham. 2001. "Preliminary Findings from the Community Hopes, Fears and Actions Survey." Working paper #3. Canberra: Research School of the Social Sciences, Centre for Tax System Integrity.

Braly, Malcolm. 1976. *False Starts: A Memoir of San Quentin and Other Prisons.* Boston, MA: Little Brown.

Breed, Bryan. 1979. *White Collar Bird.* London: John Clare Books.

Brenner, Steven N., and Earl A. Molander. 1977. "Is the ethics of business changing?" *Harvard Business Review* 55:57–71.

Brewer, Lynn. 2002. *House of Cards: Confessions of an Enron Executive* (with Matthew Scott Hansen). College Station, TX: Virtualbookworm.com Publishing.

British Broadcasting Company. 2005. "Monsanto fined $1.5 million for bribery." January 7.

Bromily, Philip, and Alfred Marcus. 1989. "The deterrent to dubious corporate behavior: Profitability, probability and safety recalls." *Strategic Management Journal* 10:233–50.

Brooks, Robin J., and Marco Del Negro. 2002. "Firm-level evidence on global integration." Paper Presented at International Monetary Fund Global Linkages Conference, April 26, Washington, DC.

Buffalo News. 2004. "Don't get trapped while reducing debt." February 17, Business, page 1.

Burnett, Ros. 1992. *Dynamics of Recidivism: Summary Report.* Oxford: University of Oxford, Centre for Criminological Research.

Business Week Online. 2001. "Arthur Andersen: How bad will it get?" December 24.

Bussman, Kai. 2003. *Coping with Economic Crime: Risks and Strategies.* Ruschlikon, Switzerland: Swiss Re Center for Global Dialogue.

Cable News Network. 2003. "Microsoft, Best Buy accused of net scam." May 8, *CNN Technology Releases,* page 1.

Calavita, Kitty. 1983. "The demise of the Occupational Safety and Health Administration: A case study in symbolic politics." *Social Problems* 30:437–48.

Calavita, Kitty, Henry N. Pontell, and Robert Tillman. 1997a. *Big Money Crime: Fraud and Politics in the Savings and Loan Crisis.* Berkeley: University of California Press.

    1997b. "The Savings and Loan debacle, financial crime, and the state." *Annual Review of Sociology* 23:19–39.

Callahan, David. 2004. *The Cheating Culture.* Orlando: Harvest Books.

Canan, Penelope, and George W. Pring. 1988. "Strategic lawsuits against public participation." *Social Problems* 35:506–19.

Carroll, Stephen J., Allan Abrahamse, and Mary Vaiana. 1995. "The costs of excess medical claims for automobile personal injuries." Rand Research, RAND DB-139-ICJ, Santa Monica, CA: RAND.

Castells, Manuel. 2004. *The Power of Identity* (2nd edition). Malden, MA: Blackwell Publishing.

Cavaglia, Stefano, Chirstopher Brightman, and Michael Aked. 2000. "The increasing importance of industry factors." *Financial Analyst Journal* September:41–54.

Christie, Nils. 2000. *Crime Control as Industry: Toward Gulags Western Style* (3rd edition). New York: Routledge.

Citizens for Tax Justice. 2003. "Surge in corporate welfare drives corporate tax payments down to near record low." *Corporate Tax Justice Analysis,* April 17. Washington, DC.

Clarke, Michael. 1990. "Control of insurance fraud: A comparative view." *British Journal of Criminology* 30:1–23.

    1992. *Mortgage Fraud.* London: Chapman and Hall.

    1993. "EEC fraud: A suitable case for treatment." Pp. 162–186 in *Global Crime Connections: Dynamics and Control,* edited by Frank Pearce and Michael Woodiwiss. London: Macmillan.

Clarke, Ronald V. 1995. "Situational crime prevention." Pp. 91–150 in *Crime and Justice: An Annual Review of Research*, Vol. 19, edited by Michael Tonry and David P. Farrington. Chicago: University of Chicago Press.

Clinard, Marshall B. 1983. *Corporate Ethics and Crime: The Role of Middle Management.* Beverly Hills, CA: Sage.

Clinard, Marshall B., and Peter C. Yeager. 1980. *Corporate Crime.* New York: Free Press.

Cohen, Mark A., and Sally S. Simpson. 1997. "The origins of corporate criminality: Rational individual and organizational actors." Pp. 33–51 in *Debating Corporate Crime*, edited by William S. Lofquist, M. A. Cohen, and G. A. Rabe. Cincinnati: Anderson.

Coleman, James S. 1982. *The Asymmetric Society.* Syracuse, NY: Syracuse University Press.

——— 1990. *Foundations of Social Theory.* Cambridge: Harvard University Press.

Coleman, James W. 1987. "Toward an integrated theory of white-collar crime." *American Journal of Sociology* 93:406–39.

Collins, Judith M., and Frank L. Schmidt. 1993. "Personality, integrity, and white-collar crime: A construct validity study." *Personnel Psychology* 46:295–311.

Colson, Charles W. 1976. *Born Again.* Old Tappan, NJ: Chosen Books.

Cooter, Robert D. 2000. "Do good laws make good citizens? An economic analysis of internalized norms." *Virginia Law Review* 86:1577–1601.

——— 2000. "Three effects of social norms on law: Expression, deterrence, and internalization." *Oregon Law Review* 79(1):1–22.

Cordilia, Ann T. 1986. "Robbery arising out of a group drinking context." Pp. 167–80 in *Violent Transactions*, edited by Anne Campbell and John J. Gibbs. New York: Basil Blackwell.

Cornish, Derek B., and Ronald V. Clarke. 1986. "Preface." Pp. i–viii in *The Reasoning Criminal*, edited by Derek B. Cornish and Ronald V. Clarke. New York: Springer-Verlag.

Corporate Crime Reporter. 2003. "Democrats, Republicans awash in funds from corporate criminals, report finds." July 3, page 1.

Couch, Carl J. 1989. *Social Processes and Relationships.* New York: General Hall.

Cressey, Donald R. 1953. *Other People's Money.* Glencoe, IL: Free Press.

——— 1995. "Poverty of theory in corporate crime research." Pp. 413–31 in *White-Collar Crime: Classic and Contemporary Views*, edited by Gilbert Geis, Robert F. Meier, and Lawrence M. Salinger. New York: Free Press.

Cressey, Donald R., and Charles A. Moore. 1983. "Managerial values and corporate codes of ethics." *California Management Review* 25:53–77.

Croall, Hazel. 1992. *White-Collar Crime*. Philadelphia: Open University Press.

Cromwell, Paul, James N. Olsen, and D'Aunn Wester Avary. 1991. *Breaking and Entering: An Ethnographic Analysis of Burglary*. Newbury Park, CA: Sage.

Croteau, David. 1995. *Politics and the Class Divide: Working People and the Middle Class Left*. Philadelphia: Temple University Press.

Cruver, Brian. 2002. *Anatomy of Greed: The Unshredded Truth from an Enron Insider*. New York: Carroll & Graf.

Dallas Business Journal. 2004. "Time for usury laws to change, comish says." June 4, page 1.

Daly, Kathleen. 1989. "Gender and varieties of white-collar crime." *Criminology* 27:769–93.

Deal, Terrence E., and Allan A. Kennedy. 1982. *Corporate Cultures: The Rites and Rituals of Corporate Life*. Reading, MA: Addison-Wesley.

Delorme, Eugene. 1994. *Chief* (edited by Inez Cardozo-Freeman). Lincoln: University of Nebraska Press.

Devine, Thomas M. 1999. "The Whistle-blower Protection Act of 1989: Foundation for the modern law of employment dissent." *Administrative Law Review* 51:531–60.

Dilulio, John J. 1991. *No Escape: The Future of American Corrections*. New York: Basic Books.

Direct Marketing Association. 2001. www.the-dma.org.

Doocy, Jeffrey H., David Shichor, Dale K. Sechrest, and Gilbert Geis. 2001. "Telemarketing fraud: Who are the tricksters and what makes them trick?" *Security Journal* 14:7–26.

Dowding, Keith. 1991. *Rational Choice and Political Power*. Aldershot: Edward Elgar.

   1995. *Preferences, Institutions and Rational Choice*. Oxford: Clarendon.

Dubber, Markus Dirk. 2002. *Victims in the War on Crime: Abuse of Victims' Rights*. New York: New York University Press.

Dudley, Susan, and Melinda Warren. 2003. *Regulatory Spending Soars: An Analysis of the U.S. Budget for Fiscal Years 2003 and 2004, Regulatory Budget Report 25*. Arlington, VA: Mercatus Center.

Dumez, Herve, and Alan Jeunamaitre. 2000. *Understanding and Regulating the Market at a Time of Globalization: The Case of the Cement Industry*. New York: St. Martin's.

Dunk, Thomas W. 1991. *It's a Working Man's Town: Male Working-Class Culture in Northwestern Ontario*. Montreal: McGill-Queen's University Press.

Dunleavy, Patrick. 1991. *Democracy, Bureaucracy and Public Choice*. Hemel Hempstead: Harverster Wheatsheaf.

Eccles, Robert G., and Dwight B. Crane. 1988. *Doing Deals: Investment Banks at Work*. Boston, MA: Harvard Business School Press.

Edelhertz, Herbert. 1970. *The Nature, Impact and Prosecution of White Collar Crime*. Washington, DC: U.S. Department of Justice, National Institute of Law Enforcement and Criminal Justice.

Ehrenreich, Barbara. 1989. *Fear of Falling: The Inner Life of the Middle Class*. New York: Knopf.

2002. *Nickel and Dimed: On (Not) Getting by in America*. New York: Henry Holt.

Eichenwald, Kurt. 2000. *The Informant: A True Story*. New York: Broadway Books.

2005. *Conspiracy of Fools*. New York: Broadway Books.

Eisner, Marc Allen. 2000. *Regulatory Politics in Transition* (2nd edition). Baltimore: Johns Hopkins University Press.

Elias, Robert. 1986. *The Politics of Victimization*. New York: Oxford University Press.

Ellsberg, Daniel. 2002. *Secrets: A Memoir of Vietnam and the Pentagon Papers*. New York: Viking.

Elster, Jon. 1989. *Nuts and Bolts for the Social Sciences*. Cambridge: Cambridge University Press.

Environmental Working Group. 2003. "Total USDA subsidies in the United States." December 23. http://www.ewg.org/farm/.

Erickson, Judith A. 1994. *The Effect of Corporate Culture on Injury and Illness Rates within an Organization*. Unpublished Ph.D. thesis. University of Southern California.

Ethics Resource Center. 2003. *National Business Ethics Survey*. Washington, DC: Ethics Resource Center.

Etzioni, Amatai. 1993. "The U.S. Sentencing Commission on corporate crime: A critique." *Annals of the American Academy of Political and Social Science* 525:147–56.

2002. "Scandals will end when penalties fit crimes." *Jewish World Review*, March 31, page 1.

Farberman, Harvey. 1977. "A criminogenic market structure: The automobile industry." *Sociological Quarterly* 16:438–57.

Farrington, David P. 1997. "Human Development and Criminal Careers." Pp. 361–408 in *The Oxford Handbook of Criminology* (2nd edition), edited by Mike Maguire, Rod Morgan, and Robert Reiner. Oxford: Oxford University Press.

Faulkner, Robert, Eric R. Cheney, Gene A. Fisher, and Wayne E. Baker. 2003. "Crime by committee: Conspirators and company men in the illegal electrical industry cartel, 1954–1959." *Criminology* 41:511–54.

Federal Emergency Management Agency. 1992. *Chicken Processing Plant Fires: Hamlet, North Carolina, and North Little Rock, Arkansas*.

Washington, DC: United States Fire Administration, National Fire Data Center.

Feeney, Floyd. 1986. "Robbers as decision-makers." Pp. 53–71 in *The Reasoning Criminal: Rational Choice Perspectives on Offending*, edited by Derek B. Cornish and Ronald V. Clarke. New York: Springer-Verlag.

Feeney, Floyd, and Adrianne Weir. 1975. "Prevention and control of armed robbery." *Criminology* 13:102–05.

Felson, Marcus, and Ronald V. Clarke. 1998. *Opportunity Makes the Thief: Practical Theory for Crime Prevention*. London: Home Office, Policing and Reducing Crime Unit.

Finney, H. C., and Henry R. Lesieur. 1982. "A contingency theory of organizational crime." Pp. 255–99 in *Research in the Sociology of Organizations*, Vol. 1, edited by S. B. Bacharach. Greenwich, CT: JAI.

Fisse, Brent, and John Braithwaite. 1983. *The Impact of Publicity on Corporate Offenders*. Albany: State University of New York Press.

Forbes, Kristin J., and Menzie D. Chinn. 2003. "A decomposition of global linkages in financial markets over time." National Bureau of Economic Research, Working Paper no. w9555.

Forst, Brian, and William Rhodes. 1980. *Sentencing in Eight United States District Courts, 1973–1978*. Ann Arbor, MI: Inter-University Consortium for Political and Social Research.

Frederick, William C. 1988. "An ethics roundtable: The culprit is culture?" *Management Review* 77:48–50.

——— 1995. *Values, Nature and Culture in the American Corporation*. New York: Oxford University Press.

Freeman, Richard B. 1995. "The labor market." Pp. 171–91 in *Crime*, edited by James Q. Wilson and Joan Petersilia. San Francisco, CA: Institute for Contemporary Studies.

Friedman, Debra, and Michael Hechter. 1988. "The contribution of rational choice theory to macrosociological research." *Sociological Theory* 6:201–18.

Friedrichs, David O. 2004. *Trusted Criminals: White-collar Crime in Contemporary Society*. Belmont, CA: Wadsworth.

Friedrichs, David O., and Jessica Friedrichs. 2002. "The world bank and crimes of globalization: A case study." *Social Justice* 29:13–36.

Fusaro, Dave. 1997. "Price fixing, bankruptcy and 200 lost jobs." *Dairy Foods* 98:9.

Ganzini, Linda, Bentson H. McFarland, and Joseph D. Bloom. 1990. "Victims of fraud: Comparing victims of white-collar and violent crime." *Bulletin of the American Academy of Psychiatry and Law* 18:55–63.

Garland, David. 2001. *The Culture of Control: Crime and Social Order in Contemporary Society*. Chicago: University of Chicago Press.

Gazette. 2000. "Cut! Cinar mas the barricade: Embattled production company stands by managers." December, 20, page D3.

Geis, Gilbert. 1967. "The heavy electrical equipment antitrust cases of 1961." Pp. 139–50 in *Criminal Behavior Systems,* edited by Marshall B. Clinard and Richard Quinney. New York: Holt, Rinehart and Winston.

——. 1975. "Victimization patterns in white-collar crime." Pp. 89–105 in *Victimology: A Focus,* edited by Israel Drapkin and Emilio Viano, Vol. 5. Lexington, MA: D.C. Heath.

——. 1976. "Defrauding the elderly." Pp. 7–19 in *Crime and the Elderly,* edited by John Goldsmith and Sharon S. Goldsmith. Lexington, MA: D.C. Heath.

——. 1999. "Is incarceration an appropriate sanction for the nonviolent white-collar offender? Yes." Pp. 152–58 in *Controversial Issues in Corrections,* edited by Charles B. Fields. Boston: Allyn and Bacon.

Geis, Gilbert, and Colin Goff. 1983. "Introduction" to Edwin Sutherland, *White Collar Crime: The Uncut Version.* New Haven, CT: Yale University Press.

Geis, Gilbert, and Lawrence S. Salinger. 1998. "Antitrust and organizational deviance." Pp. 71–110 in *The Sociology of Organizations: Deviance in and of Organizations,* edited by Peter A. Bamberger and William J. Sonnenstuhl, Vol. 15. Stamford, CT: JAI.

Gilbert, Michael J., and Steve Russell. 2002. "Globalization of criminal justice in the corporate context." *Crime, Law and Social Change* 38:211–38.

Glaser, Daniel. 1964. *The Effectiveness of a Prison and Parole System.* Indianapolis, IN: Bobbs-Merrill.

Glazer, Myron P., and Penina M. Glazer. 1989. *The Whistleblowers: Exposing Corruption in Government and Industry.* New York: Basic Books.

Gottfredson, Michael R., and Travis Hirschi. 1990. *A General Theory of Crime.* Stanford, CA: Stanford University Press.

Grabosky, Peter. 2001. "The system of corporate crime control." Pp. 137–53 in *Contemporary Issues in Crime and Criminal Justice,* edited by Henry N. Pontell and David Shichor. Upper Saddle River, NJ: Prentice Hall.

Grabosky, Peter, and John Braithwaite. 1986. *Of Manners Gentle: Enforcement Strategies of Australian Business Regulatory Agencies.* Melbourne: Oxford University Press.

Grabosky, Peter N., Russell G. Smith, and Gillian Dempsey. 2001. *Electronic Theft: Unlawful Acquisition in Cyberspace.* Cambridge: Cambridge University Press.

Green, Donald P., and Ian Shapiro. 1994. *Pathologies of Rational Choice Theory: A Critique of Application in Political Science.* New Haven, CT: Yale University Press.

Grether, Jean Marie, and Jamie de Melo. 2004. "Globalization and dirty industries: Do pollution havens matter?" Pp. 167–203 in *Challenges to Globalization: International Seminar on International Trade*, edited by Robert E. Baldwin and Alan Winters. Chicago: University of Chicago.

Guehenno, Jean-Marie (translated by Victoria Elliott). 1995. *The End of the Nation-State*. Minneapolis: University of Minnesota Press.

Gunningham, Neil, and Peter Grabosky. 1998. *Smart Regulation: Designing Environmental Policy*. New York: Oxford University Press.

Hagan, John. 1992. "The poverty of a classless criminology." *Criminology* 30:1–20.

Haggard, Merle. 1968. "Mama tried." Sony/ATV Songs, Tree Publishing.

Halle, David. 1984. *America's Working Man*. Chicago: University of Chicago Press.

Hambrick, Donald C., and Phyllis A. Mason. 1984. "Upper echelons: The organization as a reflection of its top managers." *Academy of Management Review* 9:193–206.

Harris, Jean. 1986. *Stranger in Two Worlds*. New York: Macmillan.

Hazani, Moshe. 1991. "Aligning vocabulary, symbols banks, and sociocultural structure." *Journal of Contemporary Ethnography* 20:179–203.

Hechter, Michael. 1996. "Through thick and thin: How far can theory predict behavior?" *The Times Literary Supplement*, no. 4852, March 29, 1996:15.

Hechter, Michael, and Satoshi Kanawaza. 1997. "Sociological rational choice theory." *Annual Review of Sociology* 23:191–214.

Hesselberg, Jan, and Hege Merete Knutsen. 2002. "Leather tanning: Environmental regulations, competitiveness and locational shifts." Pp. 157–97 in *Environmental Regulation in the New Global Economy*, edited by Rhys Jenkins, Jonathan Barton, Anthony Bartzokas, Jan Hesselberg, and Hege Merete Knutsen. Northhampton, MA: Edward Elgar.

Hirsch, Paul. 1986. "From ambushes to golden parachutes: Corporate takeovers as instance of cultural framing and institutional integration." *American Journal of Sociology* 91:800–37.

Hochstetler, Andy. 2001. "Opportunities and decisions: Interactional dynamics in robbery and burglary groups." *Criminology* 39:737–64.

Hochstetler, Andy, and Heith Copes. 2003. "Managing fear to commit felony theft." Pp. 87–99 in *In Their Own Words: Criminals on Crime* (3rd edition), edited by Paul Cromwell. Los Angeles: Roxbury.

Horney, Julie, and Ineke Haen Marshall. 1992. "Risk perceptions among serious offenders: The role of crime and punishment." *Criminology* 30:575–92.

Hughes, Everett C. 1971a. "Good people and dirty work." Pp. 87–97 in *The Sociological Eye*. Chicago: Aldine Atherton.

1971b. "The *Gleichschaltung* of the German Statistical Yearbook." Pp. 516–23 in *The Sociological Eye*. Chicago: Aldine Atherton.

Insurance Information Institute. 2003. *International Insurance Factbook*. New York: Insurance Information Institute.

Internal Revenue Service. 2003. *Corporate Tax Statistics: Complete Report*. Washington, DC: U.S. Government Printing Office.

Internet Fraud Complaint Center, with National White Collar Crime Center and Federal Bureau of Investigation. 2005. *IC3 Internet Fraud Report* (January 1, 2003–December 31, 2003). www.ifccfbi.gov/ strategy/2003 IC3Report.pdf. January 8.

Investment Company Institute. 1999. *Equity Ownership in America*. Washington, DC: American Council for Capital Formation.

2002. *Equity Ownership in America: Special Report*. Washington DC: American Council for Capital Formation.

Irish Times. 1997. "Investing in the Irish film industry." July 25, Sound and Vision, page 13.

Irwin, John. 1985. *The Jail*. Berkeley: University of California Press.

Jackall, Robert. 1988. *Moral Mazes: The World of Corporate Managers*. New York: Oxford University Press.

Jackson, Jerome. 1994. "Fraud masters: Professional credit card offenders and crime." *Criminal Justice Review* 19:24–55.

Jacques, Elliot. 1951. *The Changing Culture of the Factory*. London: Tavistock.

Jamieson, Katherine M. 1994. *Organization of Corporate Crime: Dynamics of Antitrust Violation*. Thousand Oaks, CA: Sage.

Janis, Irving. 1982. *Groupthink: Psychological Studies of Policy Decisions and Fiascoes* (2nd edition). Boston: Houghton-Mifflin.

Jenkins, Anne, and John Braithwaite. 1993. "Profits, pressure and corporate lawbreaking." *Crime, Law and Social Change* 20:221–32.

Jesilow, Paul, Henry N. Pontell, and Gilbert Geis. 1993. *Prescription for Profit – How Doctors Defraud Medicaid*. Berkeley: University of California Press.

Jeter, Lynne W. 2003. *Disconnected: Deceit and Betrayal at WorldCom*. Hoboken, NJ: John Wiley & Sons.

Jett, Joseph. 1999. *Black and White on Wall Street: The Untold Story of the Man Wrongly Accused of Bringing Down Kidder Peabody* (with Sabra Chartrand). New York: William Morrow.

Kagan, Robert A., Neil Gunningham, and Dorothy Thornton. 2003. "Explaining corporate environmental performance: How does regulation matter?" *Law & Society Review* 37:51–90.

Kagan, Robert A., and John T. Scholz. 1984. "The criminology of the corporation and regulatory enforcement strategies." Pp. 67–96 in *Enforcing Regulation*, edited by Keith Hawkins and John M. Thomas. Boston: Kluwer-Nijhoff.

Katz, Jack. 1980a. "Concerted ignorance: The social psychology of cover-up." Pp. 149–70 in *Management Fraud: Detection and Deterrence*, edited by Robert K. Elliot and John I. Willingham. New York: Petrocelli.

———. 1980b. "The social movement against white-collar crime." Pp. 161–84 in *Criminology Review Yearbook* (Vol. 2), edited by Egon Bittner and Sheldon Messinger. Beverly Hills, CA: Sage.

———. 1988. *Seductions of Crime: Moral and Sensual Attractions of Doing Evil.* New York: Basic Books.

Kerley, Kent R., Michael L. Benson, Matthew R. Lee, and Francis T. Cullen. 2004. "Race, criminal justice contact, and adult position in the social stratification system." *Social Problems* 51:549–68.

Kling, Jeffrey R. 2002. "The effect of prison sentence length on the subsequent employment and earnings of criminal defendants." Department of Economics and Woodrow Wilson School, Public and International Affairs Papers, 208. Princeton, NJ: Princeton University.

Kohn, Melvin L. 1977. *Class and Conformity: A Study in Values* (2nd edition). Chicago: University of Chicago Press.

Kornbluth, Jesse. 1992. *Highly Confident: The Crime and Punishment of Michael Milken.* New York: William Morrow.

Kuehberger, Anton. 1996. "The influence of framing on risky decisions: A meta-analysis." *Organizational Behavior and Human Decision Processes* 75:23–55.

Laite, William E. Jr. 1972. *The United States vs. William Laite.* Washington, DC: Acropolis.

Langston, Doris. 1993. "Who am I now? The politics of class identity." Pp. 60–73 in *Working Class Women in the Academy*, edited by Michelle M. Tokarczyk and Elizabeth A. Fay. Amherst: University of Massachusetts Press.

Lareau, Annette. 2002. "Invisible inequality: Social class and childrearing in black families and white families." *American Sociological Review* 67:747–76.

———. 2003. *Unequal Childhoods: Class, Race, and Family Life.* Berkeley: University of California Press.

Lash, Scott, and John Urry. 1994. *Economies of Signs and Space.* London: Sage.

Laub, John H. 2001. "Understanding desistance from crime." Pp. 1–70 in *Crime and Justice: An Annual Review of Research*, Vol. 28, edited by Michael Tonry. Chicago: University of Chicago Press.

Laub, John H., and Robert J. Sampson. 2003. *Shared Beginnings, Divergent Lives: Delinquent Boys to Age 70.* Cambridge, MA: Harvard University Press.

Lawson, Stephen P. 1992. *Daddy, Why Are You Going to Prison?* Wheaton, IL: Shaw.

Leeson, Nick. 1996. *Rogue Trader* (with Edward Whitley). Boston: Little, Brown.

Leonard, William N., and Marvin Weber. 1970. "Automakers and dealers: A study of criminogenic market forces." *Law & Society Review* 4:407–24.

Levi, Michael. 1987. *Regulating Fraud: White-Collar Crime and the Criminal Process.* London: Tavistock.

———. 2001a. "'Between the risk and the reality falls the shadow:' Evidence and urban legends in computer fraud (with apologies to T. S. Eliot)." Pp. 44–58 in *Crime and the Internet,* edited by David S. Wall. New York: Routledge.

———. 2001b. "Transnational white-collar crime: Some explorations of victimization impact." Pp. 341–58 in *Contemporary Issues in Crime and Criminal Justice: Essays in Honor of Gilbert Geis,* edited by Henry N. Pontell and David Shichor. Upper Saddle River, NJ: Prentice Hall.

Levi, Micahel, Paul Bissell and Tony Richardson. 1991. *The Prevention of Cheque and Credit Card Fraud.* Crime Prevention Unit paper number 26. London: Home Office.

Levine, Dennis B. 1991. *Inside Out: An Insider's Account of Wall Street* (with William Hoffer). New York: G. P. Putnam's Sons.

Levinson, Arik, and M. Scott Taylor. 2001. "Trade and environment: Unmasking the pollution haven effect." Washington, DC: Georgetown University.

Levitt, Arthur. 2002. *Take On the Street: What Wall Street and Corporate America Don't Want You to Know, and What You Can Do to Fight Back* (with Paula Dwyer). New York: Random House.

Lilly, William, and James C. Miller. 1977. "The new 'social regulation.'" *The Public Interest* 47 (Spring):49–61.

Litton, Robert. 1998. "Fraud and the insurance industry: Why don't they do something about it, then?" *International Journal of Risk, Security and Crime Prevention* 3:193–205.

Lochner, Lance. 2003. "Individual perceptions of the criminal justice system." National Bureau of Economic Research, working paper 9474. Cambridge, MA.

Lofquist, William S. 1993. "Legislating organizational probation: State capacity, business power, and corporate crime control." *Law & Society Review* 27:741–84.

Los Angeles Daily News. 2004. "Job training agency should be fired." February 13, page n1.

Los Angeles Times. 1989. "Did he do the right thing? Chairman's role in Bhopal disaster remains ambiguous." February 15, page D3.

———. 1991. "Fox's customs cleanup effort has led to a 36-fold increase in seizures of illegal goods compared with last year." September 23, page A5.

1992. "Chicken plant owner gets jail for fatal blaze." September 15, page A16.

1997. "Army's sex convictions: Now the larger question." April 30, page B8.

1999. "Cruise line fined $18 million for dumping waste at sea." July 22, page 6.

2003. "California leads nation in number of fraud complaints." January 23, part 3, page 1.

2004. "More than half avoided levies during boom years." April 11.

Lubrano, Alfred. 2004. *Limbo: Blue-Collar Roots, White-Collar Dreams.* Hoboken, NJ: John Wiley & Sons.

Luckenbill, David F., and Joel Best. 1981. "Careers in deviance and respectability: The analogy's limitations." *Social Problems* 29:197–206.

MacIsaac, John. 1968. *Half the Fun Was Getting There.* Englewood Cliffs, NJ: Prentice Hall.

Maio, Gregory, R., James M. Olson, Mark M. Bernard, and Michelle A. Luke. 2003. "Ideologies, values, attitudes, and behavior." Pp. 283–308 in *Handbook of Social Psychology,* edited by John DeLamater. New York: Kluwer Academic.

Makkai, Toni, and John Braithwaite. 1996. "Procedural justice and regulatory compliance." *Law and Human Behavior* 20:83–98.

Markowitz, Fred E., and Richard B. Felson. 1998. "Social demographic attitudes and violence." *Criminology* 36:117–38.

Maruna, Shadd. 2001. *Making Good: How Ex-convicts Reform and Rebuild Their Lives.* Washington, DC: American Psychological Association.

Maruna, Shadd, and Heith Copes. 2004. "Excuses, excuses: What have we learned in five decades of neutralization research?" Pp. 221–320 in *Crime and Justice: A Review of Research,* Vol. 32, edited by Michael Tonry. Chicago: University of Chicago Press.

Maruna, Shadd, and Russ Immarigeon, editors. 2004. *After Crime and Punishment: Pathways to Offender Reintegration.* Cullompton, UK: Willan.

Mason, Karen A. 1999. *Unpublished Qualitative Interviews of White-Collar Offenders.* Courtesy of Karen A. Mason, Washington State University.

Mathews, M. Cash. 1987. "Codes of ethics: Organizational behavior and misbehavior." Pp. 107–30 in *Research in Corporate Social Performance and Policy: Empirical Studies of Business Ethics and Values,* edited by William C. Frederick, Vol. 9. Greenwich, CT: JAI.

May, Peter J. 2004. "Compliance motivations: Affirmative and negative bases." *Law & Society Review* 38:41–68.

Mayne, Ruth, and Caroline Le Quesne. 1999. "Calls for social trade." Pp. 91–114 in *Global Trade and Social Issues,* edited by Annie Taylor and Caroline Thomas. New York: Routledge.

McCall, Nathan. 1994. *Makes Me Wanna Holler: A Young Black Man in America.* New York: Random House.

McCleary, Richard. 1992. *Dangerous Men: The Sociology of Parole* (2nd edition). New York: Harrow and Heston.

McCourt, Frank. 1996. *Angela's Ashes: A Memoir of a Childhood.* London: HarperCollins.

McDougall, Susan, and Pat Harris. 2003. *The Woman Who Wouldn't Talk.* New York: Carroll and Graf Publishers.

McGarry, Kathleen, and Robert F. Schoeni. 2000. "Social security, economic growth, and the rise of independence of elderly widows in the 20th century." *Demography* 37:221–36.

McLean, Bethany, and Peter Elkind. 2004. *The Smartest Guys in the Room: The Amazing Rise and Scandalous Fall of Enron.* New York: Penguin.

McMahon, E. J., Adrian Moore and George Segal. 2003. *Private competition for public services: Unfinished agenda in New York.* Civic Report, number 41 (December). New York: Manhattan Institute.

Melbourne Herald Sun. 2004. "Childcare porn fear: Teachers, police, doctors nabbed." October 1, page 1.

Memphis Commercial Appeal. 1992. "Jury convicts Lanier of abusing power for sex." December 19, page A1.

      2004. "Daycare kingpins guilty." May 13, page Al.

Memphis Flyer. 1998. "An offender gets his: Editorial." July 9, page 3.

Mendelhoff, John and Wayne B. Gray. 2005. "Inside the black box: How do OSHA inspections lead to reductions in workplace injuries?" *Law and Policy* 27(2):219–37.

Messerschmidt, James W. 1995. "Managing to kill: Masculinities and the space shuttle Challenger explosion." *Masculinities* 3:1–22.

Miami Daily Business Review. 1999. "Double trouble: FPL admits contacting one juror." Page A1.

      1999. "Questionable contact: FPL sets investigator on juror after $37 million verdict." May 26, page A1.

Minkow, Barry. 1995. *Clean Sweep: The Inside Story of the ZZZZ Best Scam.* Nashville: Thomas Nelson.

Mokhiber, Russell, and Robert Weissman. 2002. "Phillip Morris to Canada: Drop dead." *The Final Call,* April 4, page Al.

Morrison, James, and Peter Wickersham. 1998. "Physicians disciplined by a state medical board." *Journal of the American Medical Association* 279:1889–93.

Murray, Dennis. 2000. "Online investment scams: Coming to a screen near you." *Medical Economics* 77:184–97.

Nadler, Richard. 1999. "The rise of worker capitalism." *Cato Institute Policy Analysis* no. 359:1–30.

National Law Journal. 2004. "A less is more strategy clicks with jury in Tyson case." Vol. 26, page 1.

National Tax Payer's Union. 2002. "The first session of the 107th Congress: Brave new world, same old congress?" Policy paper no. 136. Alexandria, VA.

Needleman, Martin L., and Carolyn Needleman. 1979. "Organizational crime: Two models of criminogenesis." *Sociological Quarterly* 20:517–28.

Nettler, Gwynn. 1974. "Embezzlement without problems." *British Journal of Criminology* 14:70–7.

Network. 2000. "Open source code may be good news for criminals." May 2, page 2.

New Straits Times (Malaysia). 1997. "Manufacturers abusing tax incentive scheme." October 14, 1997, page National 17.

New York Daily News. 2003. "300 G fine for gift-giving jail biz." February 27, page 22.

New York Times. 1991a. "25 are killed and 40 are hurt in blaze at Carolina plant." September 4, page A1.

   1991b. "U.S. fines 500 mine companies for false air tests." April 5, page A12.

   1995. "Former United Way chief guilty in theft of more than $600,000." April 4, page A1.

   1999. "Cruise line pleads guilty to dumping of chemicals." July 22, page A10.

   2003a. "Indictment seen in Stewart case." June 4, page A1.

   2003b. "Favors heaped on lawmakers raise inquiries." February 17, page a1.

   2004. "Tobacco firms face U.S. in high-stakes trial." September 19 (online edition). www.nytimesee.com.

Newsweek. 1996. "Anchors aweigh." February 5, page 69.

Nichols, Lawrence T. 1991. "'Whistleblower' or 'renegade': Definitional contests in an official inquiry." *Symbolic Interaction* 14:395–414.

O'Brien, Darcy. 1996. *Power to Hurt: Inside a Judge's Chambers: Sexual Assault, Corruption, and the Ultimate Reversal of Justice for Women.* New York: HarperCollins.

Offe, Claus. 1985. *Disorganized Capitalism.* New York: Cambridge.

   1996. *Modernity and the State East, West.* Cambridge: Massachusetts Institute of Technology Press.

Office of National Drug Control Policy. 2003. *National Drug Control Strategy Update.* Washington, DC: U.S. Government Printing Office.

Ogren, Robert W. 1973. "The ineffectiveness of the criminal sanction in fraud and corruption cases: Losing the battle against white-collar crime." *American Criminal Law Review* 11:959–88.

Ostrom, Elinor. 1998. "A behavioral approach to the rational choice theory of collective action." *American Political Science Review* 92:1–22.

Ott, Steven J. 1989. *The Organizational Culture Perspective.* Pacific Grove, CA: Brooks/Cole.

Ottawa Citizen. 1994. "Taxpayers finally getting some revenge for monumental R&D rip-offs." May 1, page A11.

2000. "Police seize Cinar files from film agency." April 7, page D4.

Partnoy, Frank. 1997. *Fiasco: The Inside Story of a Wall Street Trader.* New York: W.W. Norton & Co.

Passas, Nikos. 1990. "Anomie and corporate deviance." *Contemporary Crises* 4:157–78.

2000. "Global anomie, dysnomie, and economic crime: Hidden consequences of neoliberalism and globalization in Russia and around the world." *Social Justice* 27:16–44.

Passas, Nikos, and David Nelken. 1993. "The thin line between legitimate and criminal enterprises: Subsidy frauds in the European Community." *Crime, Law and Social Change* 19:223–43.

Pate, Anthony M., and Edwin E. Hamilton. 1992. "Formal and informal deterrents to domestic violence: The Dade County spouse assault experiment." *American Sociological Review* 57:691–97.

Paternoster, Raymond, and Sally S. Simpson. 1993. "A rational choice theory of corporate crime." Pp. 37–58 in *Routine Activity and Rational Choice*, edited by Ronald V. Clarke and Marcus Felson. New Brunswick, NJ: Transaction.

1996. "Sanction threats and appeals to morality: Testing a rational choice model of corporate crime." *Law & Society Review* 30:549–83.

Pearce, Frank. 2001. "Crime and capitalist business organizations." Pp. 35–49 in *Crimes of Privilege*, edited by Neal Shover and John P. Wright. New York: Oxford University Press.

Pearce, Frank, and Steven Tombs. 1990. "Ideology, hegemony, and empiricism: Compliance theories of regulation." *British Journal of Criminology* 30:423–43.

1998. *Toxic Capitalism: Corporate Crime in the Chemical Industry.* Aldershot, UK: Ashgate.

Petersilia, Joan. 2003. *When Prisoners Come Home: Parole and Prisoner Reentry.* New York: Oxford University Press.

Philadelphia Daily News. 2004. "Police chief charged in prostitution case steps down." February 4 (online edition). http://www.philly.com/mld/philly/7872897.htm.

Piquero, Alex R., David P. Farrington, and Alfred Blumstein. 2003. "The criminal career paradigm: Background and recent developments." Pp. 359–506 in *Crime and Justice: An Annual Review of Research* (Vol. 30), edited by Michael Tonry. Chicago: University of Chicago Press.

Piquero, Alex R., and Greg Pogarsky. 2002. "Beyond Stafford and Warr's reconceptualization of deterrence: Personal and vicarious experiences, impulsivity, and offending behavior." *Journal of Research in Crime and Delinquency* 39:153–186.

Plott, Charles R. 1987. "Rational choice in experimental markets." Pp. 117–44 in *Rational Choice: The Contrast Between Economics and Psychology*, edited by Robin M. Hogarth and Melvin W. Reder. Chicago: University of Chicago Press.

Pontell, Henry N., Kitty Calavita and Robert Tillman. 1994. "Corporate crime and criminal justice system capacity." *Justice Quarterly* 11:383–410.

President's Task Force on Victims of Crime. 1982. *Final Report*. Washington, DC: U.S. Government Printing Office.

Pring, George W., and Penelope Canan. 1996. *SLAPPS: Getting Sued for Speaking Out*. Philadelphia, PA: Temple University Press.

Rebovich, Donald J. 1999. "The extent of fraud victimization: A comparison of surveys." Paper presented at the annual meeting of the American Society of Criminology, Toronto.

Rebovich, Donald J., and Jenny Layne. 2000. *The National Public Survey on White Collar Crime*. Morgantown, WV: National White Collar Crime Center.

Reichman, Nancy. 1988. "Insider trading." Pp. 55–96 in *Crime and Justice: A Review of Research*, Vol. 18., edited by Michael Tonry and Albert S. Reiss. Chicago: University of Chicago Press.

———. 1993. "Insider trading." Pp. 55–96 in *Beyond the Law: Crime in Complex Organizations*, edited by Michael Tonry and Albert J. Reiss Jr. Chicago: University of Chicago Press.

Reiss, Albert J., Jr. 1988. "Co-offending and criminal careers." Pp. 117–70 in *Crime and Justice: A Review of Research*, Vol. 10, edited by Michael Tonry and Norvall Morris. Chicago: University of Chicago.

Reiss, Albert J., Jr., and Albert D. Biderman. 1980. *Data Sources on White-Collar Law-Breaking*. Washington, DC: U.S. Department of Justice, National Institute of Justice.

Reiss, Albert J. Jr., and Michael Tonry. 1993. "Organizational Crime." Pp. 1–10 in *Beyond the Law: Crime in Complex Organizations*, edited by Michael Tonry and Albert J. Reiss Jr. Chicago: University of Chicago Press.

Ross, Edward Alsworth. 1907. *Sin and Society*. Boston: Houghton Mifflin.

Ross, Irwin. 1980. "How lawless are big companies?" *Fortune*, December 1:57–94.

Rossi, Peter H., and Richard A. Berk. 1997. *Just Punishments: Federal Guidelines and Public Views Compared*. New York: Aldine de Gruyter.

Rothschild, Joyce, and Terance D. Miethe. 1999. "Whistle-blower disclosures and management retaliation: The battle to control information about organization corruption." *Work and Organizations* 26:107–28.

Rousseau, Denise M. 1990. "Assessing organizational culture: The case for multiple methods." Pp. 153–92 in *Organizational Climate and Culture*, edited by Benjamin J. Schneider. San Francisco, CA: Jossey-Bass.

Rubin, Lillian B. 1994. *Families on the Fault Line*. New York: HarperCollins.

Ruckman, P. S. Jr. 2003. "Clemency Statistics." January 15. http://jurist. law.pitt.edu/pardons5a.htm.

Sacramento Business Journal. 2001. "Most U.S. homes now have computers." September 6, page a1.

Salt, John. 1997. "International movements of the highly skilled." *International Migration Unit Occasional Papers*, No. 3. Paris: OECD.

Salt Lake Tribune. 2004. "Idaho dentist accused of fondling heavily sedated female patients." February 1. www.sltrib.com/2004/Feb/02012004/utah/134546.asp?display=print.

Sampson, Robert J., and John H. Laub. 2003. "Life-course desisters? Trajectories of crime among delinquent boys followed to age 70." *Criminology* 41:555–92.

Samuelson, Robert J. 1995. *The Good Life and Its Discontents*. New York: Random House.

Schaefer, Brett D. 1999. "Why Congress should hold firm on reducing foreign aid." *Executive Memorandum*, no. 623. Washington, DC: The Heritage Foundation.

Schell, Bernadette H., John L. Dodge, and Steve S. Moutsatos. 2002. *The Hacking of America: Who's Doing It, Why, and How?* Westport, CT: Quorum Books.

Schell, Michael S., and Charlene Marmer Soloman. 1997. *Capitalizing on the Global Work Force: A Strategic Guide to Expatriate Management*. London: Irwin.

Schlegel, Kip. 1990. *Just Deserts for Corporate Criminals*. Boston: Northeastern University Press.

Schlosser, Eric. 1998. "The prison industrial complex." *Atlantic Monthly* 282:51–77.

Schudson, Charles B., Ashton P. Onellion, and Ellen Hochstedler. 1984. "Nailing an omelet to the wall: Prosecuting nursing home homicide." Pp. 131–46 in *Corporations as Criminals*, edited by Ellen Hochstedler. Beverly Hills, CA: Sage.

Schwartz, Richard D., and Jerome H. Skolnick. 1964. "Two studies of legal stigma." Pp. 103–17 in *The Other Side*, edited by Howard S. Becker. New York: Free Press.

Sechrest, Dale K., David Shichor, Jeffrey H. Doocy, and Gilbert Geis. 1998. "Research note: Women's response to a telemarketing scam." *Women and Criminal Justice* 10:75–89.

Sennett, Richard, and Jonathan Cobb. 1972. *The Hidden Injuries of Class.* New York: Alfred A. Knopf.

Shapiro, Susan P. 1983. "The new moral entrepreneurs: Corporate crime crusaders." *Contemporary Sociology* 12:304–07.

———. 1985. "The road not taken: The elusive path to criminal prosecution for white-collar offenders." *Law & Society Review* 19:179–217.

Shichor, David, Jeffrey Doocy, and Gilbert Geis. 1996. "Anger, disappointment and disgust: Reactions of victims of a telephone investment scam." Pp. 105–11 in *Proceedings of the 8th International Conference of Victimology*, edited by Chris Summer, Mark Israel, Michael O'Connell, and Rick Stare. Canberra: Australian Institute of Criminology.

Shichor, David, Dale Sechrest, and Jeffrey Doocy. 2001. "Victims of investment fraud." Pp. 81–96 in *Contemporary Issues in Crime and Criminal Justice: Essays in Honor of Gilbert Geis*, edited by Henry N. Pontell and David Shichor. Upper Saddle River, NJ: Prentice Hall.

Shipler, David K. 2004. *The Working Poor: Invisible in America.* New York: Alfred A. Knopf.

Shover, Neal. 1985. *Aging Criminals.* Beverly Hills, CA: Sage.

———. 1996. *Great Pretenders: Pursuits and Careers of Persistent Thieves.* Boulder, CO: Westview.

Shover, Neal, and Kevin M. Bryant. 1993. "Theoretical explanations of corporate crime." Pp. 141–76 in *Understanding Corporate Criminality*, edited by Michael B. Blankenship. New York: Garland.

Shover, Neal, Donald A. Clelland, and John P. Lynxwiler. 1986. *Enforcement or Negotiation? Constructing a Regulatory Bureaucracy.* Albany: State University of New York Press.

Shover, Neal, Glenn S. Coffey, and Dick Hobbs. 2003. "Crime on the line: Telemarketing and the changing nature of professional crime." *British Journal of Criminology* 43:489–505.

Shover, Neal, Glenn S. Coffey, and Clinton R. Sanders. 2004. "Dialing for dollars: Opportunities, justifications, and telemarketing fraud." *Qualitative Sociology* 27:59–75.

Shover, Neal, Greer Litton Fox, and Michael Mills. 1994. "Long-term consequences of victimization by white-collar crime." *Justice Quarterly* 11:301–24.

Shover, Neal, and Andy Hochstetler. 2001. "Cultural explanation and organizational crime." *Crime, Law and Social Change* 35:1–18.

Shover, Neal, and David Honaker. 1992. "The socially bounded decision making of persistent property offenders." *Howard Journal of Criminal Justice* 31:276–94.

Shover, Neal, and Aaron S. Routhe. 2004. "Environmental crime." In *Crime and Justice: A Review of Research* (Vol. 32), edited by Michael Tonry. Chicago: University of Chicago Press.

Shover, Neal, and Carol Y. Thompson. 1992. "Age, differential expectations and crime desistance." *Criminology* 30:89–104.

Simon, David R., and Stanley Eitzen. 1993. *Elite Deviance* (4th edition). Boston, MA: Allyn and Bacon.

Simpson, Sally S. 1987. "Cycles of illegality: Antitrust violations in corporate America." *Social Forces* 65:943–63.

2002. *Corporate Crime, Law and Social Control.* New York: Cambridge University Press.

Simpson, Sally S., and Christopher Koper. 1992. "Deterring corporate crime." *Criminology* 30:347–75.

Simpson, Sally S., and Nicole Leeper Piquero. 2001a. "The Archer Daniels Midland antitrust case of 1996." Pp. 175–94 in *Contemporary Issues in Crime and Criminal Justice: Essays in Honor of Gilbert Geis*, edited by Henry N. Pontell and David Shichor. Upper Saddle River, NJ: Prentice Hall.

Simpson, Sally S., and Nicole Leeper Piquero. 2001b. "Low self-control, organizational theory, and corporate crime." *Law & Society Review* 36:509–47.

Simpson, Sally S., Nicole Leeper Piquero, and Raymond Paternoster. 2002. "Rationality and corporate offending decisions." Pp. 25–40 in *Rational Choice and Criminal Behavior: Recent Research and Future Challenges,* edited by Alex R. Piquero and Steven G. Tibbets. New York: Routledge.

Sjoberg, Gideon., Elizabeth A. Gill, and Norma Williams. 2001. "A sociology of human rights." *Social Problems* 48:11–47.

Skrzycki, Cindy. 2003. *The Regulators: Anonymous Power Brokers in American Politics.* Lanham, MD: Rowman & Littlefield.

Smirich, Linda. 1983. "Concepts of culture and organizational analysis." *Administrative Science Quarterly* 28:339–58.

Smith, Russell G., Peter Grabosky, and Gregor Urbas. 2004. *Cyber Criminals On Trial.* Cambridge: Cambridge University Press.

Smith, Vernon L. 1991. "Rational choice: The contrast between economics and psychology." *Journal of Political Economy* 99:877–97.

1986. "Experimental methods in the political economy of exchange." *Science* 234:167–73.

Snider, Laureen. 1993. "Regulating corporate behavior." Pp. 177–210 in *Understanding Corporate Criminality*, edited by Michael B. Blankenship. New York: Garland.

2002. "Corporate crime: Business as usual?" Pp. 150–67 in *Critical Criminology in Canada: Breaking the Limits between Marginality and*

Condemnation, edited by Bernard Schissel and Carolyn Brooks. Toronto: Fernwood.

———. 2004. "'This time we really mean it!' Cracking down on stockmarket fraud." Presented to *Governing the Corporation: Mapping the Loci of Power in Corporate Governance Design,* September 21, Queens University, Belfast, UK.

Social Security Administration. 1999. www.ssa.gov/statistics/supplement/ 1999/tables/index.

Solow, Steven P. 2003. "Environmental crime update: What is the state of federal environmental crime enforcement?" Paper presented at the 32nd annual American Bar Association, Section on Environment, Energy and Resources, Conference on Environmental Law, Keystone, CO, March 13–16.

Sonnenfeld, Jeffrey, and Paul R. Lawrence. 1978. "Why do companies succumb to price fixing?" *Harvard Business Review* 56:145–57.

Spalek, Basia. 1999. "Exploring the impact of financial crime: A study looking into the effects of the Maxwell scandal upon the Maxwell pensioners." *International Review of Victimology* 6:213–30.

Sparrow, Malcolm K. 1996. *License to Steal: Why Fraud Plagues America's Health Care System.* Boulder, CO: Westview.

Spencer, John C. 1965. "White-collar crime." Pp. 233–66 in *Criminology in Transition,* edited by Edward Glover, Hermann Mannheim, and Emmanuel Miller. London: Tavistock.

Stafford, Mark C., and Mark Warr. 1993. "A reconceptualization of general and specific deterrence." *Journal of Research in Crime and Delinquency* 30:123–35.

State Bar of California. 2003. *2002 Report on the State Bar of California Discipline System.* Los Angeles: Author.

Staw, Barry M., and Eugene Szwajkowski. 1975. "The scarcity munificence component of organizational environments and the commission of illegal acts." *Administrative Science Quarterly* 20:345–54.

Steele, Eric H. 1975. "Fraud, dispute and the consumer: Responding to consumer complaints." *University of Pennsylvania Law Review* 123:1107–86.

Strange, Susan. 1996. *The Retreat of the State: The Diffusion of Power in the World Economy.* Cambridge: Cambridge University Press.

Strauss, Murray A. (with Denise A. Donnely). 1994. *Beating the Devil Out of Them: Corporal Punishment in American Families.* New York: Lexington.

Streeck, Wolfgang, and Phillipe C. Schmitter. 1991. "From national corporatism to transnational pluralism: Organized interest in the single European market." *Politics and Society* 19:133–63.

Strunk, Mildred, and Hadley Cantril, editors. 1951. *Public Opinion 1935–1946*. Princeton, NJ: Princeton University Press.

Sutherland, Edwin H. 1940. "White-collar criminality." *American Sociological Review* 5:1–11.

———. 1945. "Is 'white-collar crime' crime?" *American Sociological Review* 10:132–39.

———. 1949. *White-Collar Crime.* New York: Dryden.

———. 1983. *White Collar Crime: The Uncut Version,* edited with an introduction by Gilbert Geis and Colin Goff. New Haven, CT: Yale University Press.

Swartz, Mimi. 2003. *Power Failure: The Inside Story of the Collapse of ENRON* (with Sherron Watkins). New York: Doubleday.

Sydney Morning Herald. 1999. "Corporate welfare." December 7, page A18.

Sykes, Gresham, and David Matza. 1957. "Techniques of neutralization: A theory of delinquency." *American Sociological Review* 22:667–70.

Szockyj, Elizabeth, and Gilbert Geis. 2002. "Insider trading: Patterns and analysis." *Journal of Criminal Justice* 30:273–86.

Szwajkoski, Eugene. 1986. "The myths and realities of research on organizational misconduct." Pp. 121–47 in *Research in Corporate Social Performance and Policy,* edited by James E. Post. New York: JAI.

Tabarrok, Alexander. 2002. *Changing the Guard: Private Prisons and the Control of Crime.* Oakland, CA: The Independent Institute.

Tacoma News Tribune. 2004a. "Bridge builder, agency fined." February 4. www.tribnet.com/news/local/v-printer/story/4704027p-4655038c.html.

———. 2004b. "CU wants probe into sex party allegations." February 1. www.tribnet.com/sports/v-printer/story/4694169p-464549c.html.

Tampa Tribune. 2004. "Drug ring defendants include well-to-do." February 1. www.tampatrib.com/floridametronews/MGAZD7YI4QD.html.

Taxpayers Against Fraud. 2003. *Reducing Medicare and Medicaid Fraud by Drug Manufacturers. The Role of the False Claims Act.* Washington, DC: Taxpayers Against Fraud Education Fund.

Taylor, Ian. 1999. *Crime in Context: A Critical Criminology of Market Societies.* Boulder, CO: Westview.

Tennyson, Sharon. 1996. "Economic institutions and individual ethics: A study of consumer attitudes toward insurance fraud." *Journal of Economic Behavior and Organization* 32:247–65.

t'Hart, Paul. 1991. "Groupthink, risk-taking and recklessness: Quality of process and outcome in policy decision making." *Politics and the Individual* 1:67–90.

Thornton, Dorothy, Neil Gunningham, and Robert A. Kagan. 2005. "General deterrence and corporate environmental behavior." *Law and Policy* 27:262–88.

Tibbets, Steven G., and Chris L. Gibson. 2002. "Individual propensities and rational decisionmaking: Recent findings and promising approaches." Pp. 3–24 in *Rational Choice and Criminal Behavior: Recent Research and Future Challenges*, edited by Alex R. Piquero and Steven G. Tibbets. New York: Routledge.

Tickell, Adam. 1996. "Taking the initiative: Leeds' Finanical Centre." Pp. 103–18 in *Corporate City? Partnerships Participation in Urban Development in Leeds*, edited by Graham Haughton and Colin C. Williams. Aldershot, UK: Avebury.

Tillman, Robert. 1998. *Broken Promises: Fraud by Small Business Health Insurers*. Boston: Northeastern University Press.

——— 2002. *Global Pirates: Fraud in the Offshore Insurance Industry*. Boston: Northeastern University Press.

Timilty, Joseph. 1997. *Prison Journal: An Irreverent Look at Life on the Inside* (with Jack Thomas). Boston: Northeastern University Press.

Titus, Richard. 2000. "Personal fraud and its victims." Pp. 57–67 in *Crimes of Privilege*, edited by Neal Shover and John P. Wright. New York: Oxford University Press.

Titus, Richard M., Fred Heinzelmann, and John M. Boyle. 1995. "Victimization of persons by fraud." *Crime and Delinquency* 41:54–72.

Transactional Records Access Clearinghouse. 2003. *U.S. Federal White-Collar Crime Referrals for Prosecution and Prosecutions 1987–2003 (per 100 million)*. Syracuse, NY: Syracuse University.

——— 2004. "Criminal Enforcement: White-Collar Crime." Syracuse, NY: Syracuse University.

Troy, Carmelita, Ken G. Smith, and Lawrence A. Gordon. 2003. "Firms facing SEC Action." Unpublished paper. Robert H. Smith School of Management. College Park: University of Maryland.

Tversky, Amos, and Daniel Kahneman. 1981. "The framing of decisions and psychology of choice." *Science* 30:453–8.

Tyler, Tom R. 1990. *Why People Obey the Law*. New Haven, CT: Yale University Press.

Uggen, Christopher, Jeff Manza, and Angela Behrens. 2004. "'Less than the average citizen': Stigma, role transition and the civic reintegration of convicted felons." Pp. 261–93 in *After Crime and Punishment: Pathways to Offender Reintegration*, edited by Shadd Maruna and Russ Immarigeon. Cullompton, UK: Willan.

United Nations. 2004. *World Investment Report 2002. Transnational Corporations and Export Competitiveness*. New York: United Nations.

U.S. Bureau of Labor Statistics. 2003. *Current Population Survey*. Washington, DC: U.S. Government Printing Office.

U.S. Center for Disease Control. 2003. *Health, United States*. Hyattsville, MD: National Center for Health Statistics.

U.S. Congress, House of Representatives. 1991a. *Hearing on H.R. 3160, Comprehensive Occupational Safety and Health Reform Act, and the Fire at the Imperial Food Products Plant in Hamlet, North Carolina.* Committee on Education and Labor. Washington, DC: U.S. Government Printing Office.

    1991b. *The Tragedy At Imperial Food Products.* Committee on Education and Labor. Washington, DC: U.S. Government Printing Office.

    2001. *Medicare Drug Reimbursements: A Broken System for Patients and Taxpayers.* Subcommittee on Health of the Committee on Energy and Commerce. Washington, DC: U.S. Government Printing Office.

    2003. "Examples of government waste." *House Budget Committee Fact Sheet no. 72403.* Washington, DC: House Budget Committee.

U.S. Congress, Senate. 1976. *Fraud and Abuse Among Practitioners Participating in the Medicaid Program.* Subcommittee on Long-term Care, Special Committee on Aging. Washington, DC: U.S. Government Printing Office.

    1993. *Telemarketing Fraud and S. 568, The Telemarketing and Consumer Fraud and Abuse Protection Act.* Hearing before the Subcommittee on Consumers of the Committee on Commerce, Science, and Transportation. Washington, DC: U.S. Government Printing Office.

U.S. Department of Commerce. 1975. *Historical Statistics of the United States: Colonial to 1970.* Washington, DC: U.S. Department of Commerce.

U.S. Department of Health, Education, and Welfare. 1959. *Social Bulletin* (October). Washington, DC: Social Security Administration.

U.S. Department of Health and Human Services. 2002. *The National Nursing Home Survey: 1999 Summary, no. 2002–1723.* Hyattsville, MD: U.S. Department of Health and Human Services.

U.S. Department of Justice. n.d. *Victims of Fraud: Beyond Financial Loss* (video tape). Washington, DC: Office for Victims of Crime.

U.S. Department of Justice. 1986. *Tracking Offenders: White-Collar Crime.* Washington, DC: Bureau of Justice Statistics.

    1987. *White Collar Crime.* Washington, DC: Bureau of Justice Statistics.

    2000a. *Defense Counsel in Criminal Cases.* Washington, DC: Bureau of Justice Statistics.

    2000b. *Offenders Returning to Federal Prison, 1986–97.* Washington, DC: National Institute of Justice.

    2002a. *Foreign Corrupt Practices Act Antibribery Provisions: Brochure.* Washington, DC: U.S. Department of Justice.

    2002b. "Tanker company sentenced for conspiring to conceal hazardous condition and oil pollution in Baltimore Harbor." Press Release, March 8.

    2003. United States v. Mercury PCS II, L.L.C. Civil action No. 1:98CV02751. Washington, DC: U.S. Department of Justice.

U.S. Department of Labor. 2004. "Labor Department to review new allegations of workers' rights violations against Mexico." Bureau of International Labor Affairs, News release, April 15. Washington, DC: U.S. Department of Labor.

U.S. Department of the Treasury. 1999. *Preventing Check Fraud.* Washington, DC: U.S. Government Printing Office.

U.S. District Courts. 2003. *Judicial Business of United States Courts: Civil Cases Commenced.* U.S. Washington, DC: U.S. Government Printing Office.

U.S. Federal Reserve Board. 1962. *Survey of Financial Characteristics of Consumers.* Washington, DC: U.S. Federal Reserve Board.

  1970. *Survey of Consumer Finances.* Washington, DC: U.S. Federal Reserve Board.

  1977. *Survey of Consumer Finances.* Washington, DC: U.S. Federal Reserve Board.

  1983. *Survey of Consumer Finances.* Washington, DC: U.S. Federal Reserve Board.

  1989. *Survey of Consumer Finances.* Washington, DC: U.S. Federal Reserve Board.

  1992. *Survey of Consumer Finances.* Washington, DC: U.S. Federal Reserve Board.

  1995. *Survey of Consumer Finances.* Washington, DC: U.S. Federal Reserve Board.

  2004a. "Consumer credit historical data." *Federal Reserve Statistical Release.* Washington, DC: U.S. Government Printing Office.

  2004b. *Consumer Credit Outstanding, Releases.* Washington, DC: U.S. Federal Reserve Board.

U.S. Food and Drug Administration. 2004. "Merck withdraws Vioxx; FDA issues public health advisory." *FDA Consumer Magazine* 38(6):3–4.

U.S. General Accounting Office. 1992. *Food Assistance: School Milk Contract Bid-rigging.* Washington, DC: U.S. General Accounting Office.

  2000. *Medicare Improper Payments: Challenges for Measuring Potential Fraud and Abuse Remain Despite Planned Enhancements.* Washington, DC: General Accounting Office.

  2004. *Tax Administration: Comparison of the Reported Tax Liabilities of Foreign- and U.S.-Controlled Corporations, 1996–2000,* GAO-04–358. Washington, DC: U.S. Government Printing Office.

U.S. Office of Management and Budget. 2004. *Competitive Sourcing: Report on Competitive Sourcing Results Fiscal Year 2003.* Washington, D.C.

U.S. Securities and Exchange Commission. 2001. "In the matter of Arthur Andersen LLP. Order Instituting Public Administrative Proceedings, Making Findings and Imposing Remedial Sanctions." Available online at www.sec.gov/litigation/admin/34-44444.htm.

U.S. Sentencing Commission. Annual, 1997–2004. *Sourcebook of Federal Sentencing Statistics.* Washington, DC: U.S. Sentencing Commission. Available online at www.ussc.gov/ANNRPT.

2003. *Sentencing of Corporate Fraud and White Collar Crimes: Testimony of Paul Rosenzweig, Senior Legal Research Fellow Center for Legal and Judicial Studies, the Heritage Foundation.* Public Hearings of the United States Sentencing Commission, March 23, 2003.

2004. *Measuring Recidivism: The Criminal History Computation of the Federal Sentencing Guidelines.* Washington, DC: U.S. Sentencing Commission.

n.d. *The Federal Sentencing Guidelines for Organizational Crimes: Questions and Answers.* Washington, DC: U.S. Sentencing Commission.

USA Today. 2003. "Ring of identity thieves busted." November 26, page a1.

van den Haag, Ernest. 1975. *Punishing Criminals: Concerning a Very Old and Painful Question.* New York: Basic Books.

Vandivier, Kermit. 2001. "Why should my conscience bother me?" Pp. 146–66 in *Corporate and Governmental Deviance* (6th edition), edited by M. David Ermann. New York: Oxford University Press.

Vaughan, Diane. 1982. "Transaction systems and unlawful organizational behavior." *Social Problems* 29:373–79.

1983. *Controlling Unlawful Organizational Behavior.* Chicago: University of Chicago Press.

1992. "The macro-micro connection in white-collar crime theory." Pp. 124–45 in *White-Collar Crime Reconsidered,* edited by Kip Schlegel and David Weisburd. Boston: Northeastern University Press.

1996. *The Challenger Launch Decision: Risky Technology, Culture, and Deviance at NASA.* Chicago: University of Chicago Press.

1998. "Rational choice, situated action, and the social control of organizations." *Law & Society Review* 32:23–61.

1999. "The dark side of organizations: Mistake, misconduct, and disaster." *Annual Review of Sociology* 25:271–305.

Vaughan, Diane, and Giovanna Carlo. 1975. "The appliance repairman: A study of victim responsiveness and fraud." *Journal of Research in Crime and Delinquency* 12:153–61.

von Hirsch, Andrew, Anthony E. Bottoms, Elizabeth Burney, and P.O. Wikstrom. 1999. *Criminal Deterrence and Sentence Severity: An Analysis of Recent Research.* Portland, OR: Hart.

Waksal, Sam. 2003. "I was arrogant." *60 Minutes.* CBS Television. October 2.

Walker, Nigel, and Michael Argyle. 1964. "Does the law affect moral judgements?" *British Journal of Criminology* 6:571–79.

Wall Street Journal. 1995. "Firms find new ways to target bad press." November 10, page B8.

2003. "Abuses plague program to insure farmers' crops." May 5, page A1.

Wallace, J. Clifford. 1986. "Man does not live by law alone." Pp. 1–9 in *Crime and Punishment in Modern America*, edited by Patrick B. McGuigan and Jon S. Pascale. Washington, DC: Institute for Government and Politics.

Warr, Mark. 2002. *Companions in Crime: The Social Aspects of Criminal Conduct*. New York: Cambridge University Press.

Washington Post. 1991. "Virginia dairy charged with price fixing." July 31, page D6.

1997a. "Ex-judge sent back to jail in sex-abuse case appeal." August 16, page A14.

1997b. "Months of anarchy in Albania yield financial ruin, public fear: Lawlessness and tattered institutions impede return to normality." August 4, page A13.

1999. "Prison firm settles suit by D.C. inmates in Ohio." March 2, page B1.

2004a. "Banker charged in mutual fund scandal." February 4, page C3.

2004b. "IRS sharpening audit pencil, chief says." March 12, page E3.

2004c. "Microsoft settles Minnesota class-action case." April 19, page 1.

Weisberg, Herbert W., and Richard Derrig. 1991. "Fraud and automobile insurance: A report on the baseline study of bodily injury claims in Massachusetts." *Journal of Insurance Regulation* 9:497–541.

Weisburd, David. 1997. *Reorienting Crime Prevention Research and Policy: From the Causes of Criminality to the Context of Crime*. Washington, DC: U.S. Department of Justice, National Institute of Justice.

Weisburd, David, and Elin Waring, with Ellen Chayet. 2001. *White-Collar Crime and Criminal Careers*. New York: Cambridge University Press.

Weisburd, David, Stanton Wheeler, Elin Waring, and Nancy Bode. 1991. *Crimes of the Middle Classes*. New Haven, CT: Yale University Press.

Wheeler, Stanton., and Mitchell L. Rothman. 1982. "The organization as weapon in white-collar crime." *Michigan Law Review* 80:1403–26.

Wilkinson, Rorden, and Steve Hughes. 2000. "Labor standards and global governance: Examining the dimensions of institutional engagement." *Global Governance* 6:269–77.

Williams, Arlington, W., Vernon Smith, John O. Leyard, and Steven Gjerstad. 2000. "Concurrent trading in two experimental markets with demand interdependence." *Economic Theory* 16:511–28.

Wilson, James Q. 1975. *Thinking about Crime*. New York: Basic Books.

1983. "Thinking about crime: The debate over deterrence." *Atlantic Monthly* 252(3):72–88.

1997. *The Moral Sense*. New York: Simon and Schuster.

Wilson, James Q., and Richard J. Herrnstein. 1985. *Crime and Human Nature*. New York: Simon and Schuster.

Wilson, James Q., and George L. Kelling. 1982. "Broken windows." *The Atlantic Monthly* 249(3):29–38.

Winans, R. Foster. 1986. *Trading Secrets.* New York: St. Martin's Press.

Wood, Greg, and Malcolm Rimmer. 2003. "Codes of ethics: What are they and what should they be?" *International Journal of Value-based Management* 161:81–95.

World Almanac. 2003. *The World Almanac.* New York: World Almanac Books.

Wright, Bradley R. Entner, Avshalom Caspi, Terrie E. Moffit, Richard A. Miech, and Phil A. Silva. 1999. "Reconsidering the relationship between SES and delinquency: Causation but not correlation." *Criminology* 37:175–94.

Wright, Richard T., and Scott Decker. 1994. *Burglars on the Job: Streetlife and Residential Break-ins.* Boston: Northeastern University Press.

    1997. *Armed Robbers in Action: Stick-up and Street Culture.* Boston: Northeastern University Press.

Wright, John P., Francis T. Cullen, and Michael B. Blankenship. 1995. "The social construction of corporate violence: Media coverage of the Imperial Food Products fire." *Crime and Delinquency* 41:20–36.

Yeager, Peter C. 1992. *The Limits of Law: Public Regulation of Private Pollution.* New York: Cambridge University Press.

Zietz, Dorothy. 1981. *Women Who Embezzle or Defraud: A Study of Convicted Felons.* New York: Praeger.

Zimbardo, Philip G. 1972. "Pathology of imprisonment." *Society* 9:6–8.

Zimring, Franklin E. 1981. "Kids, groups and crime: Some implications of a well-known secret." *Journal of Criminal Law and Criminology* 72:867–85.

Index